Reading with Feeling

READING WITH FEELING

The Aesthetics of Appreciation

SUSAN L. FEAGIN

Cornell University Press

ITHACA AND LONDON

First published 1996 by Cornell University Press.

Library of Congress Cataloging-in-Publication Data
Feagin, Susan L., 1948–
Reading with feeling : the aesthetics of appreciation / Susan L. Feagin.
p. cm.
Includes bibliographical references and index.
ISBN 0-8014-3200-6 (alk. paper)
1. Reader-response criticism. I. Title.
PN98.R38F43   1996
801'.95—dc20   95-49163

Printed in the United States of America

The paper in this book meets the minimum requirements
of the American National Standard for Information Sciences—
Permanence of Paper for Printed Library Materials, ANSI Z39.48-1984.

Contents

Acknowledgments

This book has percolated for a long time, and many individuals and institutions assisted me along the way. I am grateful to those who commented on earlier drafts of parts of the manuscript: Robert Audi, Marcia Eaton, David Goldblatt, Garry Hagberg, Carolyn Korsmeyer, Jerry Levinson, Carol Mickett, Alex Neill, Stein Haugom Olsen, Nelson Potter, Mary Sirridge, Béla Szábados, and Dabney Townsend. I also appreciate the helpful discussions over the years with numerous individuals, more or less on the topic of this book, including Jack Bender, Noël Carroll, Donald Crawford, Berent Enc, Fred Dretske, Hank Frankel, Robert Gordon, William Hay, Kathleen Higgins, Peter Lamarque, Louis Mackey, Jenefer Robinson, Robert Solomon, and William Tolhurst. I hope I haven't left anyone out, yet I know I must have. I apologize to those I have omitted and to those whose good counsel I didn't always accept.

During a Research Leave from the University of Missouri–Kansas City in 1985–1986 I began to think in terms of a book length project; a University of Missouri Research Board grant for Winter 1994 and a sabbatical leave for Fall 1994 enabled me to complete the book. Robert Audi's National Endowment for the Humanities Summer Seminar in Reasons, Rationality, and Justification, provided invaluable background for the issues discussed in Part Two. A few passages in Chapter 8 were previously published in "Imagining Emotions and Appreciating Fiction," *Canadian Journal of Philosophy* 18 (1988): 485–500.

I thank Roger Haydon of Cornell University Press for his confidence and encouragement. I could not have produced the final manuscript without the patient and intelligent assistance of Nan Bier-smith, our department secretary.

On a different note, my friends Burton Dunbar, Tim George, Do-lores Miller, and Craig Subler have been sources of unfailing personal and professional support through some very difficult times. I thank my father, Roy Chester Feagin, for his enthusiasm and encourage-ment in my professional endeavors. Finally, I dedicate this book to my late husband, Gerald C. MacCallum, Jr. Would that he could have seen it.

S. L. F.

Reading with Feeling

Introduction

Having emotional and other affective responses to a work of fictional literature is a very important part of appreciating it, and the capacity of a work to provide such responses is part of what is valuable about it. Those who appreciate a work of literature typically become involved with it and respond to it. For example, they feel a portentous chill when Ishmael describes the "damp, drizzly November in my soul."[1] They are in turns horrified and amused when Gabriel García Márquez tells how the Patriarch ordered an offending official to be carved up and served for dinner, so that "every plate held an equal portion of minister of defense stuffed with pine nuts and aromatic herbs."[2] And they are suspicious when Rosamond Vincy is described as "clever with that sort of cleverness which catches every tone except the humorous."[3]

To appreciate a work is not merely to recognize *that* a work has certain properties, aesthetic qualities, or artistic virtues, nor merely to be able to recognize what it is about a work that gives it these qualities or its value. To appreciate a work is, in part, to get the value out of it, and "getting the value out of it" involves being affectively or emotionally moved. It is to experience the work in certain ways; it involves reading "with feeling."

I don't take such claims as these to be at all controversial. But it is

1. Herman Melville, *Moby Dick* (New York: Dell, 1959), p. 27.
2. Gabriel García Márquez, *The Autumn of the Patriarch,* trans. Gregory Rabassa (New York: Harper & Row/Avon, 1976), p. 119.
3. George Eliot, *Middlemarch* (New York: Collier, n.d.), p. 161.

precisely their "obviousness" that is a symptom there is philosophical work to do, for philosophy rushes in where common sense fears to tread, questioning what others take for granted and looking for arguments, analyses, and explanations. Why is it important or desirable to have emotional responses to fiction? Why should having such responses be respected and encouraged, rather than considered a little weird or a waste of time? After all, it's only fiction. What determines which emotions are appropriate responses to a given artwork, and why: what makes an emotion of one sort appropriate (say, fear), rather than another (say, anger or amusement)? Does assessing responses as appropriate or inappropriate compromise the personal integrity of our own responses and make the reading of literature into a job rather than a pleasure? Doesn't assessing responses tend to threaten spontaneity and hence the responses themselves? How is it even possible to become emotionally involved with something we know to be fictional? What role does imagination play, and how do we reconcile its role with assessments of responses as appropriate or inappropriate?

These questions are all prompted by the presence of emotions and other affective responses in appreciation, and they cry out for an account of that dimension of appreciation. In this book I concentrate on that dimension, placing it in the context of a philosophical account of the nature of appreciation itself, and tracing implications for its value or importance.

This book is an exercise in philosophy, and it develops a philosophical account of *appreciation*. It is therefore not an exercise in literary criticism. Though I provide examples throughout to illustrate the philosophical points I wish to make, my objective is to focus attention on deeper issues about the nature of appreciation and affective response, rather than on the particular examples chosen to illustrate the issue. Perhaps a little trickier is the distinction between the philosophical work I do and literary theory and theories of interpretation, or theories of reading. I do not propose or defend a particular theory of interpretation or criticism, nor am I "against theory."[4] I have argued in the past in support of pluralism with respect to theories of interpre-

---

4. See Stephen Knapp and Walter Benn Michaels, "Against Theory," *Critical Inquiry* 8 (1982): 723–742; repr. in W. J. T. Mitchell, ed., *Against Theory: Literary Studies and the New Pragmatism* (Chicago: University of Chicago Press, 1985): 11–30.

tation, and that commitment certainly informs the discussion here.[5] Its presence is felt most strongly in the final chapter, where I discuss a special value of appreciating and of learning to appreciate fictional literature.

My topic is not interpretation but appreciation. One cannot appreciate without interpreting, but I am interested in appreciation in a way that abstracts from the particular interpretive commitments of intentionalism, formalism, reader-response theory, Marxism, feminism, and what have you. Is this abstraction possible? I suggest thinking about it in the following relatively crude way. Think of theories of interpretation as theories of meaning, and think of meaning as having strictly cognitive content. Whatever justifies or warrants or explains how one reached an interpretive conclusion will be, in itself, insufficient to explain or warrant an *affective response*. I'm interested in that "gap," as it were, between cognition and affect. What do we need to appeal to in order to explain and warrant emotions and affects, beyond what explains and warrants our cognitive conclusions?

We may interpret the passage where Rosamond Vincy is described as "clever with that sort of cleverness which catches every tone except the humorous" in different ways, and different interpretations may well lead to different kinds of affective responses. We may see her as a victim of the materialistic values eagerly pursued by her thoroughly bourgeois parents. We may see her as an intelligent young woman whose energies have been misdirected toward the superficial goals promoted by socially sanctioned standards of femininity. We may see her simply as a bad person: manipulative, shallow, and selfish. For each of these interpretations, many different responses are possible. Is she the object of our pity, or of scorn? Do we hate her, have compassion for her, hold out hope for her, or revile her? Do we desire her destruction, rehabilitation, or forgiveness?

There are two major philosophical tasks concerning affective responses. One is to *explain* how they are even possible, how they *can* arise in reading fiction. The other is to explain what *warrants* a response. In this book, the first task occupies Part One, and the second Part Two. Both explanation and warrant depend in part on the meaning or interpretation of a work—its cognitive content. But a work's cognitive content is not the whole story, for something is needed to

5. Susan L. Feagin, "Incompatible Interpretations of Art," *Philosophy and Literature* 6 (1982): 133–146.

explain and warrant emotional or affective responses, rather than merely a cognitive or intellectual recognition of what a work means or says. Thus, I do not abstract from theories of interpretation under the illusion that they are irrelevant; I abstract from them in the sense that whatever they do provide, they don't go far enough to explain and warrant affective responses.

I have presented a picture of interpretation that is cruder than is required for accuracy; many theories of interpretation accommodate emotional and affective responses. Most obviously, reader-response theory places a large value on affective response. But one thing that is missing in most reader-response theory is attention to the notion of warrant: what warrants or justifies one's responding in the particular way one does, to what one does? Rosamond makes some readers angry but leaves others cold. The pretty angle at which she tilts her head strikes some readers as endearing but makes others go ballistic. It is crucial to the whole structure of this book that affective responses can be assessed. As I hope will be apparent from Part Two, assessing emotions and affects makes assessing beliefs look like child's play. The bulk of my discussion is directed toward showing *how it is possible to make such assessments at all,* that is, what it is about emotions and other affects that occur as part of appreciating a literary work which enables us to make assessments of them. This investigation requires pushing beyond the meanings of works toward our appreciative responses to them. One might call this effort an exercise in aesthetic epistemology: what warrants responses, and how does one know they are warranted?

I deal here only with appreciating fictional literature, in particular, with literature as *read* by an appreciator, rather than, for example, as viewed (as at a performance) or heard (as at a recital). Included in the category of fictional literature are works consisting mainly of discursive prose and dialogue—novels, short stories, and plays intended primarily to be read (such as those of George Bernard Shaw). My decision to limit the study to fictional literature was a strategic choice. It was not made because I believe fictional literature to be in some sense unique, or because I think it can be separated off in some clear way from other forms of fiction or other forms of representation. Indeed, I would hope and expect that many aspects of the analysis I offer can be extrapolated not only to other verbal art forms—such as poetry and nonfiction, for example, essays on travel or culture—but to other media as well (those typically involving narrative, such as film).

I prefer to concentrate on one art form since there are significant differences among media with respect to the ways they generate emotions and affects. For example, it has been argued that emotional responses to films or paintings involve "wired-in" reactions to visual stimuli,[6] and that pictorial systems of signification may operate in very different ways from the verbal.[7] In order to avoid potential confusion, I think it is wiser to start with a fairly narrowly defined range of works and generalize where appropriate. In addition, affective responses to literature depend virtually exclusively on thoughts, imagination, and cognition. Typeface, layout, and size of the volume are not (generally) considered relevant objects of appreciation of the novel or short story *as literature*.[8] This relative independence of the appreciation of fiction from sense experience provides a special challenge when one is trying to understand affective and emotional responses to it. Aristotle recognized these challenges when he observed that it is not necessary to have a visual spectacle to respond to a tragedy; we can respond just in reading it. His own theory of tragedy centered on the cognitive sources of tragic emotions, while acknowledging the impact of the visual and auditory. Most of my discussion will address the role of such things as thoughts and imaginings, and the properties of the verbal array that generates them in order to address the special challenges accounting for emotional responses to fictional literature faces. At the same time I acknowledge that some novels, relatively old (Laurence Sterne, *Tristram Shandy*) and relatively new (Michael Ende, *The Neverending Story*), incorporate visually significant elements into the text. These works expand the paradigmatic structure of a novel and border on "mixed media."

There are also strategic reasons for limiting my discussion not merely to literature, but to fictional literature in particular. One standard account of the rationality of emotions is that they are rational when one is justified in believing the cognitive component of the emotion.[9] This position in turn depends on a particular theory of emotion, namely, that having an emotion requires having a proposi-

6. See, e.g., David Best, *Feeling and Reason in the Arts* (London: Allen & Unwin, 1985).
7. See Nelson Goodman, *Languages of Art: An Approach to a Theory of Symbols* (Indianapolis: Bobbs-Merrill, 1968).
8. W. J. T. Mitchell, "Spatial Form in Literature," in W. J. T. Mitchell, ed., *The Language of Images* (Chicago: University of Chicago Press, 1974), esp. pp. 282–283, argues persuasively for the relevance of certain visual phenomena to appreciating fiction.
9. Jerome A. Shaffer argues for this position in "An Assessment of Emotion," *American Philosophical Quarterly* 20 (1983): 164. He takes support from David Hume, *A Treatise of Human Nature* II.3. iii (Oxford: Clarendon, 1888), p. 416. See also notes 12 and 13.

tional cognitive component—generally a belief—of a particular sort. For example, being afraid requires believing that one is in danger; having pity requires believing that someone is suffering serious but undeserved misfortune; and being proud requires believing that one is responsible for what one is proud of. Thus, fear would be justified when one is justified in believing that one is in danger, pity when one is justified in believing someone has suffered undeserved misfortune, and pride when one is justified in believing one has accomplished something very worthwhile. As fiction, however, literature does not have the purpose of justifying or warranting such beliefs.[10] My concentration on fiction forces an examination of the ways one can be warranted in responding emotionally or affectively which appeal to factors other than beliefs.

At one point in our philosophical history practically the only type of emotion discussed as a response to fictional literature and other works of art was an "aesthetic experience" or "aesthetic emotion." As the inadequacies of theories of aesthetic experience and aesthetic attitude became increasingly obvious, the door opened to understanding responses to literary fiction and works of art in general as akin to, if not identical with, ordinary "real-life" emotions and feelings, desires and aversions, sympathetic and empathic imaginings— rather than on a separate, rarified plane of "aesthetic experience." They could be discussed—as Plato and Aristotle discussed responses to epic, tragedy, and comedy—as pity, fear, suffering, and amusement. (I am reminded of a comment by one of my professors in graduate school, to the effect that if you study aesthetics in reverse chronological order, you at least have the appearance of progress.) As something akin to "real-life" responses, responses to fiction could then be seen as contributing to our understanding of the world and of ourselves.

---

10. I have in mind a conception of fiction as a mode of discourse, like that developed by Peter Lamarque and Stein Haugom Olsen, *Truth, Fiction, and Literature: A Philosophical Perspective* (Oxford: Clarendon, 1994). See esp. pp. 21–23.

Roger Seamon defends the view that authors can and do make assertions in fiction. See Roger Seamon, "Acts of Narration," *Journal of Aesthetics and Art Criticism* 45 (1987): 369–379. I am sympathetic with his position, but it does not affect my point, since (a) it does not follow that even if fiction contains assertions that our beliefs in them warrant responses in the same way, and (b) appropriate affective impacts of nonassertions will also need to be accounted for. Again, there may be a great deal of overlap with nonfiction. See also John W. Bender, "Art as a Source of Knowledge: Linking Analytic Aesthetics and Epistemology," in John W. Bender and H. Gene Blocker, eds., *Contemporary Philosophy of Art: Readings in Analytic Aesthetics* (Englewood Cliffs, N.J.: Prentice Hall, 1993).

But there is a "down side" to assimilating responses to fiction to "real-life" emotions. Some years ago Colin Radford argued that, contrary to popular opinion, there were good reasons to believe that emotional responses to fiction are irrational and incoherent.[11] His position depended on a cognitive theory of emotions: having an emotion requires having a belief of a particular sort. Radford proposed that either one didn't have such beliefs when responding to fiction (in which case it would follow by definition that one did not have the emotion), or one has irrational beliefs (since what one is reading is fiction) and hence irrational emotions. Various attempts have been made to respond to Radford's charges, including appeals to imagination, different sorts of beliefs, and redefinitions of emotion.

One reason philosophers have found this dilemma of continuing interest is that the problem has an intuitive appeal and not just a theoretical basis. For example, when I described this project to an acquaintance, he remarked, "It's like my daughter said when she was watching *Jaws*, 'I know the shark's only rubber, Dad, so why am I afraid?' " Such queries about the cogency of emotional and affective responses to fiction have an equally pervasive yet more virulent cousin: even if such responses aren't irrational, what is the *point*? Why bother?—it's only fiction. If you like that kind of thing, fine—but why should kids spend time in school studying it (and why should not doing well at it keep them off the honor roll), and why should adults spend their time reading fiction unless they find it particularly entertaining, like choosing to go to a movie or watch a TV show? One doesn't need to be familiar with a sophisticated theory of mind to feel the force of questions like these and the ones that Radford raised. They are challenges to those involved in literary studies, philosophy of art, and art theory; they are mounted by ordinary citizens against assertions that reading, studying, and appreciating literature has the value it has. They deserve to be addressed.

My interest in the topic of this book began with an interest in Radford's paradox, and I, like some others, believed that I had a quick and easy solution to it. But I came to realize deeper and more extensive issues were involved—not only about the nature of emotions, but about various capacities and abilities of the human mind, about the nature of appreciation, and about how judgments or assessments of emotions, as well as other affects, are possible at all. And

11. Colin Radford, "How Can We Be Moved by the Fate of Anna Karenina?" *Proceedings of the Aristotelian Society*, supp. vol. 49 (1975): 67–80.

there are questions of value. The common opinion, at least among teachers and theorists of literature, is that emotional and other affective responses to fiction are valuable and important. I believe this common opinion is right, but I also realize we are a long way from being able to explain *why* to anyone who is not already convinced. In order to do so, we need to explore how explanations and justifications of affective responses feed into an account of appreciating a work and how this relates to the value and importance of reading and appreciating fictional literature in general.

In important respects, then, this book is broader in scope than studies that explore only *emotional* responses to fiction.[12] My concerns spring not (or not merely) from the charge that emotional responses to fiction are irrational or incoherent, but from problems about how to explain and assess the appropriateness and importance of *any* affective response to fictional literature at all. Affective responses include not only emotions properly so-called (e.g., anger, fear, pity, and pride), but also moods (being melancholy, excited, contemplative, bored), desires (various attractions and aversions), and "feelings" or "affects" that include some hard-to-classify experiences (tension, uneasiness, excitement, tingles, surprise, bewilderment, anxiety). They also include affective imaginings, that is, imagining being in these states or engaging in these processes. Affective imaginings involve not merely imagining *that* someone feels anguish or distress, but imagining (what's it like to have?) the anguish or distress. These imaginings typically occur within an activity described as, for example, imagining being (or what it's like to be) a certain person or sort of person, or in a certain situation or sort of situation. Though to distinguish imagining having an emotion or feeling from actually having that emotion or feeling is a tricky business, we can at least be assured that both actual and imaginal experiences have affective components. Some drives and desires (curiosity, lust, hunger, ambition) also have an affective quality to them, as do attitudes and frames of mind (opti-

12. See, for example, the following: Bijoy H. Boruah, *Fiction and Emotion: A Study in Aesthetics and the Philosophy of Mind* (Oxford: Clarendon Press, 1988); Kendall Walton, *Mimesis as Make-Believe: On the Foundations of the Representational Arts* (Cambridge: Harvard University Press, 1990), pt. 2; Gregory Currie, *The Nature of Fiction* (Cambridge: Cambridge University Press, 1990), chap. 5. There is also a spate of articles on the topic beginning with the symposium by Colin Radford and Michael Weston, "How Can We Be Moved by the Fate of Anna Karenina?" *Proceedings of the Aristotelian Society*, supp. vol. 49 (1975): 67–93; and including Peter Lamarque, "How Can We Fear and Pity Fictions?" *British Journal of Aesthetics* 21 (1981): 291–304; William Charlton, "Feeling for the Fictitious," *British Journal of Aesthetics* 24 (1984): 206–216; and many others.

mism, hostility, wariness); and, of course, emotions or feelings may result from adopting these attitudes or frames of mind. My concern is thus with a broad range of affective components of appreciation—not just emotions properly so called, but also moods, desires, feelings, drives and attitudes or frames of mind, as well as imaginings of states that include affective components.

I see the dilemma that Radford raised about the rationality of emotional responses to fiction as only a part of this larger picture. I assimilate emotional responses to other affective responses to fiction in an effort to develop an account of their etiology, justification, and value. In the process I look to the work that has been done on this issue in aesthetics, and also consider work on emotion and other affects that has been produced in the philosophy of mind, as well as theories of justification, warrant, and assessment in general that have emerged in epistemology.[13]

One other preliminary remains to be addressed before beginning. I have used the phrase "works of fictional literature and other works of art" in connection with aesthetic experience and aesthetic emotion above. The contested character of the concept of art and the aesthetic today is obvious, and I have no interest in grounding my own views on an outmoded notion of the fine arts or the aesthetic. Indeed, to focus on literature is in a way to work on the cusp rather than with paradigm cases of art. The fine arts have not included literature other than poetry until approximately the last hundred years, and, of course, the category of the fine arts has itself been exposed as a concept that emerged in western European civilization relatively recently. The novel is datable back only to the mid–eighteenth century, significantly, about the time of the solidification of modern aesthetic theory and the identification of a set of fine arts.[14]

I am sympathetic to the view that it should not be assumed that the

13. Seminal work in philosophy of mind includes Robert M. Gordon, *The Structure of Emotions: Investigations in Cognitive Philosophy* (New York: Cambridge University Press, 1987); Ronald de Sousa, *The Rationality of Emotion* (Cambridge: MIT Press, 1987); and Patricia S. Greenspan, *Emotions and Reasons: An Inquiry into Emotional Justification* (New York: Routledge, 1988). In ethics, see Neil Cooper, *The Diversity of Moral Thinking* (Oxford: Clarendon, 1981); and Allan Gibbard, *Wise Choices, Apt Feelings: A Theory of Normative Judgment* (Cambridge: Harvard University Press, 1990). In epistemology see work by Robert Audi, John Pollock, Keith Lehrer, Hilary Kornblith, Ernest Sosa, and Alvin Plantinga, again, among many others.

14. The locus classicus of the argument for this conclusion is P. O. Kristeller, "The Modern System of the Arts," *Journal of the History of Ideas* 12 (1951): 496–527; and 13 (1952): 17–46. Notably, Greek and Latin fictional prose narratives and "romances" are often now referred to as "ancient novels."

concept of art has application in other cultural contexts, at least without serious qualification. Furthermore, to discuss virtually any verbal or material object *only* as an art object is seriously to misrepresent it.[15] I have no doubts that insistence on employing the concepts of art and the aesthetic in questionable arenas has at least de facto contributed to attitudes and beliefs that repress and discriminate on grounds of class, gender, and race. Indeed, I view the concept of art as extremely problematic and have doubts about the utility of trying to define it. I am not, however, sympathetic with the view that we should abandon the concept of art when categorizing and discussing the verbal and materials products made by a wide variety of people in a wide variety of cultures, and especially our own. What I have to say on its behalf needs to be compared with its drawbacks; until the case is made, the comparison cannot be made.

The kinds of activities I describe as involved in appreciating fictional literature are activities that would typically be described as involved in appreciating fictional literature *as works of art.* It can be argued that such activities have *instrumental value,* for instance, for enhancing one's moral awareness or personal understanding. However, I contend that it is appropriate to see such activities as, *ceteris paribus,* valuable in themselves, in a way not depending on their instrumental value. This value that they have in themselves reflects, I demonstrate, a value that is intimately connected with our identification of their sources—fictional literature—as works of art and with our belief that it is valuable to appreciate fictional literature as works of art. Thus, I intend to show that there *is* value in appreciating works of literary fiction as works of art, through an analysis of what explains and justifies affective responses to them.

The task of Part One is to *explain* affective responses to fiction, insofar as they occur as part of appreciating a work of fictional literature. In the first chapter I argue that appreciation is the exercise of an ability, or, actually, a set of abilities. Exercising these abilities requires interacting with an object—a set of written words. They are like abilities that require merely a "perceptual" interaction with an object, such as solving arithmetic problems and playing chess (skill at chess inheres in knowing what moves to make; someone else could move the pieces according to instructions). Other abilities require physical interactions

15. See my "Paintings and their Places," *Australasian Journal of Philosophy* 73 (1995): 260–268.

with an object, such as playing the piano and hitting a baseball. Still other abilities don't require interacting with an external object at all, such as saying the times tables or reciting a poem or mathematical formula from memory.

Not only does appreciation involve skilled interaction with an object, but part of what leads us to identify this activity as an ability is how one experiences the object. When you perfect your baseball swing and hit a ball well, it may be accompanied by a certain kind of feeling. Having this feeling is not part of the skill, however, even if it is coextensional with the exercise of the skill. With appreciation, on the other hand, having thoughts, feelings, and emotions when reading are part of what makes it important to identify the activity as an ability.

In Chapter 1 I distinguish elicitors—the sequence of words one has an affective response to—and conditioners—the past experiences and current psychological states or conditions that affect what one responds to and how one responds. Using this terminology makes it explicit that appreciation involves interacting with a work, in particular, the features that elicit (and some that condition) responses, not simply reacting to it. I explain elicitors and conditioners in relation to some passages from literary works and the complex affective responses that figure in appreciating them. I then discuss some of the important, salient features of appreciation in general, in particular, that it is a temporally extended activity—a process or activity—and that it incorporates the notion of success. To appreciate something is an activity the exercise of which involves a kind of achievement, in the sense of engaging in skilled activity as a process, rather than in the production of a product.

Chapter 2 explores appreciation by looking at the nature of the *desire* to appreciate a work. If appreciation is an ability or skilled activity, the desire to appreciate will be a desire to exercise that skill. That is, it is a desire *to do*, rather than a desire *that* something be the case. In the first section of Chapter 2 I examine this distinction and discuss why we need to posit the existence of two structurally different kinds of desires. Appreciation also involves the philosophically troublesome fact that one virtually never—or, at least, not often —knows what one will be doing, except in a generalized way, in exercising the ability. That is, having the desire to appreciate will typically not include having a mental representation of the particular emotions, feelings, thoughts and imaginings one has in the process of, and that are partly constitutive of, appreciation. A desire to appreciate includes a cognitive and affective involvement commonly known as "getting into it," and it also includes a reflective component, where one reflects on and assesses the relevance and appropriateness of what one has been doing, that is, the extent to which one has been exercising the skills involved in an ability to appreciate a work.

Chapters 3, 4, and 5 explore the nature of the activities involved in appreciation: as we read, our psychological condition or sensitivities to what we read next are changed. We use a capacity to shift or slide into different mental gears as we read. This shift happens to some extent automatically and to some extent intentionally, most often without our knowing what the affective consequences of the shift will be. It would be an extremely cumbersome cognitive system that required the formation of an intention or belief (about what to do) every time a cognitive subprocessing system were altered. Nevertheless, cognitive and affective shifts and slides are, to a large extent, even if indirectly, under our control: we can learn to shift gears. To this extent, then, we have control over our emotions and feelings. Without such control at some level, it wouldn't be appropriate to call appreciation an ability or skill.

Aestheticians working in the late twentieth century have the advantage and the burden of access to numerous works in philosophical psychology and philosophy of mind on the nature and "logic" of emotions, as well as on the nature of other psychological phenomena. Emotional responses to fiction, like emotions in general, cannot be understood independently of their relationships to other mental phenomena, such as beliefs, desires, sensations, qualia, reasoning, thinking, and imagination. They are also related in significant ways to the psychologically robust phenomenon of human action, as well as psychologically more dilute phenomena such as physiological and neurological change. And, of course, emotional responses to fictional literature are predicated on a sensitivity to literature itself. As a philosophical examination of affective responses to fiction, much of this book concerns what we might call aesthetic psychology and aesthetic epistemology: the nature of and warrant for responses.

Underlying most of what follows is the fundamental idea that appreciating fiction (and art in general) requires that we develop and exercise abilities to generate feelings and thoughts in systematic ways that turn out not to be our usual patterns of feeling and thought. I have found the work of Robert Gordon on mental simulation of use in explaining the nature of these processes.[16] Though Gordon uses mental simulation to develop a theory of belief ascription, I have used it to explain certain kinds of imagination, in particular, imagination as used when empathizing with fictional characters. As a model for understanding mental processes, it can help us understand what goes on when one does respond affectively to fictional literature and its similarities to what goes on when one responds to ordinary "real-life" situations. In Chapter 4 I explain how a psychological simulation effected through making mental shifts accounts for the phenomena of empathizing with fictional characters, and in Chapter 5 I deal with sympathy and other affective responses.

Part Two has to do with *assessing* emotions and other affective responses to fiction. Despite the fact that these are the most technically demanding chapters of the book, the results are admittedly only partial and inconclusive. Yet I have tried to make some headway in this very tricky area. Assessing affects—simply as affective responses, rather than in terms of a cognitive component they may have—is problematic in ways that assessing beliefs and emotions that have belief components is not. In trying to say something constructive about assessing affects, I begin by using two strategies that minimize some of the problems inherent in assessing their affective side. First, I draw on coherentist models for the assessment of beliefs, in which beliefs are assessed as members of a whole set or group of beliefs. According to coherentism, all beliefs are evaluated in light of one's other beliefs. When applied to affective responses, the implication is that responses are not assessed independently of one's other responses, but as part of a whole set of responses that, ideally, constitute appreciating a work to some degree. This way of proceeding has a singular advantage: it makes us focus less on the quality or character of, and grounds for, a single individual response, and more on a whole collection of responses which often have great complexity and subtlety as a set. Why is this an advantage? Admittedly, it makes assessing any individual response much more complicated. It has the merit, however, of reflecting the complexity of the value of appreciating fiction and the complexity actually inherent in assessing whether what one is doing is appreciating a work. It also avoids the simpleminded approach of trying to find particular features that always warrant a particular kind of response.

16. Gordon, *The Structure of Emotions*, chaps. 3 and 4.

The second strategy I have adopted to try to minimize the difficulties of assessing affects is to begin by looking at how to assess beliefs about the appropriateness, relevance, and warrantedness of a response. Such beliefs can be assessed, as per the coherentist model, as part of a network of beliefs about the appropriateness of one's responses. This focus on beliefs enables us to assess them in terms of other beliefs, as we would other beliefs according to the coherentist model.

One of the reasons this area is so tricky is that there are myriad kinds of assessments to be made, and they haven't been sorted out carefully from one another. I am, of course, concerned with assessing emotional and other affective responses to fiction with respect to their role in appreciation, which raises questions about relationships among rational, moral and aesthetic assessments. In addition, one may assess whether it is or isn't appropriate to respond at all, what kind of response is appropriate, how to justify beliefs about whether responding at all, or responding in a given way, is appropriate, and whether responses may be warranted yet inappropriate. At the risk of tedium, in Chapter 6 I delineate a number of different kinds of assessments of emotions and other affective responses to fictional literature. Part of the lesson to be learned from recognizing the variety of kinds of assessments that are possible is to understand how complex assessing emotions and other affects is. Unless we keep clear on what kind of assessment we are making, we will end up hopelessly muddled.

But assessing beliefs about anything, and especially about affective responses to fiction, merely in terms of other beliefs has its limits. Epistemically, it has been argued, beliefs ultimately need to be grounded in either experience of or facts about the world. That is, it will not do to have a network of mutually supporting and reinforcing beliefs if that network is not grounded in some kind of reality. Aesthetically, this means that our responses need to be tied in appropriate ways to the work. But what are these "appropriate ways"? What kinds of phenomena ground affective responses to fiction? Particular theories of appreciation, interpretation, and criticism provide different answers to these questions. My quest is a philosophical one, however, and relatively indifferent to the particular claims of individual theories. My question is, how is it possible for affective responses to fiction to be grounded at all—by anything? The question is not what particular features of a work ground a particular response. For this question invites a still further question: *why* do those particular phenomena ground a response, or that particular response? This query, in turn, leads to the more abstract, philosophical question: what makes it possible for responses to be grounded at all, what kinds of things provide grounding, and why?

In Chapter 7 I explain one reason for thinking responses are grounded in features of a work. This reason is not totally independent of a particular theory of appreciation, that is, it is not independent of what we should appreciate in a work. Such grounding plays an important role in the process of appreciation, given the nature of the mental skills involved in it, as explained in the first five chapters of this book, and the value of appreciation, as explained in the final chapter. Drawing on some insights of Patricia Greenspan, I argue that there is a way to ground *responding at all*, rather than not having a response.[17] I call this "passional grounding."

We are still a far cry from answering the obvious question of what warrants having one emotional or affective response to a particular passage of a work or to a work as a whole, rather than another? Why is amusement warranted in relation to a certain passage, rather than apprehensiveness? Why pity rather than fear, or sympathetic shame rather than anger? Why melancholy and ennui, rather than delight and excitement? These are all questions about what I call type warrant, that is, how particular types of emotions and affects can be warranted.

It would be nice to pawn these questions off on individual theories of interpretation or criticism. But just as there are general questions about how any individual belief can be justified, and not just questions about how this or that scientific theory lends justification to this or that belief, so also there are general questions about how any individual emotion or affect can be warranted, and not just questions about how this or that theory of interpretation or criticism might claim this or that response to be warranted. It would make things easier if we had an account of the variety of emotions and affects, their respective components, and how they are distinguished from one another, so that an account of warrant could be developed in relation to all their relevant aspects. (Recall the wide variety of affective responses involved in appreciation as described earlier.) The philosophical literature has perhaps necessarily yet unfortunately concentrated on cognitive components as the distinguishing characteristics of a fairly limited number of emotions and has consequently obscured not only

17. Greenspan, *Emotions and Reasons*, chap. 4.

their affective aspects, but also the status of affects that do not have cognitive components. Interestingly, as discussed in Chapter 8, there are notable cases where psychological research has used responses to fiction—specifically, films—to explore the potential relevance to individual emotions of noncognitive aspects. Rather than beginning with the study of "real-life" emotions and extrapolating to responses to fiction, some research has gone the other way around. Moreover, there is no available typology of affects available, and most people's affect vocabulary is pitifully inadequate. I find myself at a loss to describe most of the feelings I have when reading fiction. If one can't even identify them, how is one to defend having such feelings, as appropriate, relevant, or warranted—or defend the sensitivities that give rise to them?

The complexity of affective phenomena defy, for all practical purposes (i.e., for what counts as practical in the world of literature, the purposes of criticism), giving an account of what warrants an emotion or affect which consists in anything more than a sketch or pointer. Nevertheless, there is not a lot of background information or experience we can assume, across the board, for readers of fictional literature—especially when the literature comes from traditions that are culturally or historically unfamiliar. In addition, certain properties of what has been read earlier in a work are relevant, temporally and nontemporally, to one's responding to what one does in the way one does. Given the appeal of what I call the "simple answer fallacy" (see Chapter 6), there is a temptation to throw up one's hands and say, "Warrant doesn't even apply in the case of emotions and affects, or sensitivities." On the contrary, I believe it does apply, and I take a small step towards explaining how in Chapter 9 by utilizing a distinction between epistemic emotions and factive emotions. Admittedly, this distinction does not carry us very far in the search for warrant for particular emotions and sensitivities, what I call type warrant. However, it does explain one respect in which it can be given.

The most highly developed models we have for assessing any mental states or activities are those developed for the purpose of assessing beliefs. Virtually all of those models, however, share one feature that is ruinous to understanding how to assess affective responses to fiction: they represent justification as a *nontemporal* phenomenon. That is, the actual timing and sequencing of one's access to the world, and hence of one's past experiences, is not taken to be relevant to the justification of belief. Rather, one is to pool all the relevant evidence culled from past as well as recent experience in order to form a belief that is, rationally speaking, justified by the whole *collection* of information. Interestingly, defenses of emotional responses to fiction that rest on defending a belief in the cognitive component of an emotion play right into the nontemporal character of warrant or justification assumed by standard accounts of epistemic justification.

However, the timing and sequencing of one's access to successive portions of a literary work *are* relevant to warranting one's emotional and affective responses. This assertion is clearly true in the case of something like suspense, but the temporal character of the activity of reading makes the timing and sequencing of access to the work relevant in a much larger number of cases than one might initially think. Furthermore, once our attention is shifted to temporal rather than nontemporal factors, we can see how temporal factors change one's sensitivities to what one reads next. It is not that one acquires a batch of evidence to warrant forming new beliefs, but rather the timing and sequencing of one's experiences of what one reads warrant shifting into a different mental state or condition, that is, developing a sensitivity. Thus, assessing emotions and affects turns into assessing sensitivities, figuring out what warrants one's having the sensitivity one does, that is, what warrants one's coming to be in a mental state or condition such that one will respond in a particular way to a given state of affairs. Chapter 10 explains and defends how sensitivities can be temporally warranted. Furthermore, because temporal warrant does not necessarily depend on cognitive content, it is relevant to warranting *affects* as well as emotions.

Why does it matter whether the sensitivities that give rise to emotions and affects are warranted or not? The answer to this question is, of course, that appreciation is a skill or ability. In the process of a skilled performance, various moves must be warranted. Appreciation requires both intellectual and affective skills. One must be responsive in both ways to what one successively encounters in the environment —to what one reads. The nature of what one reads, in conjunction with beliefs and past experiences, warrants how one responds.

I explain what I conceive to be the value of learning to appreciate fictional literature, and hence of developing such skills, in Chapter 11. In short, the value is in developing a certain mental *capacity* I call affective flexibility. Whereas an ability is the power to do something, a capacity is an underlying condition that enables one to acquire, acquire more easily, or perfect an ability to a higher degree. Affective flexibility is the affective analogue of the intellectual flexibility that underwrites abilities to understand different points of view and the physical flexibility that underwrites physical abilities to perform various physical movements. Enhanced flexibility may simply be the result of adding a number of abilities to one's repertoire. But acquiring specific abilities may also alter one's condition "deeper down," so that, simply in acquiring an ability, one's capacity for acquiring, acquiring more easily, or perfecting other abilities may be enhanced. These are preconditional capacities; so too is affective flexibility.

I do believe in the value of affective flexibility, but I don't believe appreciating fictional literature is the only way to develop it. I also believe that its value should be put in perspective. Huge numbers of people throughout history have lived perfectly satisfactory lives with no appreciation of fictional literature at all, given that most of them couldn't even read. Furthermore, the extent to which people's lives have been unsatisfactory (John Stuart Mill's claims about his own life notwithstanding) is rarely directly due to the absence of their ability to appreciate fiction (or art or poetry). In light of the horrors and abuses and tragedies that people have had to suffer throughout history, reveling over the niceties of a phrase by Henry James, or the obscurities of James Joyce, or the antics of Laurence Sterne, may indeed seem like a frivolous diversion—a "let them eat cake" response to racial oppression, sexual abuse, mass starvation, and ethnic torture and genocide. Indeed, it is in part because of these realities that stressing the importance of the kinds of *aesthetic* values I do appears to be so much bourgeois callousness, an indulgence that perpetuates the denigration of people who, having been forced to live lives that are only marginally human, share the additional ignominy that they fail to appreciate fictional literature.

I cannot gainsay these points, yet they do not entail that there is no such thing as aesthetic value. Indeed, the extent to which the importance and value of being able to appreciate fiction pales in relation to these other realities manifests the extent to which we live in a seriously defective world. Any society should strive to create conditions such that its members have time, opportunity, inclination, and ability to pursue something other than the unholy triumvirate enumerated by Nelson Goodman, "survival, conquest, and gain."[18] To be in a position to debate the point—as I and the readers of this book clearly are —is to be in a position of comparative luxury and comfort. Concerns with mere survival take priority over pursuit of enhanced imaginal capacities, but it doesn't follow that the latter should be looked on as

18. Goodman, *Languages of Art,* p. 256.

lacking value. Instead, that pursuit is something that many around the world, and within our own society, are not privileged enough to enjoy. But denigration of what some people are in no position to enjoy does not show respect or support for those people. Quite the contrary: it refuses to acknowledge the importance of what they lack and thereby underappreciates how deficient their circumstances really are.

There are also those who are in fact very comfortably situated who deny the importance of appreciating fiction as works of art, at least beyond whatever potential it has for providing personal enjoyment. These are the philistines, who are bemused by the very idea that art might do something other than entertain (or participate in schemes of political repression). An adequate response to such people requires more than just a reassertion (in moving language?) of one's conviction that great literature and the arts in general have made significant contributions to (Western?) civilization and constitute the foundation of "our" cultural heritage. This book as a whole attempts to explain the kinds of mental abilities appreciating fiction employs, and the final chapter proposes a broader mental benefit from acquiring and exercising those abilities. That is, it responds to the philistine with argument.

PART ONE

EXPLANATION

Chapter One

Abilities

Ontologically, what type of phenomenon is appreciation? There are many well known ontological categories: things or objects, events, properties, facts or states of affairs, processes, activities, tasks, achievements. Unfortunately, none of these adequately captures the nature of appreciation. The task of this chapter is to explain, ontologically, what kind of phenomenon appreciation is.

One fact that complicates the ontological picture is that appreciation involves at least three components: affective (the main object of my attention), theoretical, and reflective. The theoretical component consists in interpreting a work, and the reflective component consists in reflecting on the relevance and appropriateness of and warrant for one's affective responses. Both activities can and should alter how and whether one responds to a work and what aspects of it one responds to. Their presence ensures that one is not merely *reacting* to a work, but rather *responding* to it. Affective responses that are part of appreciating a work cannot be understood apart from these other components of appreciation.

Appreciation involves, as I indicated in the introduction, "getting the value out of" something. It thus involves interacting with an external object, a verbal text, and it entails doing something successfully. What one does successfully, however, is not to produce a product or end result; one *performs an activity* successfully. Part of the essence of this activity is that it is temporally extended, in that it involves responding to sequentially presented portions of text. To appreciate fiction is to exercise abilities: the concept of ability is the ontological clue to the nature of appreciation. It accommodates the fact that appreciation involves interacting with an object (section I), that it is temporally extended (section II), and especially that it involves success (section III). In the final section I examine the ontological nature of the particular sort of ability that appreciation is in more detail.

I: Abilities, Objects, and Elicitors

Exercising some abilities requires physically interacting in certain ways with one or more external objects. Bowling, hitting a baseball, playing the piano, and making a pot on a potter's wheel are all such abilities. Other abilities, however, do not require physically interacting with an external object, but require instead that one be able to move, or not move, one's own body in certain ways, such as the ability to do a backbend, headstand, or cartwheel. Still other abilities require neither specific physical movements nor physical interaction (as opposed to perceptual acquaintance) with an external object. These include the ability to play chess or solve randomly presented math problems. In these cases, an "output system" is needed to communicate the result of one's deliberations or the contents of one's memory, but the ability to play chess is quite independent of having the physical ability to move the chess pieces around (someone else could move the chess pieces according to your instructions), and the answers to math questions can be delivered orally, in writing, or in Morse code. A final set of abilities requires no acquaintance with an external object at all, either physical or perceptual, beyond any acquaintance needed to acquire the abilities in the first place. Such abilities include the ability to go through the "times tables," recite a memorized poem, make puns, or calculate the day of the week for any month, day, and year one might think up.

The ability to appreciate a work of fiction falls into the third set of abilities: it requires perceptual acquaintance with an external object, a literary work, without requiring physical action or interaction with it.[1] In the case of fiction, the object consists of a set of inscriptions that need to be interpreted. No physical interaction is necessary, but men-

---

1. Some of what I say here is anticipated in Harold Osborne, *The Art of Appreciation* (New York: Oxford University Press, 1970), chap. 1. On skills, see also James D. Wallace, *Virtues and Vices* (Ithaca: Cornell University Press, 1978), chap. 2. Cf. Stein Haugom Olsen, *The End of Literary Theory* (Cambridge: Cambridge University Press, 1987), pp. 121–137.

tal interactions—both cognitive and affective—are involved. The extent of one's ability to appreciate depends, in part, on how one is able to interact mentally with the relevant kinds of objects.

Here is the first stumbling block to understanding emotional and other affective responses to fiction and their role in appreciation: interpretation. Emotions and affects are often considered part of interpretation: one doesn't interpret and then respond, but rather one reads with feeling. The import of a work and the significance of a particular passage may reside partly in the affective component of experience, not just in its "meaning" or cognitive component. Unfortunately, this fact tends to fuse the ontology of appreciation, on the one hand, with the ontology of interpretation, on the other. This fusion, in turn, tends to blind one to the distinctive characteristics of appreciation. Interpretation and appreciation are ontologically dissimilar; these dissimilarities are explored in section III. In this section I examine a feature they share: they both involve interaction between a reader and a set of inscriptions.

Given that appreciation involves (at least) a perceptual interaction between a reader and an object (i.e., a set of inscriptions), how does one characterize that relationship? When responses occur in response to particular portions of a text, the particular portion of the text one responds to *elicits* the response. A variety of factors, such as one's current psychological state or condition, memories of past experiences, beliefs and background knowledge will *condition* one's responses. Conditioners—these states and conditions of the individual doing the reading and appreciating—affect both how one responds and what one responds to.

Consider a response I had the first time I read a particular passage of *To the Lighthouse* by Virginia Woolf. The passage appears about two-thirds of the way through the novel and is enclosed, as here, in square brackets: "[Mr. Ramsay, stumbling along a passage one dark morning, stretched his arms out, but Mrs. Ramsay having died rather suddenly the night before, his arms, though stretched out, remained empty.]"[2] I read this passage with surprise. The book had not provided any hint that Mrs. Ramsay, one of the most significant characters in the novel—perhaps *the* most significant character—was going to die. And then, information about her death is inserted by-the-by in a minor clause of a sentence that is actually about something else

2. Virginia Woolf, *To the Lighthouse* (New York: Harcourt, Brace & World, 1927), p. 194.

—well, some*one* else, *Mr.* Ramsay, of course! The sentence appeared
on the top of the left-hand page, so I flipped back to see if I had
mistakenly turned two pages at once, exhibiting my incredulity that
she would die so suddenly (and, as it were, parenthetically). In this
context "incredulity" captures an affect, a certain feeling I have, a
sort of mental resistance to accepting something I believe I have good
reason to accept. Skimming back over the text, I discovered I hadn't
missed a page—that was the first time her mortality was mentioned.

For the sake of argument, let us agree that surprise and incredulity
are appropriate responses to this particular passage. But what exactly
is it that I respond to? It is, minimally, the particular phrase, "Mrs.
Ramsay having died rather suddenly the night before" (though, maxi-
mally, it might be the whole sentence). The phrase, or perhaps the
sentence, elicited the response. The elicitor is the *linguistic unit* to
which one responds. Elicitors may be of varying magnitudes: a single
word, a phrase, a segment of a sentence, a whole sentence, or perhaps
an entire (relatively short) paragraph. The limitations on what can
count as an elicitor are the limitations on what can occupy the "phenomenal present," that is, whatever can be experienced as a single
entity or unit. It should not be assumed that everyone has the same
capacities for taking in some extended passage as a unit or even that
it remains the same for a person at all times. What one has the ability
to perceive as a single unit affects one's capacity to appreciate some
works. Further, what does in fact elicit a response—that particular
unit of language—may or may not end up counting as an aesthetically
or artistically significant feature of the work. Just as the letter sequence "cat" may not be a semantically significant unit of the word
"catatonic" (but it may be significant in the context of a pun), a given
bounded sequence of letters or words may not be aesthetically or
artistically significant in a work of fiction.

Experiences do not come divided up into discrete chunks, arising
out of easily definable sets of verbal stimuli. At least, this is not how
experience is *experienced.* But letters and words are discrete units and
are "accessed" by reading during fairly clearly specifiable periods of
time. It does not follow from the fact that what elicits the response is
a discretely identifiable chunk of prose that one's response will be a
discretely identifiable chunk of experience. The effects of a quite
specific thing may be vague and amorphous; they will leech into other
experiences and be affected by prior experiences. It will prove important to understanding appreciation to be able both to point to the

source or generator of the experience and to describe the character and process of experiencing the work.

As small a unit as a single word may elicit a response. Even a single letter can constitute a significant unit and clearly does so with much poetry. Since letters are the smallest unit of (alphabetic) language, they are the smallest conceivable units that could be elicitors in works of fiction. However, what constitutes a significant unit in so-called "mixed media" works, such as concrete poetry and some novels, can include things other than units of language, such as the shapes of (parts of) letters, their spatial relationships to one another on the page, and so on. What constitutes aesthetic or artistic significance in a unit of language will of course differ with different inscriptional systems, such as those employed by Chinese as opposed to alphabetic languages. My examples in this book will all be from alphabetic languages and primarily though not always in English.

Speaking of English, I suppose it's a cheap trick to choose as an example of a word that is an elicitor one that is not only used but actually mentioned and singled out for discussion, but it does have the advantage of being a relatively clear-cut case. Harriet Doerr's 1978 Booker Prize–winning novel, *Stones for Ibarra,* is a tale of a San Francisco couple's self-transplantation to a remote village in Mexico, as they retrace a great-aunt's steps, and embrace that great-aunt's dreams. In describing how the people in the village of Ibarra viewed the couple, Doerr writes, "At last the village found a word that applied to the North Americans. It was a long word, *mediodesorientado,* meaning half disoriented."[3] It is significant that the villagers didn't already have a readily available word to apply to their visitors. The *mediodesorientación* was not only experienced by the couple from San Francisco, but the couple's presence engendered the condition in the inhabitants as well. In the text, the word is, of course, in Spanish, and its obvious English kin assures that when we read it we ourselves are (only) half-disoriented.

This occurrence of the word may produce a mild case of what it describes, which is also a major theme of the work, the multifarious embodiments of *mediodesorientación.* Many of them are cases where we might not even notice the slightly skewed perspective, such as the reference to the San Francisco couple as North Americans. But notice also the various manifestations of *mediodesorientación* in the following

3. Harriet Doerr, *Stones for Ibarra* (New York: Viking Penguin, 1978), p. 24.

passage, "Every day for a month Richard has reminded Sara, 'We mustn't expect too much.' And each time his wife has answered, 'No.' But the Evertons expect too much. They have experienced the terrible persuasion of a great-aunt's recollections and adopted them as their own. They have not considered that memories are like corks left out of bottles. They swell. They no longer fit."[4] This passage describes several waves of *mediodesorientación*. The Evertons become half-disoriented not only because they are immersed in an alien cultural milieu but also because of the way their own minds behave. There is conflict between their expectations or inclinations to believe and their knowledge of the likelihood their beliefs will be inaccurate; there is conflict between what is apparently memory (which is supposed to be our record of the past) whose influence they feel and the fact that they know it cannot be relied on.

Entire sentences can function as elicitors. Sentences, paradigmatically—that is, according to textbook definitions—contain "a single, complete thought," and the punctuation that defines the boundaries of a sentence can also define the boundaries of the expression and context of the thought. However, Gabriel García Márquez's *The Autumn of the Patriarch* furnishes an idea of what lies *beyond* the limits of what can be elicited by a sentence considered as a unit. The novel is written in a highly idiosyncratic style, with sentences often extending for ten to twenty pages and with the final chapter consisting of only a single sentence. These sentences, as you might expect, do not contain merely a single complete thought. Indeed, it's not clear they contain any complete thoughts, but rather numerous ideas and thought fragments. Moreover, from phrase to phrase there are shifts with respect to speaker and point of view which express conflicting attitudes in rapid succession. The learned "rule" that a sentence is supposed to express "a single thought," and the common experience of any given sentence expressing only the thought of a single person or from a single point of view affect (condition) our responses to these sentences as we (automatically) try to compact the minutely articulated but varied content into a single experienced present. We cannot do it, at least I cannot, and I suspect García Márquez does not expect us to be able to. But the sentences create a tension between what we are impelled to do and what we can achieve, as well as between the horrors recounted within the prose and the leveling of the emotional surface

4. Doerr, *Stones for Ibarra*, p. 3.

by the equal treatment given to conflicting and competing states of consciousness.[5]

Punctuation marks, as well as typographical features such as italics and spatial isolation such as indentation, typically function as cues for picking out significant units of a text.[6] Responses to *The Autumn of the Patriarch* are complex: they depend on our having internalized the understanding that we are dealing with a single sentence and all that traditionally represents, but they also depend on our *in*ability to integrate all we read within that sentence into a coherent thought or even a coherent set of thoughts. The novel is partly about language, about how language is used to tell stories, about how our experiences are affected by the language we use to tell the stories, as well as about the eponymous patriarch. Punctuation clearly does not define the elicitor in this case. Indeed, one reason for the disturbing character of the prose is that we are not given the usual cues for picking out what is an aesthetically or artistically significant unit of the text; that is, a unit we can respond to *as* a unit. The limits of the unit are de facto established by the arbitrary limits of the phenomenal present, though also by certain phrasings and recognitions that there has been a shift in point of view. The arbitrariness of the unit and shifts in point of view are features of García Márquez which make him a postmodernist author —his subversion of the usual conventions for experiencing a work as a unity, with a "logical" set of relations among its (identifiable) parts.

Elicitors are identified only with respect to their boundaries and what Nelson Goodman calls "correctness of spelling."[7] Sameness of spelling is at least a necessary condition for reidentification of a given elicitor. What one responds to is a part of the world, namely, a particular inscription of a unit of language. What one reads is the inscription, not something in one's own mind (though it may be transformed by one's own mind), and not something created in the reading (although there may be great variations in how one reads and in what one reads it *as* being or saying).

5. See discussions by George R. McMurray, *Gabriel García Márquez* (New York: Ungar, 1977), pp. 130–136; and by Regina Janes, *Gabriel García Márquez: Revolutions in Wonderland* (Columbia: University of Missouri Press, 1981), chap. 5.

6. See Part Two for a discussion of what warrants responding to a particular linguistic construct as a unit, i.e., what warrants one's responding to that particular elicitor.

7. *Languages of Art: An Approach to a Theory of Symbols* (Indianapolis: Bobbs-Merrill, 1968), pp. 131–135. Also Nelson Goodman and Catherine Z. Elgin, *Reconceptions in Philosophy and Other Arts and Sciences* (Indianapolis: Hackett, 1988), chap. 3, esp. pp. 58–59.

Elicitors are also to be identified in ways that allow different people, or the same people at different times, to respond to the same linguistic unit in different ways. A complete, non-question-begging specification of the features to which one responds will never entail that there is only one possible way that a normal adult human being might respond or react. (If one grants the admissibility of multiple interpretations, as I do, a complete, non-question-begging specification of the elicitor will not entail there is only one way one is supposed to respond.) This observation would not even bear stating except for the great temptation to explain the fact that two people have different responses or reactions to a work by alleging that they are responding or reacting to different qualities, aspects, or features of it. This may be the case, but there is no reason to suppose that it must be so. The error is to equate the fact that how one responds or reacts may be affected by, say, past experiences or memories (i.e., conditioners), with the idea that what one is responding to is to be identified in part by these past experiences or memories.

Admittedly, we do say such things as, "I'm responding to the fact that I've read so much of this sort of thing before," or "I'm responding to difficulties I've had with the sorts of people described in the novel," but the point is more clearly and accurately made by saying that these past experiences are influencing how I respond to this here now. Past experiences, including "real life" encounters as well as what one has read and what one remembers of both, may influence how I respond to something here and now, as well as whether I respond to this or that aspect of my current environment. In other words, one responds to a portion of a novel or short story at a given time, even though one's responses no doubt will be and ought to be affected by what one has already read in the work, as well as by its relationships to other works of literature, one's past experiences, and general knowledge.

Another example should help illustrate the contrast between elicitors and conditioners. The phrase "the host of the beast" occurs repeatedly in Heinrich Böll's *Billiards at Half-Past Nine*, and it comes to have a haunting effect, with an accompanying sense of mystery and horror. The effect is due in part to understanding the Satanic implications of "the beast" in *Revelation* 13, where "the beast" is described as rising out of the sea, cursing God, fighting against God's people, and as eventually worshiped by all people on earth. In addition, understanding of the host as the consecrated bread and wine of the Eucharist, the sacrament commemorating the Last Supper, or communion, as well as background knowledge about a contrasting phrase also provided in the text, "the lamb of God," will likely affect how one responds to the phrase, "the host of the beast," and whether one responds to it at all. These associations link the phrase "the host of the beast" with a sense of ritual, mystery, and horror, and its repetition encourages mantralike and mystical allusions that are reinforced every time the phrase is used. The phrase elicits affective responses at different points in the novel; a slightly different response, or responses of different intensities, will likely be elicited each time one reads it, due to repetition and of course the altered contexts in which each occurrence of the phrase appears. (The repetition—the fact that the phrase has been used previously in the book—is part of what constitutes that altered context.) Our capacity to respond differentially to different occurrences of the same word or phrase may in this way be crucial to appreciating a novel or other fictional work.

In summary, then, elicitors of a response, what one responds to, are different from (1) one's past experiences and activities, and from (2) one's current psychological states or conditions—such as beliefs, memories, and sensitivities. (1) and (2) are conditioners; they affect how one responds to a given elicitor, *whether* one responds to a given unit of language, and what (the "boundaries" of the elicitor are that) one responds to.

II: Appreciation as a Temporally Extended Activity

Here is an obvious fact: reading takes time. It takes time not merely in the obvious sense that it takes a while to bring it all off, as it takes time to solve a math problem, or paint the living room, or get a haircut. Rather, reading takes time in the sense that it requires responding *sequentially* to a number of things, in the way that it takes time to see a film, listen to a piece of music, or play a game of monopoly. One progresses through a novel sequentially, and readers are only gradually exposed to various structural features, plot developments, and revelations of character. It is a mistake to think of this as an unfortunate fact of life that we just have to put up with when we read, as if things would be so much better if the whole novel could be presented to us all at once. It is essential to the nature of reading that it is a temporally extended activity.

Nothing significant would be lost if we could solve the math problem, paint the room, or get the haircut instantaneously. It is a certain product or result that we want, and for many of us, the quicker we achieve the result the better. But when listening to a piece of music, we don't want to hear all the notes at once,[8] nor do we want to see all the frames of a film at the same time.[9] The idea is not to get it over with as quickly as possible. Similarly, something significant would be lost if we were to be presented, *per impossible*, with the fictional work all at once. The fact that reading takes time structures the very possibilities inherent in (and the values of) our involvement with and experience of the medium—in short our appreciation of it.

Affective responses to a work occur within the "real time" it takes to read it and within sequentially different limitations on and expansions of our access to information about the work and what it contains. Any account of how we do respond to different aspects of a work in appreciating it (and how we ought to or shouldn't respond to appreciate it) will have to do so in light of these facts. The conditions of "real time" and limited access restrict what may affect or inform (and what may reasonably be expected to affect or inform) one's response at any given point. What happens in a novel after the point I have reached in my reading is not available to me at the time, and I cannot (reasonably be expected to) take it, or the relationships between it and what I am reading now, into account when I respond.[10] Some of the significance of aspects of the writing and of what is being said may not even be revealed until later on in the novel or short story, and I may not have any reason to believe, at the time, that they are significant. We may at a given point in our reading have reason to believe that certain aspects are significant, or significant in certain ways, when in fact they are not. Hence, pressures of "real time" and limited information can also broaden the basis on which we respond

8. This example was stolen from a quip by Dennis Stampe.

9. Hiroshi Sugimoto has taken a series of photographs of old theaters in which the exposure time of the photograph is the same as the length of a specific film projected in each theater. The screen comes out solid white and the rest of the theater is dimly lit by the film.

10. I am speaking here of first-time readers, and I will continue to make such readers my focus. See Matei Calinescu's stimulating critique of Roman Ingarden's "classical paradigm" of reading as having a "linear and irreversible temporal perspective," in *Rereading* (New Haven: Yale University Press, 1993), pp. 34–39. Calinescu argues that *re*reading, rather than reading, should be given normatively privileged status. If reading is taken to be uninterrupted, undertaken at a single sitting, and of uniform speed, then there is indeed a problem with taking reading as the ideal for appreciation. But reading, on my account, also includes reflection and some reconsideration and perhaps even rereading of certain passages. Thus, my emphasis is on the first-time reader rather than on some idealized model of reading.

beyond the boundaries of what actually turns out to be significant. These later discoveries constitute some of the delights of reading, some of the surprises, and at times, some of the disappointments. Finally, with any reasonably complex work, there is a lot more to what I read than I am capable of assimilating and perhaps even noticing when I read it. Appreciating certain aspects may even preclude our appreciating others at the same time or during the same reading.[11] Squeezing everything we can out of each sentence before going on to the next one also takes time, and affective responses will likely be constricted if not altogether extinguished by such obsessiveness.

We lose a sense of the importance of reading and of appreciating what we read if the only experiences we are willing to validate are the experiences of those who have repeatedly read and studied a work. My remarks in the previous paragraph are made with first-time readers in mind, and I will continue to make such readers the focus of my attention. We need not spend our whole life studying Henry James in order to appreciate *anything* about his novels (and if we do need to spend a lifetime at it, why should people who do other things with their lives bother to read Henry James at all?). Ignoring the sort of appreciation that first-time readers enjoy in favor of the appreciative experiences of those who study and read a work repeatedly is one manifestation of a professionalized view of appreciation, the danger of which is to lose sight of the importance of appreciation for nonprofessionals.[12] I concentrate on first-time readers to try to avoid the kinds of biases that creep in with a more professionalized view of appreciation. One of these biases is a tendency to "flatten out" access to information about the text, a tendency to see the reading of every sentence as informed by knowledge of what appears in the text, both before and after.

The understanding of reading as a temporally extended activity and of appreciation as necessarily extending through and over time

11. We come to be attuned to various kinds of differences as we acquire reasons for believing those differences have significance. For instance, consider the process called "normalization" when learning to understand a spoken or written language. We tend to overlook phonemic distinctions in a foreign language we don't yet know when they are not semantically significant in our own language, even if they are semantically significant in that language.

12. Though the amount of information and experience available to scholars is clearly greater, I believe that the basic principles at work remain the same. Whether there are values scholar/professionals derive from reading fiction that are different in kind rather than in degree from those we expect to accrue to nonprofessional readers is not an issue I address in this book.

competes with a product-oriented view of appreciation. The product-oriented view is that there is a resultant product, "an appreciation," that is produced only after sufficient involvement with the total work. The desire to sum everything up in what we might call "an appreciation" is a compelling one and explains our tendency to see anything short of a complete, correct understanding or experience of a work as a failure to appreciate it. But this view is surely mistaken: appreciation admits of degrees. It admits of degrees not merely in the sense that an experience may have more or fewer good-making qualities (e.g., richer, more informed, more perceptive, more imaginative) but in the sense that we may appreciate some aspects—at some points in time—but not others. Because of the temporally extended nature of the activity, we can talk about our responses at given points in time, to that with which we are presented (the elicitors) at that or some previous point in time. Reading fiction is more like playing a game of tennis than solving a math problem, in that reading and playing can be assessed differently at different points in time, depending on how we respond to that with which we are presented at a given point in time. However, reading and playing tennis are different in that with tennis there is a kind of "product"—winning or losing—that is different from the process of playing. We may play badly and still win, or play well and still lose. But appreciation has no such product; its value lies, to borrow a metaphor, in "how you play the game."

Recognizing that appreciation is a particular sort of temporally extended activity is a beginning, but we need to know more about appreciation than this. In particular, appreciation also entails a kind of success. Highlighting differences between appreciation and interpretation helps reveal this feature of appreciation more clearly.

III: Appreciation Involves Success

It is not easy to state the differences between appreciation and interpretation. Neither is merely a passive reception on the part of the reader of what is "really there"; both require a reader's active involvement. Both take time to develop. Both admit of degrees: one can have a more or less encompassing interpretation or appreciation, or interpret or appreciate different aspects of a work. Both can carry implications about a work's value: the interpretive claim that a given passage is not flat and boring but subtly expressive implies praise, just as an appreciation of its subtle expressiveness (experiencing it as subtly expressive rather than as flat and boring) involves experiencing this particular good-making characteristic. Finally, both seem to admit a process/product distinction, at least grammatically: one can engage in a process of interpreting or appreciating a work, or one can come up with "a product," an interpretation or an appreciation of a work.

Are these apparent similarities real? Though both interpretation and appreciation may contain normative implications, the notion that one has *succeeded* in doing something is built into the concept of appreciation in a way it is not built into the concept of interpretation. There is no such thing as a "misappreciation," something that is an appreciation but incorrect or inappropriate; there are only failures to appreciate. But a misinterpretation is still an interpretation. Neither "to interpret" nor "an interpretation" entails that one "gets it right," or even that one hasn't gotten it wrong (whatever one's account of "getting it right," or whatever one's view about whether there is more than one way to "get it right").[13] Some other modifier must be added to indicate how successful one's interpretive efforts are. Exactly which words should be used to describe success when interpreting a work is a subject of much debate. If one admits multiple interpretations, "true," "right," and "correct" (and their contrasts, "false," "wrong," and "incorrect") seem too restrictive; "relevant," "permissible," and "satisfactory" indicate too minimal an accomplishment; "imaginative," "interesting," "plausible," and "fruitful" don't necessarily imply that one "got it right."[14]

An interpretation is a product, something one can have, hold on to, summarize, and communicate to others. This product can be written up in a book and is subject to the preceding sorts of evaluative

13. Talk of "getting it right" and what is "really" there is not intended to exclude the possibility of multiple interpretations. They can be handled by saying that the properties a work "really" has are relativized to a perspective, point of view, or interpretative strategy that yields one of the acceptable interpretations. See my "Incompatible Interpretations of Art," *Philosophy and Literature* 6 (1982): 133–146. A view such as William Empson's in *Seven Types of Ambiguity* (New York: New Directions 1966), that appreciation involves apprehending the relationships among "levels" of meaning is really a single interpretation view. A "complete" appreciation, on this view, requires that one understands all the various ambiguities in the work, and that one responds in light of that understanding. The ambiguities do not support alternative interpretations but are recognized to exist within a single interpretation.

14. I tend to prefer the term "appropriate," but that's not the issue here. It is, however, no accident that I chose the same term to pick out the sorts of responses (e.g., disgust but not amusement) that figure in appreciating a given work. See Chapter 2 and "Incompatible Interpretations of Art."

judgments. An appreciation, despite grammatical appearances, is not a product, not a result of (much less an evidentially warranted conclusion on the basis of) what was gained through a process. The activity of appreciating a fictional work does not lead to a separable product, it is constitutive of it. Judgments of success or failure do not describe a separable product, but how (well) one performed during the process.

The fact that appreciation entails success in a way that interpretation does not reaffirms differences between the way interpreting a work and appreciating a work take time. Interpretation takes time in the way solving a math problem, painting a room, or getting a haircut takes time. Interpretation takes time because it deals with something sufficiently complex that one cannot take it in, or accomplish it, all at once. The time it takes to develop an interpretation is the time it takes to gather relevant data and put them together into a meaningful picture or account of the whole. The time-consuming nature of interpretation is also secured by the fact, if it is a fact, that interpretations are "deep," in Arthur Danto's sense; that is, they derive in part from factors that are not apparent on a work's surface.[15] The difficulty of access to the totality of what is being interpreted makes interpretation something it takes time to do, because one must think beyond the surface qualities of what is presented.

Any relevant information in the whole work or about its literary or cultural context is fair game for interpretation, as may be information about the course literature takes after it is written. One might plausibly say that readers are simply not justified in committing themselves to an interpretation, that is, in endorsing one interpretation or another, until they have read the whole work and have acquired sufficient background information about it and understanding of it (which may itself require significant amounts of rereading) that bear on its interpretation, no matter how plausible other interpretations may seem (or how justified readers are in tentatively accepting them, say, as a working hypothesis) before their researches are over. However, it is quite implausible to hold such a position about appreciation, as is especially clear with respect to the emotional or affective responses,

---

15. Arthur C. Danto, "Deep Interpretation," in *The Philosophical Disenfranchisement of Art* (New York: Columbia University Press, 1986): 47–67. I understand this notion of interpretation to be compatible with Annette Barnes's account of interpretation in *On Interpretation: A Critical Analysis* (Oxford and New York: Basil Blackwell, 1988). I assume that it is this sense of "deep interpretation" to which Susan Sontag objects in her famous essay "Against Interpretation," in *Against Interpretation and Other Essays* (New York: Dell, 1961).

moods, imaginings, and vague feelings that are partly constitutive of appreciation. If responsible readers had to wait for the results of all these interpretive researches before they responded, they would virtually never respond at all.

One factor that confuses our understanding of appreciation is the fact that appreciation involves interpretation. Insofar as appreciation involves interpretation, it inherits interpretation's characteristics as essentially nontemporal and product-oriented. Interpreting a work is something we are to do during the process of reading, and the adequacy and cogency of our interpretation, the product (the interpretation, even if it is partial) we have produced at any given point in time, will affect the character of our experience of the work. What, then, of the foregoing claim that we would not be justified in endorsing a given interpretation until we had engaged in a fair amount of rereading and research? If appreciation *depends on* interpretation, so that interpretations are developed during the process of appreciation, as they surely seem to be, doesn't this require that we judge appreciation by the more stringent requirements that apply to interpretation?

During the process of reading, a person comes to have various beliefs, or hypotheses, about the characters and events in a novel and their significance. One also develops beliefs about why the tale is being told the way it is and how that affects the meaning, or significance, of the work. If these sorts of beliefs and at least some of the thinking and speculating that goes into developing them are part of developing an interpretation, then developing an interpretation constitutes part of appreciating a work. This assertion doesn't require that one judge appreciation by the same standards that one judges interpretations—meaning by "interpretations" the *final products* of one's inquiries about the meaning and significance of a work and its parts. It may mean, however, that judgments about what is reasonable to believe about a work's meaning and significance at various times during the reading will affect whether experiences and responses affected by those beliefs count as appreciating a work.

I have so far argued that, considered as an ability, appreciation involves a temporally extended, sequential interaction with an object and that it involves success. Let us look more closely now at the nature of the ability to appreciate.

IV: Exercising Abilities

Gilbert Ryle's well-known distinction between tasks and achievements
might initially seem helpful in characterizing the ontological status of
appreciation. Appreciating a work of fictional literature would seem
to be an achievement, since it entails success. Achievements and failures are correlative; one's identification of something as an achievement or failure is essentially normative, involving an evaluative
judgment. But, according to Ryle, with an achievement "some state
of affairs obtains over and above that which consists in the performance, if any, of the subservient task activity." [16] But this characteristic
is precisely what I have claimed appreciation lacks: there is no product "over and above" the performance of the constituent activities. As
Ryle points out, "It is a consequence of this general point [i.e., that
achievements involve a state of affairs over and above the performance of subservient task activities] that it is always significant,
though not, of course, always true, to ascribe a success partly or
wholly to luck." [17] Because the product that is achieved is separable
from the process or task undertaken in achieving it, the achievement
can, in principle (however unlikely in practice), occur through luck.
But this possibility is definitely not true of appreciation: the process
and the product cannot be separated in this way. One cannot end up
with "an appreciation" of a literary work "by luck"; one has to go
through the appropriate processes, since the appreciating occurs in
those processes.

That one does not and cannot achieve a desired product "by luck"
is in general true of exercises of ability when exercising an ability
involves going through a particular process rather than ending up
with a particular product. The extent to which one achieves a goal by
luck is precisely the extent to which ability has not been used; luck
and ability constitute alternative explanations of how a desirable result is achieved. Luck is beside the point when the point—the desired
objective—is to exercise ability. Similarly, the point is not to come up
with something—product, effect, or result—that, it turns out, can
only be acquired by developing certain abilities, as when developing
an ability of a certain sort is the only avenue for achieving a given
result. For then the ability would still be a means to the production or
acquisition of the separable product.

16. Ryle, *The Concept of Mind* (New York: Harper & Row, 1949), p. 150.
17. Ryle, *Concept*, p. 150.

Ryle's account of achievements does not adequately characterize appreciation, but what about his account of tasks? His notion of tasks that are serial performances comes closest. A serial performance is one "the execution of which requires continued application; doing the second step requires having done the first step."[18] Furthermore, these stages do not necessarily bear the relationship of means to ends but, as Ryle delicately and somewhat mysteriously puts it, "some other relation": "We do not eat the first course in order to eat the second, or begin to hum a tune in order to finish humming it."[19] These fit the notion of temporally extended activities that are not identified by the production of a separable product, but Ryle's account falls notably short of what it is to exercise an *ability*. Ryle says that with a nonsudden task, such as a serial performance, what is crucial is that one is, for example, "ready to perform step three when the occasion arises."[20] But what is it, what internal condition of the organism, makes it the case that one is ready to perform that step? There needs to be some explanation why some people sometimes are in that state and others aren't. Having the ability can ensure that one is in, crudely put, the right psychological states at the right time to do the right thing. Ryle's failure to allow a place for internal, psychological explanations of exercises of abilities makes his account inadequate.[21]

Ryle was concerned primarily to combat the view that "knowing what you are doing" involves doing two things, doing it and being consciously aware of your doing it. On this point I am in sympathy with him. However, Ryle was also sufficiently under the thrall of behaviorism that he avoided internal psychological explanations even when they were necessary. Explanations of abilities, "knowing how,"

18. Ryle, *Concept*, p. 176.
19. Ryle, *Concept*, p. 176.
20. Ryle, *Concept*, p. 177. Ryle is here actually addressing the issue of what it is to "have in mind" what is to be done next when one is engaged in a task. To have it in mind, Ryle holds, is simply to be in the relevant dispositional state. Though his focus in this passage is a little different from mine, I don't think I am misrepresenting his views.
21. Ryle, *Concept*, p. 25: "I try to show that when we describe people as exercising qualities of mind, we are not referring to occult episodes of which their overt acts and utterances are effects; we are referring to those overt acts and occurrences themselves." Many of my ideas about dispositional explanations (e.g., as expressed in Chapter 3) owe a debt to chap. 2 and chap. 6, secs. 4 and 5, of Ryle's *Concept of Mind*. However, the essential role of internal mechanisms to the view I advance in Chapter 3 is very much at odds with Ryle's and other predominantly behaviorist approaches. Though behaviorism is not in vogue in general, it is tempting with respect to the concept of ability, i.e., when having an ability is analyzed in terms of overt success rate rather than as an internal psychological condition.

need to be given in terms of the internal psychological states and conditions that enable the behavioral accomplishments, which overt accomplishments (the results that could be produced by ability or by luck) in turn provide the observable evidence, even if the evidence were never absolutely conclusive, for attributing abilities to people.

Appreciation entails success, though appreciation is not an achievement in Ryle's sense of entailing a separable product. What is in fact an achievement in Ryle's sense is having an ability. To have an ability is to be in a special kind of psychological state or condition that enables one to accomplish certain things with a certain degree of reliability and success. The "separable product" is the psychological condition, having an ability. It could be obtained, in principle, by luck —some people seem to be "born with it"—but others have to acquire it. Mozart was clearly born with a psychological condition that made it a lot easier to compose and perform music. And it may indeed be that some people are born with a sort of mind that makes it harder, or easier, for them to appreciate fiction.

Having an ability is different from exercising that ability. Having an ability is a psychological condition that enables one to perform with some degree of success, and when one exercises that ability it necessarily follows that one has performed with some degree of success. One may fail to use the ability one has and hence not succeed, or not succeed to the extent of one's ability. It is only when one has an ability—only when one has made that achievement (by hard work and/or partly by luck)—that one can exercise it. That appreciating fiction is something one can have an ability to do is commonly brought out explicitly by speaking of whether one is *able* to appreciate individual works or works of certain kinds. To be able to appreciate contemporary South American fiction, or *One Hundred Years of Solitude*, or eighteenth-century picaresque novels, or *Tom Jones*, is (in part) to be able to have (appropriate) responses to (significant features of) works of that kind.

Kendall Walton has argued that "appreciation of representational works of art is primarily a matter of participation [in authorized games of make-believe]."[22] "Participation in a game" captures the idea of appreciation as a temporally extended activity in the right sense, that is as engaging in a process rather than orienting towards the production of a product. In Walton's view, as in mine, affective

---

22. Kendall Walton, *Mimesis as Make-Believe: On the Foundations of the Representational Arts* (Cambridge: Harvard University Press, 1990), p. 213.

responses occur as a part of that process. In addition, to characterize appreciation as requiring participation in an *authorized* game of make-believe captures a sense in which it involves success, for not just any game of make-believe readers play with fictional literature constitutes appreciating it.

I do think, however, that the characterization of appreciation as an "authorized game"—with certain principles or rules of the game that readers implicitly accept when they respond to fiction—is less than ideal. Partly, it fosters the impression that there is a product akin to winning that constitutes appreciative success, whereas the success of appreciation is the extent to which one exercises abilities in a temporally extended way. Moreover, the *degree* or extent of one's ability is not a matter of acting according to rules: it is not the case that the greater one's ability, the more one abides by the rules. In understanding, psychologically, the ability to appreciate a work of fiction, it is no more illuminating to say one is following rules (i.e., one is playing an authorized game of make-believe), than it is to say that in being good at bowling one is following rules. To be able to play a game well is not simply to learn to follow the rules; it is to function successfully while following the rules. How successful that functioning is constitutes the degree of one's ability to play a game. But there is no separation in Walton's view between playing an authorized game of make-believe in relation to fiction and playing the game well.

Ontologically, what sort of thing is appreciation? It is an ability, specifically, an ability requiring a perceptual interaction with an external object, where inscriptions need to be interpreted. It is an ability necessarily involving temporally extended activity. There is no separately identifiable product of the ability, but it is manifested by the nature of our mental engagement with a text. In the following chapter I examine the attitude that underwrites this engagement.

Chapter Two

Desires to Do

In this chapter I propose that there is, psychologically, a structural difference between two types of desires, "desires that" and "desires to do." Desires *that* are, simply, desires that some state of affairs obtains. They include such desires as the desire that the plumber arrives as scheduled, that I get to Lawrence without my car breaking down, and that I finish the paper I've been working on. They are desires whose objectives are results. Desires *to do*, on the other hand, are urges or inclinations to engage in some sort of activity. They include the desire to fix the plumbing (not merely the desire that it be fixed), the desire to drive to Lawrence (not merely the desire that I get there), and the desire to work on the paper (not merely the desire that I finish it). Desires to do include both desires to engage in overt physical actions and desires to engage in what we might call "mental actions": I desire to plan my garden for this spring (planning is, of course, a "mental action," whereas planting involves overt physical actions); I desire to run over my lecture for tomorrow in my mind ("running it over in my mind" is mental; giving the lecture is not merely mental); I desire to spend some time thinking about my troubled relationship with a friend ("thinking about it" is mental; doing something about it is overt and not merely mental).

That a desire to appreciate is a desire to do might not be surprising. The necessity of "active involvement" on the part of readers of literature and appreciators of art in general is by now an old idea. However, it has not been underwritten by a philosophical account of the nature of the sort of desire or mental attitude on the part of readers that encourages active involvement. The following examination of the desire to appreciate as a specific kind of desire to do informs us about the object of that desire, which is appreciation itself. In particular, it explains why the kinds of mental shifts and slides I discuss in Chapters 3 through 5 are essential to appreciation and also why the kinds of judgments or assessments of what one is doing that I discuss in chapters 6 through 10 are also a part of the process of appreciation. It helps to illuminate why it is so difficult to defend the affective responses that arise during the process of appreciation, and it has implications for why it is valuable to develop and to exercise the ability to appreciate fictional literature. This chapter is concerned primarily with developing the relevant aspects of a philosophy of mind for understanding the nature of what it is one desires when one desires to appreciate a fictional work. I say little about fiction here, though I speak a great deal about desires to appreciate fictional literature.

In the first section I distinguish between desires that something be the case and desires to do something, and I argue that desires to appreciate a work of fictional literature are desires to do. They are, in short, desires to exercise an ability of the sort described in Chapter 1, as a temporally extended exercise rather than as a way to produce a product. For most desires, one has a way of characterizing, mentally, what one desires. Sometimes called a mental representation of the object of desire, it ensures that one's mental state is cognitively sophisticated enough to count as a desire, rather than a need, compulsion, or reflex. Desires *that* have propositional representations of the object of desire, and desires to *do* have what I call enactive representations of what is desired. I discuss these objects of desire in section II. However, there is a group of desires to do that do *not* have such representations, except in a very abstract way. I call these "norep" desires, and the desire to appreciate is one of them. The fact that one doesn't know in advance what specifically one will be doing when one fulfills one's desire to appreciate, coupled with the fact that appreciation occurs in the activity and not in a product separable from the activity, shows why certain kinds of judgments are part of the appreciative process and has implications for why appreciation is valuable.

I: Desires That and Desires to Do

Desires are easily confused with other types of mental states and phenomena. In particular, they need to be distinguished from "wired-in" states and behavior patterns—attractions and repulsions, drives such as hunger and thirst, fixated action patterns, and randomized flexings and stretchings. Each of these "wired-in" states or behavior patterns may be present in organisms that do not have a psychology cognitively sophisticated enough to be in states or have urges that are desires. Some philosophers have thought that "wired-in" attractions to certain kinds of shapes, colors, sounds, and so on are the foundation on which aesthetic appreciation is built.[1] These kinds of attractions are evidenced in the wider animal kingdom, such as when birds pick up brightly colored scraps of paper to build a nest, or when animals are sexually attracted to certain colors, patterns, or movements in potential mates. Grounding appreciation in these kinds of psychophysiological phenomena bases it on a passive response rather than activity and involvement. If we are to make sense of appreciation as an ability, we clearly need to move beyond this primitive notion of what it is to have a desire to appreciate.

Desires are psychological phenomena with *cognitive* components that distinguish them from purely physiological dispositions, needs, reflexes, and drives. Unless organisms have something like "innate ideas," desires will all be acquired by virtue of patterns of reinforcement and discouragement provided by experience, unlike needs, reflexes, and drives. "Desires that" are propositional attitudes. A propositional mental representation of *what* is desired, what is sometimes called a desire's "intentional object," accounts for the goal-oriented character of one's behavior. For one to have a *desire*—that

1. David Best claims two kinds of "natural" responses, instincts and mimicry, are "the roots of the concept of art." Reasons for responding in particular ways to particular works of art are, he claims, "given their meaning" by these "natural responses." See his *Reason and Feeling in the Arts* (London: Allen & Unwin, 1985), pp. 4–5, 9. With respect to the aesthetics of nature, Jay Appleton argues that "all humans probably share some innate preferences for certain types of natural landscapes." The rationale for this is that something about their genetic make-up drew hominids to savannahs, and this genetic structure survives in us today. It would hence explain our attraction to parks, since they are reminiscent of the trees scattered through the grassland in a savannah. See *The Symbolism of Habitat: An Interpretation of Landscape in the Arts* (Seattle: University of Washington Press, 1990), p. 15.

particular attitude—the representation of what is desired must play a role in the functioning of the organism so as to warrant saying someone desires that that be the case rather than that one has some other attitude towards the proposition, such as a belief that something is or will be the case, or merely that one has an idea of something's being the case (i.e., an "unasserted thought" that such-and-so is the case).

The mental representation of what is desired, one's goal, serves as a basis for comparison with perceptions of or beliefs about how the world *is*. One can then "compute" what needs to be done to eliminate the difference between the latter and the former.[2] It may even be necessary to have another sort of belief, and as the belief that what one desires is good or that it would make a contribution to something good. This belief would make it explicit that the mental representation of what is desired does provide the standard for judging what one perceives or believes things actually to be like. Thus, William Lyons has argued that one's beliefs about a situation cause one's evaluations of it, and one's evaluations or evaluative beliefs cause one's desires.[3] On this view, desires are propositional attitudes towards states of affairs; the fact that the functional role of the mental representation is to enable one to figure out what to do to eliminate the difference between the way one perceives the world to be and how one wants it to be ensures that one's attitude is one of desire (as opposed to aversion, or belief, or simply one of having an "unasserted thought").[4]

Since propositions are the sorts of things that can become conclusions of arguments, one's desire that one thing be the case rather than some other is open to rational debate. That is, in principle, one can defend desiring that *p* (rather than *q*, *r*, or *s*). And it would seem that if one can defend desiring *what* one desires (in Lyons' terms, if the evaluation—the belief that such-and-such is good—on which one's desire is based is defensible), then it would follow that one is rationally

2. For a description and critique of a cognitive account of desires see Andrew Woodfield, "Desires, Intentional Content, and Teleological Explanation," *Proceedings of the Aristotelian Society*, n.s. 82 (1982): 69–87.

3. See William Lyons, *Emotion* (Cambridge: Cambridge University Press, 1980), pp. 56–57, 96. Michael Stocker has argued against this view in "Desiring the Bad: An Essay in Moral Psychology," *Journal of Philosophy* 76 (1979): 738–753.

4. Roger Scruton developed the notion of "entertaining an unasserted thought" and its implications for describing and defending emotional responses to fiction in *Art and Imagination: A Study in the Philosophy of Mind* (London: Methuen, 1974).

justified in desiring it. For it certainly seems that it is rational to desire what one is justified in believing is good.[5]

This model for desires *that* shows them to function as cognitive states in a comprehensible manner, and it provides a pretty clear account of how to understand their objects and rational defensibility. The desire to appreciate is not, however, a desire *that* something be the case. Some desires are desires to *do* things. To understand desires to do, consider the following example. I am teaching a very young child how to tie a bow with his shoelaces. The child is in the middle of trying to tie a bow, with laces looped loosely over and around each other, and he just needs to pull on two of the loops to complete the task. I see what he needs to do: just go like "that." But the child doesn't see it. As I watch him fumbling and coming oh so close but not quite getting it, I have an almost overwhelming urge—a desire—to pull those loops and finish tying the bow. Occupational therapists who work with stroke and accident victims learn early on that you simply don't watch as patients struggle to accomplish their task. Otherwise, the urge to complete the task for them is too excruciating. It may even prove impossible to resist, in which case the therapist ends up doing the task *for* the patient. Of course, that misses the whole point. The point is not simply to get the shoe tied, or the task accomplished, but to have patients develop the ability to do it for themselves. It has been my experience that computer whizzes who are supposed to explain how to perform a particular task on the computer quickly succumb to the temptation to do it for you: they do it (really quickly) and somehow expect you to follow what they're doing closely enough to know how to make it work yourself. Yeah, right.

Physical desires to do are urges to do things, and as anyone who has had such desires knows, they are not only states of mind but also propulsions of body. They are in part physical urges to do what are in part physical things.[6] Human beings are not only decision-making machines, but creatures of flesh, blood, muscle, and nerve endings, whose experiences (e.g., as children) influence dispositions to behave

---

5. In presenting this view I have not distinguished between having some reason to believe it is good and having reasons to believe it's good *tout court*. Though this distinction is certainly important when it comes to judging the rationality of a desire, it is not necessary to enter into this complication for an exposition of the view.

6. This view is somewhat similar to Richard Swinburne's "favored account" of desire as an organized readiness to act of which one is aware in "Desire," *Philosophy* 60 (1985): 429–445.

long before we are capable of making evaluations or judgments about what is good in any full-fledged sense (and hence long before we are capable of forming desires that this or that be the case, or that we behave in a given way). Desires to do can thus arise independently of any beliefs in the goodness, as distinguished from the pleasantness, of what we desire to do.

Desires to do may take the form not only of bodily urges but also of mental urges. They are in part mental urges to engage in mental activity. These urges are harder to sort out phenomenologically, yet they play an important role in our mental lives. Typical sorts of mental urges are desires to fantasize—about driving a new sports car, soaking up the sun on a Greek Island cruise, or basking in the limelight at a professional meeting. Not all mental urges are as frivolous, however, as desires to fantasize. There are urges to solve a problem (not just a desire to know the solution), design a device (not just a desire to have such a design), and figure out the underlying basis for a person's peculiar behavior patterns (not just a desire to know what it is). These are all desires to do, where the doing is a matter of engaging in mental activity rather than overt physical activity.

Desires to do something and desires that something be the case are, respectively, akin to what Wayne Davis has called appetitive desires and volitive desires.[7] Appetitive desires are urges, yearnings, cravings, or appetites, but they are not identical with drives such as hunger and thirst. Desires and needs are not always coordinate: some people have a desire to eat when they are not hungry (no physiological need); others can get so wrapped up in what they're doing that they don't notice that they are hungry (when there *is* a physiological need). Some people never know when they are tired; others have the urge to sleep (appetitive desire) even though they're not tired (they lack the physiological need). But, Davis argues, appetitive desires are also distinct from volitive desires, in that the "objects" of appetitive desires (what one desires to do) are viewed with pleasure (such as eating a chocolate mousse), or at least relief from discomfort (such as rubbing a sore muscle), but the objects of volitive desires (such as getting those term papers graded) need not be viewed with pleasure.[8]

What is the activity one desires to engage in when one desires to appreciate a work of fictional literature? For most desires there is a

7. Wayne A. Davis, "The Two Senses of Desire," *Philosophical Studies* 45 (1984): esp. pp. 181–186.
8. Cf. Davis, "Two Senses," p. 183. Also, Frank Jackson, "Internal Conflicts in Desires and Morals," *American Philosophical Quarterly* 22 (1985): 105–114.

reasonably specific answer to this question, as I will explain in the following section. Appreciation, however, does not admit of this sort of answer, and this fact has implications for the components of the ability involved, the rationality or reasonableness of what we do in the process of exercising that ability, and the value of the ability.

II: Representations of What One Desires to Do

The trick to understanding desires to do is not only to understand their structural distinctness from desires that, but also, as mentioned above, to keep them from collapsing into drives such as hunger and thirst which most commentators agree are not desires.[9] Drives display physiological needs that show up as sensory disturbances or discomforts, at least when people are self-monitoring. They do not, qua drives, involve beliefs about states of affairs that will satisfy them. They do not, qua drives, involve intentional objects. But when such phenomena as hunger and thirst become psychologically enriched with an awareness of the reason for one's discomfort, the belief that food and drink will relieve the discomfort, or with an urge to perform specific acts (not just physical movements) of eating or drinking, they become desires.

It would seem, then, that for a (mental or physical) urge to do to count as having a desire, there must also be something like a mental representation of the action one desires to perform that would play a role analogous to the role played by the propositional representation in relation to desires that something be the case. We can call what plays the role of a mental representation when one desires to *do* something an "enactive" representation in order to distinguish it from the propositional representations of what we desire when we desire *that* something be the case.[10] The distinctive character of enactive representations is best illustrated by an analogy with visual memory.

9. Davis, "Two Senses," p. 193. Also see Frank Jackson, "Weakness of Will," *Mind* 93 (1984): 14; and N. J. H. Dent, *The Moral Psychology of the Virtues* (Cambridge: Cambridge University Press, 1984), pp. 47–51.
10. In *The Thread of Life* (Cambridge: Harvard University Press, 1984), chap. 3, Richard Wollheim uses "iconic" to mark a similar phenomenon in the context of discussing what it is to imagine being someone. As he recognizes, however, "iconic" is not entirely felicitous, as it is too strongly identified with visual images, "snapshots," or static representations in general.

Visual perception is a process during which we become aware of objects and events in the external world. Part of what occurs during the process of perception is something we call "having a visual experience," and these visual experiences may be "retained" in the form of iconic memories. Iconic memories, among other things, make recognition (of a visual array) possible and serve to identify what we seek out. Similarly, proprioception and kinesthetic perception are processes during which we become aware of the position and movements, respectively, of our own bodies, and, as with visual memories, we can have enactive memories of bodily positions and movements. Because we have these memories, we can gradually come to monitor and control the position of our body and our movements and form desires to do things, where what we desire to do involves, as part of what we desire to do, moving in particular sorts of ways. In addition, with practice and experience, the enactive representation of what we desire to do becomes more and more acute and sophisticated.

The presence of an enactive representation, like a propositional representation, ensures that the inclination or urge to act is partly constitutive of a psychological state, as opposed to simply a physical dispositional state or a physiological need or drive. Enactive representations may function in two different ways. First, they may function as objectives to be pursued, in which case the desire to do is not structurally distinct from desires that something be the case. Suppose I desire to do a cartwheel. If I have done cartwheels before, I may already have an enactive representation of, as one would ordinarily express it, what it feels like to do one correctly, a representation ensured by kinaesthetic memories of past experiences. This enactive mental representation could identify what I want to do as a goal or objective. When I desire to do a cartwheel it is not simply "doing a cartwheel" in the abstract that I desire, but I desire to perform an action that, when performed properly, has certain kinesthetic features. It is (partly) by virtue of these features that I identify what I want to do. Similarly, I may desire to hit a softball solidly. There is a certain "feel" to getting a good solid hit, a "feel" that what you've done has when you've done what you wanted to do and by virtue of which you wanted to do it. In these cases it is not the doing of the cartwheel or the hitting of the softball that I desire; rather, I desire that I do x, where x is at least partly characterized by an enactive representation of what I desire to do. When an enactive mental representation serves as an objective or goal to be pursued, the desire to do is not structurally distinct from desires that something be the case.

I may desire that I do a cartwheel in the first sense, without really wanting to do one. In such a case, I may very well feel somewhat divorced from my body: I want "that" my body does something, but *I* don't have any special desire to do it.[11] But desires to do in the second sense do not involve this divorce between the attitude of desire and one's physical or mental urges or inclinations. Desires to do in the second sense involve an enactive mental representation of what one desires to do that informs one's physical and mental being and behavior in a way that (at least helps to) create an urge to move one's body in a given way.[12] For this reason, desires to do in the second sense are structurally distinct from desires that. The *activity* involved in the actions, the doing, not merely the accomplishment of a purpose, reinforces the desire to do. Crudely, the activity of fishing, not just the catching of fish, reinforces the desire to go fishing; the activity of reading, not just what is learned or remembered as a result of the reading, reinforces the desire to appreciate.[13]

Having a desire to do in the second sense, whether physical or mental, does require that one's body or mind is inclined to or that one has an urge to do this or that, but this is only part of the story. For what one's body or mind is disposed to do is identified not only in bodily terms, but also as a kind of action. What one desires to do is identified in part because one has a certain cognitive comprehension of it—it is not merely a movement (such as one's arm's moving about) but an action of a given sort (alerting a friend to your whereabouts). To have a desire to perform an *action* (not merely to make a movement) is to be inclined or to have an urge to perform it. This inclination is not simply a physiological state or condition: the (enactive) representation of the action one is inclined to perform informs the condition one is now in, that is, how one's body has an urge to move or what one's mind has an urge to do. Movement sequences (moving an arm about) will be psychologically linked with an action identifica-

11. See Bruce Vermazen, "Aesthetic Satisfaction," in Jonathan Dancy, J. M. E. Moravcsik, and C. C. W. Taylor, eds., *Human Agency: Language, Duty, and Value: Essays in Honor of J. O. Urmson* (Stanford: Stanford University Press, 1988).

12. For simplicity of exposition, I sometimes only use examples of desires to do physical things.

13. See Fred Dretske, *Explaining Behavior: Reasons in a World of Causes* (Cambridge: MIT Press, 1988), chap. 5.

tion (alerting a friend to one's whereabouts). Thus, desires to do are rarely unadulterated by desires that—one reason it is difficult to separate and analyze desires to do as distinct psychological phenomena.

In a healthy individual, desires that and desires to do will be, in large part, coordinate. One develops inclinations to perform, or at least habits of performing actions that are inherently unpleasant because one realizes they satisfy a desire *that*. However, when desires to do *not-p* alter and erode a desire that *p* in the face of better reasons for continuing to desire *p*, we call this rationalization. Desires that and desires to do, then, play different rational roles: rationally justified "desires that" have much more legitimacy as instigators of desires to do than desires to do have as instigators of desires that. This is in large part because of the ease of developing desires to do independently of beliefs, a fortiori justified beliefs, about the goodness or value of doing that particular thing (remember the shoelace-tying example given earlier).

Activities, and hence the desires to perform them, can be partially defended as desirable simply on account of their pleasurableness, of course, but not only is appreciating fiction not always pleasurable in a straightforward sense, but we generally take the value of engaging in the activity as something more. I argue in the final chapter that this value depends on a feature of the desire to appreciate which I explore in the following section: there is no specific enactive representation of what one desires to do.

III: Desires without Representations of What Is Desired

The desire to appreciate falls into a problematic subcategory of desires to do. Sometimes one desires to do things even when there is no enactive representation of what one desires to do or when the enactive representation is so sketchy or superficial that it does not provide the details of the actions to be performed the way an enactive representation of a cartwheel informs the desire to do a cartwheel. I call these "norep desires." But how is it possible to have an urge to do something when, quite literally, one doesn't have an (enactive) idea of what it is one desires to do? Curiously, many desires take this shape: desires to contemplate, to imagine, to fantasize; desires to be challenged or tested; and desires to experience and explore. All are desires that may take the form of urges to do where one doesn't know what one will be doing when acting out of the desire.[14]

Among the clearer cases of such desires are those where one desires to exercise an ability when the ability involves responding to or interacting with something in one's environment and when one doesn't know quite what the environment will present. It is unlikely that a desire to exercise an ability will persist as a desire to do unless one has confidence in one's ability. Indeed, the desire to exercise an ability can be combined with a desire to enhance (or sustain) that ability. But the latter is not always a desire to do: it can take the form of a desire *that* I come to have or retain an ability, without (as per Davis's appetitive desires) being accompanied by pleasure, that is, without a desire to do (in the second sense) the things that are required to develop or sustain the ability.

Curiosity also provides an interesting case. Curiosity can be a desire *that* I know, such as wanting to know a particular fact or the answer to a particular question, such as the name of the eighteenth president of the United States. But curiosity can also be a desire to do, for example, when it is piqued by seeing the mouth of a cave when one is hiking through a hillside. One might also want to know what's in the cave (a desire *that* I know), but it might just as well be the case that one wants to know what's in the cave because one desires to explore it, rather than that one desires to explore it because one wants to know what's in it. The exploratory urge may serve, psychologically, to generate a desire *that*, a desire to know, just as much as the desire to know can generate a desire to explore.

It is characteristic of curiosity (as a desire to do) that one does not have an idea of what specifically one will be doing (the mental or physical actions one will be performing) in doing what one wants to do in satisfying the curiosity. Nevertheless, doing the finding out, *doing* those things, is, as we say, part of what one wants. It is different from curiosity where one has a desire to know a particular thing, such as to acquire a particular item of information, where it is not part of one's desire that one wants to find it out for oneself. Curiosity as a

---

14. In "Startle," *Journal of Philosophy* 92 (1995): 53–74, Jenefer Robinson argues that examining the less cognitively endowed "startle response" can help us better understand the noncognitive aspects of emotions, e.g., the bodily nature of the responses and the respects in which they do not flow from cognition. Similarly, excessive concentration on the cognitive aspects of desires has drawn attention away from enactive desires, and desires to do without specific representations of what is desired.

desire to do is not wanting to know the answer to a question but wanting to figure out for oneself what the answer is. If this is the case, one will not have done *all* that one wanted if someone just tells one the answer. It may be that my *curiosity* has been satisfied (I've found out what I wanted to know), but *I* have been left unsatisfied (I didn't get to do the finding out).[15] The implication is that there is something more to *me*, my own identity, than merely getting what I want: it requires also my involvement as an agent, my doing something.

A desire to appreciate a work of fictional literature doesn't involve merely wanting to know various facts about the work, what it's like, what happens to the characters or how it ends, what it's role has been in the history of literature, or how it reveals certain cultural attitudes. The desire to appreciate is a desire to get the good out of a work, whatever that good might be. Just as the desire to know what's in the cave may be generated by a desire to explore, so also a desire to know various sorts of things about the work and the world of the work may be generated by a desire to appreciate. And appreciation requires using one's abilities to make a work "work"—to make it work for you, the reader—by making whatever mental adjustments are necessary to do this. Making those mental adjustments is the activity one must engage in to appreciate; *those* things are what one must have an urge to do, even though one doesn't know quite what one will need to do to appreciate the work, much less what emotions or affective responses will attend them.[16] I offer a fuller discussion of the nature of these mental adjustments in Chapter 3.

Since there is no enactive representation of what one desires to do, judgments about whether what one is doing is "working" help to distinguish cases of genuine desires to do from lower-order phenomena such as so-called "searching and orientation behaviors" and randomized movements. Even the term "searching and orientation behavior" attributes cognitively inflated properties to an organism displaying those behaviors, because the terms "searching" and "orientation" imply intentions, or at least consciously controlled processes,

15. See Vermazen, "Aesthetic Satisfaction," pp. 201–218, for a discussion of the linkages between desires and the *person*'s being satisfied.
16. David Pugmire, "Real Emotion," *Philosophy and Phenomenological Research* 54 (1994): 113, contends that when one's desire is "to attain to a sentiment," then the desire does not involve a direct concern for the alleged object of that sentiment. Similarly, a desire to have a particular emotion or affective experience does not involve a "direct concern" for the work, and thus per se no desire to appreciate *it*. (See also Chapter 6, sec. II.)

even though adding the term "behavior" tends to take the intentional import of "searching" and "orientation" away. The terminology thus obscures the distinction between these behaviors and manifestations of norep desires to do. (Indeed, the terminology is reminiscent of behaviorism's ambivalent attitude towards mental phenomena in general, characterized by a desire to eliminate reference to the unobservable but also by a desire to recognize the existence of cognitively sophisticated mental activity and intentional actions. In its most extreme, this ambivalence manifests itself by such bizarre descriptions as "The organism is exhibiting language behavior," as if adding the word "behavior" automatically picks out a phenomenon whose essential characteristics are observable.)

Are little laboratory rats and mice really searching around and orienting themselves? Are they guided by *desires* to find out what is around and to understand their relationship to their environment? Of course not; they have certain genetically coded, fixed action patterns that are automatically elicited when the animal is in certain kinds of environments. Some of these action patterns function as "scanning" mechanisms, just as, in humans, saccadic movements of the eyeball both ensure that new supplies of visual data are continually forthcoming and avert "retinal fatigue." Exploratory behavior in animals typically takes the form of fixed action patterns, whereas in humans it more commonly takes the form of randomized movements, such as the stretchings and flexings exhibited by human infants.[17] Fixated behavior patterns and genetically elicited random activity both often serve useful functions—for instance, to gather information or facilitate physical and cognitive development. Insofar as they do serve these functions they are purpo*sive*, though the behaviors are not purpose*ful*.

Fixated behavior patterns and random movements may serve an organism well and manifest beneficial genetic adaptations to an environment without the benefits being represented in the "psyche" of the organism as a goal or end to be achieved. An organism may be "hard-wired" so that certain results are achieved even though what in fact ensures that the organism achieves them does not involve any explicit mental representation—any sense on the part of the organism itself—of those results as ends or goals. The appearance of cognitive sophistication can be "unmasked" by changing the environment

17. See *The Encyclopedic Dictionary of Psychology*, ed. Rom Harré and Roger Lamb (Cambridge: MIT Press, 1983), p. 226.

so that a fixated behavior pattern is no longer beneficial.[18] If an organism were genuinely guided by a goal or purpose, when it became clear that an action pattern no longer achieves that purpose, the behavior would stop. Pathological human conditions such as those of compulsive hand washers are similar in this respect to "wired-in" behavior patterns: they do not change when altered circumstances eliminate their benefits or even make them harmful. The problem is not that compulsive hand washers are excessively fastidious and suffer from misplaced priorities, as if they have an unrealistically high ideal of very clean hands. To interpret their behavior in this way represents it as more rational than it is: it makes clean hands a goal rather than hand washing a compulsion.

One reason for attributing purposes, ends or goals that are psychologically real and somehow "in" the organism, to individuals, is to explain how organisms reorient themselves in the face of a changing environment. The self-reflexiveness of this expression entails that an organism has the ability to control its own behavior. If it doesn't reorient itself, at least after a reasonable period of time, when changed circumstances make the behavior no longer effective, an explanation for the behavior should not be couched in terms of what that organism represents to itself or uses as an end, goal, or object to be achieved. The explanation for the behavior is not rational: the organism does not act that way for reasons—on the basis of beliefs that such-and-such behavior will lead to such-and-such an end or goal, or in light of some notion of the behavior as an end in itself. "Fixated" behaviors may be either "wired-in" or persist out of habit. Having a habit may be purposeful, but when it persists beyond its utility, and especially when it consistently interferes with the achievement of one's goals or interests, it loses its rational basis and justification.

Since fixed action patterns are fixed genetically, they are not susceptible to rational control. Thus, even if one recognized that the behavior were counterproductive, one could not alter it. Some perceptual processes, due to their modularity (i.e., relative impenetrability to higher order reasoning) provide examples. Knowing that the two lines in the Müller-Lyer illusion, or "arrow illusion," are of equal lengths does not prevent them from looking like they are different

18. A well-known example of a purposive adaptation whose lack of purposefulness is "unmasked" occurs in Daniel C. Dennett's discussion of the "digger wasp," *sphex ichneumoneus,* in *Elbow Room: The Varieties of Free Will Worth Wanting* (Cambridge: MIT Press, 1984), pp. 10–11.

lengths. Habits have advantages that accrue from the fact that the action or action sequence is elicited automatically without the disadvantage of being irreversible. There are definite advantages to developing at least some habits: speed and relative constancy (what we might call "perseverance" if it didn't have so much of the smell of a moral virtue about it). The acquisition of skills also often depends on one's having certain patterns of automatically elicited behavior. If one always had to decide, prior to acting, whether a certain kind of action or movement would work towards one's goal, then deliberation would have to occur at each stage along the way. This requirement in itself could prevent one's behavior from being effective. Habits, skills, and relatively fixated behavior patterns are useful when speed and unswerving commitment are more advantageous than what one could do if one took the time to deliberate about whether to engage in different behavior.

Appreciation requires adjusting oneself psychologically in ways one often can't anticipate. It requires shifting one's point of view and developing and utilizing various sensitivities. This psychological activity is required not merely when reading a new work but during the process of reading a single work. I explore the character of these different "doings" in the following three chapters. Because the doings are mental, and in particular because the mental shifts and slides we make often take place at a preconscious level, there tends to be less awareness of the active role an appreciator plays. Similarly, the judgments readers make about whether their attitude or point of view makes the work succeed are often not explicitly recognized. In Chapter 6 I describe the role that such judgments play in the process of appreciation; in this chapter we have come to see why they are essential to that process. They are part of the assurance that the goal is the normatively loaded phenomenon of appreciation when there is no enactive representation of what one desires to do.

The absence of an enactive representation of what one desires to do raises a question about the rationality or reasonableness of desires to do and the desires they generate. There are no reasons that are agents' reasons for doing the specific things they will be doing, since they don't know in advance what they will be doing. A goal may be to appreciate a work, of course, but without an enactive representation of what one desires to do, it is not clear that there is a rational way to embed desires to do and the desires that they generate into a rational construction of one's ends or goals. Having a capacity to develop desires to do, however, even though one doesn't know specifically what one will be doing, is a desirable capacity in an intelligent being. Intelligence requires that one doesn't act *only* when one has a belief—much less a justified belief—about the best way to behave to achieve a given goal or set of goals in a given situation. Intelligence is not served by allowing preconceptions to handicap one's understanding of what are essentially new situations calling for new types of behavior. Preconceptions may harmfully narrow one's horizons.[19] Ignoring preconceived goals and established ideas can be a useful method for gathering information when one has little relevant knowledge to begin with. Randomizing devices act as a kind of generator of activity when no specific object attracts or repels someone and in the absence of goals or purposes to guide behavior in a *well-informed* way, so that one does not single-mindedly scurry down the road in the wrong direction.

Thus, it may be a good design feature of an organism to have the capacity to act out of desires to do without having reasons for doing the specific things one does when acting out of those desires (apart from the fact that one desires to do them). Having this capacity for desires to do can—though not always will—enhance the well-being of the organism. If the possession of a given sort of capacity enhances the well-being of an organism, making use of it counts toward making the behavior arising out of it rational or reasonable. Making use of such a capacity is not sufficient for making one's behavior rational or reasonable, for only certain exercises of the capacity enhance well-being, and others may be downright harmful. But it doesn't follow from this that one shouldn't indulge desires to do. What does follow is that such desires should be indulged with moderation, with occasional reflection on the larger-scale implications of the behavior.

Wanting to appreciate a work of fiction is structurally like having curiosity of an amalgamated type, where one wants not merely to know what it is about the work that is good or bad, or what it means or says, or what happens, but where one wants to find this out or figure it out for oneself. These wants manifest themselves, appropriately enough, in a desire to read the work. Reading, like many of life's biddings, requires a combination of applying what was learned in the past with a sensitivity to what is new. Appreciating requires trying things out, experimenting, doing things whose effectiveness is not

19. Cf. Alvin Goldman, "Epistemics: The Regulative Theory of Cognition," *Journal of Philosophy,* 75 (1978): 519, on how problem solvers often get caught in a rut or "loop" because they tend to think of new hypotheses in terms of ones that have recently worked.

assured in advance. Reading the work is necessary for appreciating it, since, *ex hypothesi,* one wants to get the good out of it in the experience of it and not merely to know what is good about it or how to interpret it. One rather wants to find out or discover what this is for oneself, even though one doesn't know in advance what one will be doing in doing this.

Building on the account of appreciation as a temporally extended activity developed in Chapter 1, I have suggested here that the desire to appreciate is a desire to do, a desire to engage in activity, rather than a desire that something be the case. Appreciation requires the mental flexibility to make psychological shifts in sensitivities and point of view. But these "doings" that partially constitute appreciation are not predictable in advance; there is no enactive mental representation of what one will be doing in appreciating a work. Judgments about the relevance and appropriateness to appreciation of what one is doing ensure that one is acting out of a desire (to do) even though there is no enactive representation of what one desires. Such judgments are thus essential to the activity one desires to do precisely because of the lack of an enactive mental representation of what is desired. Furthermore, the lack of an enactive representation of what is desired also creates problems for defending the rationality or reasonableness of what one is doing at the enactive level, since one quite literally doesn't know what that is. The justifications that can be given are in terms of the ends or goals—appreciation—rather than the specific doings that compose it. The following chapter describes a psychological model for understanding the doings that one engages in during the process or activity of appreciation.

Chapter Three

Mental Shifts, Slides, and Sensitivities

In the previous two chapters I proposed that the ability to appreciate a fictional work of literature is a set of abilities and that a desire to appreciate is a desire to do. In particular, desires to appreciate are norep desires, desires not involving representations of the specific activities one engages in when acting out of such a desire. The next step is to examine in more detail important types of psychological processes involved in what one does in acting out of a desire to appreciate, that is, the sorts of things one will be doing of which one doesn't have any specific mental representation.

I explain in section I the nature of mental "shifts" and "slides," and in section II I describe what the human mind must be like to make those shifts, noting that explanations for these shifts and slides do not always involve appeal to changes in one's system of beliefs or desires. Section III explores how mental shifts and slides change our *sensitivities* to what we read. "Sensitivity" is used here in a semi-technical sense to refer to a dispositional state or condition of an individual, such that the individual will respond affectively in a given way in response to given stimuli. In Chapter 4 I show how harnessing one's affective and cognitive potential for making mental shifts and slides, and hence altering our sensitivities, enables us to empathize with fictional characters. Chapter 5 shows how the generation of sympathy, as distinguished from empathy, and other kinds of responses can be understood by a similar model. Empathizing and sympathizing with fictional characters and having the other sorts of responses described in Chapter 5 are exercises of abilities involved in appreciating fictional literature. In this chapter I describe the psychological foundations on which those abilities are built.

I: What Are Mental Shifts?

Consider the following metaphors: as a reader I "get wrapped up in a story," I "get into" the story and "outside" of myself. These metaphors use a shift in spatial perspective to indicate a change in cognitive and emotive orientation. They indicate a mental shift, a change in attitude or "point of view," that governs the way we think and feel about things. In the process of reading a novel or short story we become psychologically adjusted in different ways as we read: we mentally shift, or slip into, different "gears." Sometimes we intentionally do something that effects this shift. Sometimes we can identify what it is about the text that is responsible for our making the shifts, such as a defiance of our expectations for the medium or genre, changes in voice or diction, and conflicting descriptions of what is apparently the same individual or event. Explication of the multitude of ways literary works can elicit a shift in a reader's perspective, point of view, and conceptual and affective orientation to the text is part of the stock-in-trade of critical analysis.

Some novels and short stories are justly famous for having a first sentence that not only draws readers into the spirit and tone of the work—mentally shifting readers "into" the story—but also virtually encapsulates, epigrammatically, some important insight contained within it. The first sentences of Jane Austen's *Pride and Prejudice* and Charles Dickens' *A Tale of Two Cities* come to mind; others will have their own favorite examples. One of mine is from Heinrich Böll's short story "The Thrower Away": "For the last few weeks I have been trying to avoid people who might ask me what I do for a living."[1] The first person introduces readers to the perspective of the narrator, who is being a little mysterious but also confessional, hinting that we will discover something about his personal emotional world that explains this peculiar behavior.

First sentences don't always shift us abruptly into a new frame of mind; sometimes we gently slide "into it." Furthermore, introductory passages of novels and short stories are often ambiguous: we don't

1. Heinrich Böll, "The Thrower Away," in *18 Stories*, trans. Leila Vennewitz (New York: McGraw-Hill, 1966), p. 11.

know the location, time period, characteristics of speakers, or surrounding events. For example, Angela Carter begins her 1972 novel,
The Infernal Desire Machines of Doctor Hoffman in the following way:

> I remember everything.
> Yes.
> I remember everything perfectly.[2]

How did you read this passage? When I first read it, I read it as
someone who was, more or less, trying to convince *herself* that she
really did remember everything. Her interest in persuading herself is
the reason for the repetition and the short punchy phrases (to ward
off challenges). That is, I read it with a kind of psychological insistence, a need to reaffirm the fact that "I" really did remember everything; *everything;* really. This reading was partly due to, or
conditioned by, my having read her slightly earlier novel *Love,* in
which the protagonist was dysfunctional in a number of ways and
troubled by doubts. (*Love* begins: "One day, Annabel saw the sun and
moon in the sky at the same time. The sight filled her with a terror
which entirely consumed her and did not leave her until the night
closed in catastrophe for she had no instinct for self-preservation if
she was confronted by ambiguities."[3]) My reading may also have been
due to the fact that I assumed that the narrator was speaking in a
female voice (an assumption that, as it turns out, was false).

But one can read the initial lines from *The Infernal Desire Machines*
in a very different way, as a series of calm, self-confident rational
assertions, perhaps even expressed in response to questions, where
someone else asks—orally, or perhaps just through skeptical looks—
for reconfirmation that one is sure of one's memory. On this reading,
the "doubt" comes not from the speaker but from an imaginary audi-
tor, and the repetition reflects not one's own doubts but the expressed
or implied doubts of the person being addressed.

The issue here is not which, if either, reading is correct or appropriate. It is an illustration of how we can engage in "mental shifts"
that effect different experiences of a segment of text. This passage
can be experienced in quite different ways—as consumed with self-
doubt or as confident assertion—different experiences we can pro-

2. Angela Carter, *The Infernal Desire Machines of Doctor Hoffman* (1972; repr., *The War
of Dreams* [1973; New York: Penguin, 1982]), p. 11.
3. Angela Carter, *Love* (1971; rev. ed. London: Chatto and Windus, 1987; Penguin,
1988), p. 1.

duce with fairly minimal conscious mental effort. Moreover, these
shifts can be made without any alteration in the text, or in our belief
system about relevant parts of the world (e.g., Angela Carter's intentions) or the text (e.g., the sorts of personality traits the narrator is
revealed to have later in the novel). This is a very important fact
about mental shifts: they can be inaugurated without changes in our
beliefs and desires but simply by ideas about, prompted by comments
about, how one might "see" or experience the text differently.

Here is another example of a mental shift from Tobias Smollett's
satirical eighteenth-century novel *Roderick Random*. The faithful ser-
vant Strap is preparing to shave Roderick, when Roderick tells him
something surprising. "It would require the pencil of Hogarth to
express the astonishment and concern of Strap on hearing this piece
of news."[4] I read the assertion as following a standard eighteenth-
century practice for expressing the dramatic nature of Strap's reaction by appealing to the power of a pictorial representation. But
Smollett follows with this: "The basin in which he was preparing the
lather for my chin dropped out of his hands and he remained some
time immovable in that ludicrous attitude, with his mouth open and
his eyes thrust forward considerably beyond their station, but, re-
membering my disposition, which was touchy and impatient of control, he smothered his chagrin and attempted to recollect himself."[5]
Well, clearly it does *not* require the pencil of Hogarth to express
Strap's astonishment. Smollett's pencil has done very well—better
than Hogarth would do, given the ability of language to include the
temporal dimension. Language can be explicit about how Strap "remained some time in that ludicrous attitude" and about the alterations in his face as he attempted to hide his chagrin, in a way that a
painting cannot be. We are surely prompted by Smollett's description
to read the claim about Hogarth as ironic. Though the claim about
Hogarth repeats a commonplace that it takes a great painter to "describe" such a reaction, Smollett does not simply echo that commonplace but challenges it. He doesn't announce that he's challenging it
but demonstrates its falsity in the very next sentence. (And Smollett
would probably not be at all displeased to find the line about Hogarth
was read initially as a straightforward assertion.) The line about Hogarth, then, can be read and experienced in at least two ways, either

4. Tobias Smollett, *The Adventures of Roderick Random* (New York: New American Li-
brary/Signet Books, 1964), p. 312.
5. Smollett, *Roderick Random*, p. 312.

as a candid expression of the power of the painter or as ironic. Making the appropriate mental shifts, we can read it either way.

This type of shifting back and forth between different "perspectives" is familiar in the visual realm as "aspect perception." Mental shifts go beyond mere aspect perception, however, because they affect one's experiences of and responses to not only words that are currently being read but also what one reads in the future. In the Carter example, it affects how we "read" the narrator's later remarks, and in Smollett, it make us sensitive to later claims about the relative powers of writers and painters. A mental shift results in our being in a different psychological condition, a condition that leads us to perceptually, cognitively, or affectively respond differently to the environment. That is, a mental shift alters our dispositional state. It is analogous to being in a certain gear when driving an automobile. *Shifting into* third gear, that event, puts an automobile into a new state or condition. Psychologically, slipping or shifting into a "new gear" gets us into a condition that results in processes and activities that wouldn't take place if we weren't in that "gear." *Being in* third gear is a state or condition of an automobile, but it is a state that has a major effect on how a car runs and what it will do. The car's being in that gear explains why a certain sort of process or activity goes on as the car moves. Psychological analogues to being in third gear include being in a given frame of mind, taking a certain kind of mental perspective or point of view, and having a given emotional sensitivity. Our attitude or frame of mind, point of view, or cognitive or affective sensitivity can lead to our seeing or experiencing things as being a given way.[6] Being in this or that psychological condition affects how we interpret or analyze what we see or read.

Changes in context and experience serve not only to widen our mental storehouse of sensations, ideas, and so on but also to alter the way we respond to the same or similar features of the environment in the future. Sometimes affective shifts are elicited by a new explicit, specific bit of information, or a statement of a new idea, leading us to experience things, emotionally, in a different way. Affective shifts may also be initiated by bringing to mind, or *raising the level of salience of*, an idea or bit of information we had all along. A shift can, in turn, alter our cognitive orientation—the sequence of thoughts and ideas,

6. It may also be understood as partially comprising the way one sees or experiences things, so that the attitude or point of view is defined in part in terms of what one is in fact doing. It is not necessary to debate these ontological tangles about the nature of attitudes or points of view here.

and the kinds of reasoning processes that go through our mind—as well as our affective responses.

Sometimes shifts change how we will process or respond to a single, fairly specifically describable feature or set of features of the environment so that that feature or set of features is experientially integrated in a different way or so that it "triggers," say, a new idea or feeling. This shift would be a relatively localized change or "mental shift." For example, in Heinrich Böll's short story "Murke's Collected Silences," Murke is irritated by the unremitting tastefulness of the furnishings in the building where he works. "He suddenly felt a desire to take the sentimental picture of the Sacred Heart which his mother had sent him and see it somewhere here on the wall. . . . The tawdry little print was highly colored, and beneath the picture of the Sacred Heart were the words: *I prayed for you at St. James' Church.*"[7] We are locally sensitized to the occurrence of those italicized words without our even knowing it, until they occur again at the very end of the story, and we experience a recognition and resonance with what went before. At the end of the story Murke is able to perform a surprising professional feat to come to the aid of the Assistant Producer. Murke's professional competence contrasts with his act of quiet vandalism, as the Assistant Producer pulls out the piece of paper he found on his door, saying "'Funny, isn't it, the corny stuff you can come across in this place? I found this stuck in my door.' . . . *I prayed for you at St. James' Church.*"[8]

Other changes are due to a more global alteration in the way a whole range of phenomena are processed by "lower order" systems in the psyche. These include changes in mood, attitude, perspective or point of view, as well as the adoption of a new set of values and objectives, bringing about far-ranging changes in what kinds of things one notices and how one perceives them.[9] Whether a shift is localized or global is a matter of degree. Moreover, it may be quite difficult to tell on any particular occasion whether the change in one's condition

---

7. Böll, "Murke's Collected Silences," in *18 Stories*, p. 129.
8. Böll, "Murke's Collected Silences," p. 149.
9. Neil Cooper, *The Diversity of Moral Thinking* (Oxford: Clarendon Press, 1981), argues that morality does not consist merely in "maxims and precepts," but also requires a "vision of the world." Works of art, he points out, can lead to a kind of "gestalt shift" so that one sees oneself and one's life differently (pp. 236–242). Claudia Card emphasized the importance of this point to me in discussion. Early feminist efforts at "consciousness-raising" were not only directed toward focusing people's attention on phenomena that were ordinarily not noticed but also designed to make people affectively more sensitive to these phenomena. See the discussion of sensitivities below.

is of a sort that affects only a fairly narrowly defined or localized phenomenon, or whether it will affect one's experiences in a broader, more global way. Some global shifts may be reducible to a specific set of localized shifts, and some may involve a few localized shifts but not be reducible to them.

Different dispositional states also last for different periods of time. On the one hand, a mental shift may alter one's condition permanently, so that one becomes "locked in" to a given condition forever after. Some experiences are so traumatic that their memory infuses virtually all of one's future actions, effecting a shift of global proportions. On the other hand, one's condition may be changed only for a fleeting moment. In Chapter 10 I argue that timing or temporal factors may warrant one's responding to what one does, as one does. Here I discuss timing as a factor that explains our responses, one that has largely been ignored in relation to fiction. That one has "shifted gears" may not even be noticeable at the time when the shift is made, because the factors on which it comes to operate are not present then but only later. One may think it is a localized shift when it is more global, and vice-versa. One just doesn't know, from introspection, what cognitive and affective changes go on as one reads.

Many mental shifts are more like slides than shifts. Experience over time gradually changes how a certain phenomenon is interpreted or how it functions (e.g., how much importance it assumes) within the complex network of activities and processes that go on in one's mind. For many explanatory purposes, "mental slides" can be treated like "mental shifts": they are changes in one's psychological condition that effect minor changes in one's pattern of thought or the character of one's experiences. In "Murke's Collected Silences," evidence of Murke's quiet resistance to "the system," gradually mounts: from the "existential exercise" he performs on the elevator each morning, to his sticking a tacky religious card on the Assistant Producer's door, to the subversive substitution of the wrong snippet of tape spliced into a radio lecture, to taking home scraps of tape cut out of lectures to be broadcast, which is strictly against the rules. There may be no sudden shift but only a gradual change in how one feels about and relates to the central character.

II: Psychological Capacities for Making Mental Shifts

Any fairly complex yet efficiently organized system will employ some kind of hierarchical arrangement of activities, so that some processes can take place more or less automatically, without deliberation, and typically without one's even having to be aware of what's going on.[10] In this section I argue that this automaticity does not prevent a certain amount of intentional control. I also suggest, however, that it is a mistake automatically to impute beliefs—either conscious or preconscious—about the outcomes of one's mental shifting, even when it is intentional.

It is incontrovertible that there are mental processes outside conscious awareness that underlie, for example, language production and comprehension and exercises of skill. Similarly, many ways in which past experiences affect how new stimuli are processed and what cognitive, emotional, or affective connections they have are characteristically not accessed by, and often not even accessible to, conscious awareness.[11] Indeed, the automaticity of some mental processes is partly responsible for their typically remaining hidden from our introspective view. How stimuli are processed is affected by other beliefs, memories, desires, ideas, character and personality traits, and heaven knows what else. What *is* typically accessible to awareness, such as a perception, idea, or experience, is the *outcome* of a complex

10. See Philip N. Johnson-Laird, *Mental Models: Towards a Cognitive Science of Language, Inference, and Consciousness* (Cambridge: Harvard University Press, 1983), p. 451. Influential on Johnson-Laird was Herbert Simon, *The Sciences of the Artificial* (Cambridge: MIT Press, 1969), chap. 7, "The Architecture of Complexity." The importance of an understanding of the mind as a hierarchically arranged system is reflected in recent modularity theories of mind and their notion that the processes of modular units are relatively inaccessible to, and unchangeable by, higher-order processes. See especially Jerry Fodor, *The Modularity of Mind: An Essay on Faculty Psychology* (Cambridge: MIT Press, 1983). See also Noam Chomsky, *Modular Approaches to the Study of Mind* (San Diego: San Diego State University Press, 1984). Connectionist models of mind are decidedly less hierarchical than modular models, but they also display a kind of hierarchical structure, in the sense that there is sequential processing of information. Even though much processing is done in parallel, the different "parallel" strands also display sequencing. Nothing I say here is intended to prejudice a case against connectionist models of mind.

11. What I say here is clearly in opposition to the Cartesian view that what is mental is accessible to introspection. Lower-order activity or processing can occur without one's being aware of its occurring (i.e., without being aware of the activity or process as it is going on, or that it is going on) or aware of what sort of activity or process is going on. Further, the notion of consciousness is itself problematic and perhaps not univocal. Ned Block, for one, has distinguished several kinds of consciousness. See his review of Daniel C. Dennett, *Consciousness Explained*, in *Journal of Philosophy* 90 (1993): 181–193.

psychological process. Whatever perception, idea, or affective quality of experience results that one is aware of is often (if not always) in itself insufficient for knowing either what kind of activity or process had that result, or what went into the process eventuating in that result.

An example of this "automatic" activity is the sort that underlies the selectivity of attention and thought processes. "Real-time" constraints on the process of reading, as discussed in Chapter 1, ensure that one will not be able to explore all ways of apprehending and thinking about a chunk of text during any given "nonobsessive" session of reading. Nothing can elicit a response unless it has been "selected" out, that is, unless it emerges as a unit or entity at some level within the hierarchy of psychological operations which entity is then itself used psychologically, or "processed" in some way. Numerous factors influence what happens during these operations and hence what selections are eventually made and what is done with them after they are made. These factors include properties of the perceived text as well as one's character and personality traits, goals, desires and concerns, and recent and remote past experiences. The effectiveness of any of these factors may, of course, remain hidden to readers themselves; readers are not always in the best position to notice what explains why they notice what they do, or why they "process" what they do in the way they do.[12]

Mental shifts and slides may themselves occur "automatically": changed contexts and new experiences affect patterns of salience and how one experiences or responds to a given passage. Yet, despite the automaticity of the selectivity of attention and much mental processing, psychological shifts can also be effected intentionally by readers. Particularly striking examples of intentional changes in the mental processing of visual stimuli are provided by "double-aspect"

---

12. The influence of context on comprehension is well known, both for auditory and visual linguistic input. In speech perception, there may well be a phonemic module that organizes sounds into meaningful units so that the sound is unavailable to conscious awareness before it is so organized. Duplex perception—the simultaneous evocation of speech and purely auditory percepts—is rare. See D. H. Whalen and Alvin M. Liberman, "Speech Perception Takes Precedence over Nonspeech Perception," *Science* (10 July 1987); pp. 169–171. In reading, of course, the situation is different because the stimulus is visual, not auditory. Though the rarity of duplex perception is in less doubt, similar phenomena do exist. We have a tendency to "not see" repeated words or words with minor variations ("or" for "of") from the ones we expect. These are the things that make proofreading difficult. Thus, the processing of visual linguistic information also involves a higher level of mental organization which is at least more immediately accessible to conscious awareness.

figures, such as the duck-rabbit and Necker cube. Looking at a drawing of a Necker cube, one can see the lower square as representing
the front face of a cube or as representing its back face. With a little
practice, it is possible to acquire control over this "flipping" so that it
is possible to tell oneself, "this is the front face of the cube," and the
rest of the lines will fall into their perceptual places.

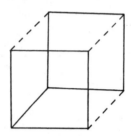

It would come as no surprise that spontaneous or automatic mental
shifts and slides occur even though the psychological mechanisms
responsible for effecting those changes remain completely unknown
to us. But they can also be consciously and intentionally effected
without our knowing anything about, psychologically, *how* we can do
it. That is, we can effect a change in "lower-order" processing without
knowing anything about how that processing is conducted. We all
know that the channels on a television set can be changed by someone
who knows nothing about electronics or about what goes on inside
the TV when that change is effected. All we need to know, given the
"user-friendly" design of most televisions, is which buttons to press.
One noteworthy fact about the human mind is that, to a large extent,
we can press, as it were, our own psychological buttons without knowing the character of the lower processes we are in effect changing.
Human minds, unlike TV sets, don't come with a set number of
channels ready to deliver a finite number of preprogrammed options,
and I think it's fair to say that human minds aren't nearly as "user-
friendly" as most TV sets. It is possible, however, to gain control over
many aspects of the mind's operation. Acquiring control over the
"flipping" does not require knowing either the "program" or "rules"
governing how the sensory stimuli become integrated to produce
such experiences, or how, neurophysiologically, this integration happens.

One other feature of this "flipping" and its multifarious manifestations in affective responses to fictional literature bears emphasizing.

Mental shifts can be effected without our knowing and without our even having beliefs about what role various parts of the text will play when we make the shift. Notice that this observation is different from claiming that we don't have to know the *mechanisms* that become operative when we make a mental shift or the rules that come into operation. Rather, we don't have to know how the various "data" or "stimuli" will be integrated into the experience. It is the difference between having to know what rules will become operative (what principles will govern the integration of the stimuli), and having to know how the stimuli will figure in the experience (phenomenologically, what role they will play).[13]

Look at the Necker cube again. I don't have to tell myself, before I can see the Necker cube as a representation of a three-dimensional figure with the lower left square representing the front face, "the dotted lines represent the visible edge of a cube receding to the right," and "the upper square represents the back face"; that is, I don't have to know or command what role each aspect of the figure is supposed to play in my perceptual experience. My mind simply operates in such a way that it "interprets" as many segments of the drawing as possible in a coherent way, without my having to think through in advance how the various portions of the image will be made to "fit" or integrate with the new interpretation. I do not have to know, in advance, how all the "parts" of the sensory experience will become integrated into the new "gestalt" or even whether they *can* be so integrated.

Although it's pretty clear that conscious awareness of how all the parts will integrate in order to make the perceptual shift is not necessary, one might think that some kind of preconscious or unconscious "knowledge" of, or at least beliefs about, how this integration can and will occur might be necessary before one can actually make the shift. The argument would be that the ability to make a specific mental shift would be inexplicable unless one had preconscious knowledge of, or at least beliefs about, how it was to be done. Thus, the preconscious knowledge or belief would explain how one could make the shift.

Two different positions need to be distinguished with respect to

13. Why this difference is important will become clearer in Chapter 3 (secs. II and III). There I argue that one can psychologically simulate what goes on in another person's mind, or what would go on in one's own mind in a different set of circumstances, without having anything approaching a complete set of beliefs about how each aspect of one's sensory input will be processed. That is, simulations do not require developing a theory about the relevant aspects of that person's psychology.

the necessity of preconscious belief.[14] First, the philosophical version of the view: preconscious belief is necessary to make a mental shift because there is no other way to explain how the shift can be made. Notice that this philosophical version makes a claim not merely about human psychology, but about any psychology; it in effect asserts that no psychological system can have a design that allows for mental shifting without involving such preconscious beliefs. The philosophical version of the necessity of preconscious belief needs to be distinguished from the empirical version of the view, which holds that the human mind does in fact work in such a way that preconscious belief about how all the "data" will be integrated into the new perceptual experience is in fact used to effect a mental shift. The empirical version is not the (philosophical) claim that a mind couldn't work without preconscious belief but rather the empirical claim that the human mind in fact doesn't work without it.

Even though the philosophical version has a certain plausibility with respect to simple visual arrays that are accessed, more or less, all at once, it loses that plausibility when considered in relation to literary texts, which are accessed through time, bit by bit. Due to the temporal nature of reading, we make mental shifts that affect how the prose we read subsequently will affect us before we even know what those words will be. That is, we put ourselves into a "mindset," a different dispositional state, that affects how what we encounter later will or will not move us. Thus, the mental shifts and slides we make while reading constitute a way of "trying things out," a kind of experimentation where we don't know, nor even hypothesize, what the results will be. We don't know how, or even if, we will respond to the text to be read next. We don't know whether our current psychological condition will create a useful pattern of salience and sensitivity to nuance, or whether it will prevent appreciative experiences of the work. Long periods when we continue to read but remain unmoved should signal us to try shifting into a different mode, attend to different details, or adopt a different point of view.

There is one more consideration in refutation of the philosophical version of the necessity of preconscious belief which bears mentioning. The philosophical version holds that a preconscious belief about what role given "stimuli" will play in our experience is necessary

14. For ease of exposition, I consider only the position that preconscious belief is needed, and not the position that preconscious knowledge is needed. If the weaker position that belief is needed can be shown to be faulty, then, a fortiori, the view that knowledge is needed will be shown to be faulty.

before it is possible to make a mental shift wherein the "stimuli" play that role. The advocate of this version then needs to explain where we get that belief. Presumably, such beliefs don't appear ex nihilo and without justification. And here is the problem for the necessity of preconscious belief, because whatever explains how we come up with such beliefs could also explain how we can make the mental shift without introducing preconscious belief as an intermediary. Consider the following analogy with the process of induction. Suppose one sees an F connected with a G, and then another F connected with another G. Upon seeing a third F one may well think "G," without ever having formed the belief "whenever there is an F there is a G" which mediates psychologically between one's past experiences of Fs and Gs, on the one hand, and one's thought of G upon one's third sighting of an F, on the other. It may be that the repeated exposure to Fs followed by Gs puts one in a dispositional state such that, upon encountering a future F, one thinks, "G." Indeed, the effectiveness of stimulus-response conditioning as an explanation of lower-order animal behavior depends on the fact that such behavior does *not* require anything as cognitively sophisticated as the formation of a belief, that is, a propositional attitude. This fact is a good reason to avoid automatically construing such mental states as tacit or implicit beliefs—as a kind of belief.

When one sees the square to the bottom left of the Necker cube as the front face of the cube, one intermediary belief about how the "stimuli" figure in one's experience would be something like the following: the dotted lines represent visible edges of a cube receding to the right. Let us call this belief *B*. When one achieves the mental shift that sees the bottom left square as the front face of the cube, the issue is whether one needs first to have formulated *B* to effect this shift, since the advocate of preconscious belief claims *B* is needed to explain how the shift can be made. My objection is that coming up with *B* itself needs to be explained. How does one acquire that belief? It certainly appears to me, through an examination of my own experience when I make such mental shifts, that I discover what role the various "stimuli" play *after* making the shift. But appeals to the phenomenology of experience, though they bear some weight, are notoriously inconclusive. Perhaps there is a "preconscious" or "unconscious" belief to that effect, of which I am unaware.

My argument against the necessity of preconscious belief does not appeal to the phenomenology of experience but to the following fact: if one does form the belief *B,* something about one's past experiences or encounter with the visual array led one to come up with the belief *B*. These past experiences or visual encounter leave one in state *S*. Just as the repeated encounters with *F*s followed by *G*s could leave one in a dispositional state that explains why one thinks *G* after encountering a future F without forming an intermittent belief, "All *F*s are *G*," so also an encounter with the visual array of the Necker cube could leave one in a psychological state *S* that explains how one can make a mental shift to see the Necker cube with the lower left square as the front face without forming *B*, the intermediary belief that the dotted lines represent the visible edge of the cube receding to the right. The state *S* might explain what makes the perceptual shift possible without generating the intermediary preconscious belief of how a particular feature is to be integrated into that new perception.

In fact, it is certainly implausible to assume that our minds take preconscious note of every possible perceptual role that a given "datum" might play. And, if our minds don't form beliefs about every possible role, why, we might ask, would we take note of some possible perceptual roles rather than others? Whatever explains why we arrived at and stored a preconscious belief about a given possible perceptual role—whatever explains why we selected out that possible perceptual role to store information about—could also explain why the relevant perceptual shift was made, even if we didn't, prior to that perceptual shift, store a preconscious belief about its possible perceptual role. That is, "taking note of" a possible perceptual role could be constituted by the visual stimuli's serving to generate a perceptual shift rather than by our storing a preconscious belief about this possible role.

It might be the case that there is no explanation for why one's mind stores, preconsciously, a particular bit of data or information (e.g., about possible perceptual roles of a given feature) for future use. It is possible that the mind "stores up" such information randomly, as a kind of "search" mechanism to gather up what might possibly be of use but whose usefulness one is not in a position presently to anticipate. However, if it's possible for the mind to engage in random preconscious selectivity, why isn't it also possible for the mind to make random mental shifts? The shifting would itself then be a kind of experiential exploratory activity without a prior basis or source in the form of stored information about possible roles of various perceptual features that would explain why one made that shift.

In reading fictional literature, mental shifts are elicited by what we read. They are also effected consciously and deliberately on the basis of things we know or believe. And they are generated somewhat randomly as we "try out" various points of view or modes of approach to see what *does* help to make sense of the text. Multiple experiences of a given passage of text may combine, as in the Smollett example, to enhance appreciation. Smollett plays a little joke on the reader—first letting us take the use of a phrase at face value ("It would take the pencil of a Hogarth . . .") and then showing us how we've been fooled. "Getting into it" requires a willingness to experience these twists and turns, to double-back and double-check, and to try again. What it does not require is sufficient familiarity with the work to know, in advance, that we are adopting the right psychological condition or frame of mind and how that and our responses should occur during the course of a work. Put very bluntly, we don't have to know the whole work to appreciate a part of it.

When we make a mental shift, psychological adjustments occur, more or less automatically, lower down in the hierarchy of "programs" that process linguistic "stimuli."[15] Though we can describe the conscious effects of mental shifts—perceptions, ideas, or emotions and other affective responses—and though we have some techniques for producing them intentionally, the average person really doesn't know what in particular goes on at that preconscious level that constitutes implementing the executive order to make this psychological shift. We do not know how the "program" works, what constitutes its implementation, how it is changed, nor often even what kind of outcome it will produce.[16] Indeed, knowing what the "program" is and how it works may not even help to initiate or achieve this shift. But even if we have no idea what's going on deep down in the dark recesses of the psyche which constitutes implementing a shift in perspective or attitude, people can and often do make it happen. Decisions, choices, and intentions are, at least sometimes, sufficient to ensure that a given sort of psychological process does take place so

15. I have adopted talk of programs because I think it is a useful metaphor for capturing differences between the kinds of psychological processes that can take place. "Running a program" allows for more cognitive richness than the metaphor of "being in a given gear." It is only a metaphor, and one that makes me a bit nervous because programs are sets of rules governing behavior. I do not mean to imply that there is an explicit representation of a rule that plays a role in the perceptual process, even if that process is describable by rules.

16. See Richard Wollheim's discussion of how one can perform an action intentionally and yet discover what one intended to do by looking at what one has done, in "On Drawing an Object," in *On Art and the Mind* (Cambridge: Harvard University Press, 1974): 3–30.

that we end up having a given sort of perception, idea, attitude, or experience.

The affective shifting and sliding I have discussed in this section constitute an important part of the activity of readers during the process of reading. The automaticity of much of this activity, which keeps the activity relatively hidden from our introspective view, makes it harder to appreciate its significance for the process of appreciating fictional literature. Our relative ignorance of what goes on during affective shifts and slides has a similar disadvantage. Nevertheless, our minds subtly or blatantly change and adjust as we read, as we try to make sense of our ever-expanding access to the work. Some of the mental shifts and slides, cognitive and affective, are due to additional cognitive "input." But the same "input" can be processed in different ways to yield different affective results. I have argued that it is not always appropriate to attribute beliefs, even preconscious beliefs, to explain why such shifts and slides are made, for to do so represents the process in a way that is overly cognitive. In the case of empathy in particular, as explained in the following chapter, appealing to such beliefs seriously misrepresents the nature of the mental process or activity.

In the following section I explore the importance of *temporal* aspects of what generates psychological shifts and slides during appreciation. Both the timing and duration of past experiences—including access to various parts of a text—help to explain why one responds to what one does as one does. These temporal factors, rather than cognitive factors such as belief, go a long way to explaining why we are in states such that, upon reading a specific passage of text, we respond in a given way.

III: Sensitivities

One sort of thing that can change through psychological shifts and slides is what I call sensitivities. A sensitivity is the psychological state or condition that makes it the case that one will have a particular kind of emotional or affective response to a certain sort of phenomenon or situation, or, to what elicits the response. The character or kind of sensitivity one has—what condition constitutes having that sensitivity —is identified in part in terms of the psychologically effective properties of what one is responding to and in part in terms of the character of the response one has. Sensitivities, in so far as they "reveal" themselves at all, "reveal" themselves by the emotions or affects one has. This assertion should not be taken to imply, of course, that one's sensitivities will always be visible to others, or even that they will always be apparent to oneself; one may be very good at hiding them or not very good at discerning one has them. More than one sensitivity may be manifested by the same sorts of emotions or affects, but only in so far as they are elicited by different phenomena. It is certainly possible, however, and commonly the case that different sorts of experiences can generate the same sensitivity, that is, get one into a condition such that one will respond to a particular sort of phenomenon in a given way.

Sensitivities are acquired and lost: they undergo a great deal of fluctuation even during the course of a day and even more during a week, month, or the span of a lifetime. Recent past experiences, memories, beliefs, and desires can all affect one's sensitivities, as can how much sleep one has had, how hungry one is and whether one is taking any medication. Sensitivities are to some extent under one's control, though some can prove to be quite intractable. Training through processes of sensitization and desensitization can be used to alter at least some standard sensitivities, though some can also be turned "on" or "off" more or less at will. Control over one's sensitivities might have to be gained indirectly, by one's making a more global mental shift in "mental set"—by changing the focus of attention or the goal towards which one is oriented—so that something will not strike one as being as poignant, or humorous, or whatever, as it would were one to persist in the same psychological "gear."

The sequencing and timing of a certain set of recent past experiences may explain why one responds to what one does, in the way one does—in short, why one has the sensitivities one has. The sequencing of a set of experiences is the systematic order in which they occur, for example, if they occur in increasing or decreasing intensity. The timing of a set of experiences comprises several factors: the duration or length of time an experience lasted, the (relative and absolute) length of time between various (relevant) past experiences, and the length of time between those experiences and the present moment.

The example from Heinrich Böll's *Billiards at Half-Past Nine* discussed in Chapter 1 illustrates how sensitivities can change with repeated exposure. But repeated exposure can affect sensitivities nontemporally, just by piling up past experiences regardless of when they occurred. In contrast, consider the following situation in which the actual timing of the past experiences provides a major part of the explanation for why I had a particular sort of response to a particular sort of situation. It explains why I had the response I did to this sort of situation by explaining why I came to have the sensitivity I had, how I came to be in the condition such that I would respond in this way to this sort of situation. The situation is that I am tired after a long day of work. I have prepared my dinner, and I'm just about to sit down at the table for a relaxing and satisfying meal. The phone rings. ("We will be in your area installing new energy-efficient windows for some of your neighbors. Do you own your own home there in Fairway?") I hadn't gotten such phone calls at dinnertime in years. I give my stock response to telephone solicitations and proceed with dinner. The following evening, just as I've started in on my evening meal, the phone rings (carpet cleaning this time). The third evening as I'm carrying my plate of food to the table at dinnertime I feel a little apprehensive. We all know why: good old-fashioned conditioning.

Suspense is a good example of a response in which temporal factors play an important role. Language that incites ideas of possible harm, or even disaster, and pauses and delays in relating the eventual results while not allowing the relevant concerns to fade from consciousness all contribute to suspense. The so-called paradox of suspense occurs when second and third time readers—called "recidivists" by Noël Carroll—experience suspense even though they know what is going to happen.[17] A paradox arises, of course, only if one supposes that suspense requires actual uncertainty about what will happen. But one's knowledge of what will happen may be deliberately taken "off line" by a reader, so that it does not interfere with the response. Hence, even if one does know what will happen, the timing and sequencing of what one reads can condition one's responses in pretty much the same way they do when one doesn't know what will happen. Though Carroll also dissolves the paradox by appealing to unasserted thoughts rather than beliefs, he underplays the role of timing. He points out that in film theory the main position has been that suspense in a film is created when a time period is "distended" and outcomes "delayed" in relation to what one expects in real life. But something like suspense, though more commonly known as tension or anxiety, also occurs in real life, and it is inexplicable according to this account.

17. Noël Carroll, "The Paradox of Suspense," delivered at the 1994 American Philosophical Association Central Division Meeting, Kansas City, Mo., 6 May, 1994.

The relation between real-life time and the timing in fiction does not explain suspense. Whatever serves to keep ideas and concerns in mind while delaying knowledge of the eventual result, or keeping that knowledge "off line," creates suspense in both.[18]

The telephone ringing just at dinnertime the previous two evenings made me sensitive to a certain kind of situation. That is, the repeated, recent occurrence of a given sort of event (the telephone ringing) in a certain kind of situation (I am at home, just about to sit down to dinner) generated in me a psychological condition such that I would affectively respond to that kind of situation. The psychological condition may be relatively short term, of course. If the situation-type I am sensitive to doesn't occur within the next day or so—say, if I go *out* to eat the following two nights—the "spell" may be broken so that I am no longer sensitive to it. The fact that an effect in one's underlying psychological condition can be short term shows that timing is an important part of the explanation for your having the sensitivity. Experiences may have longer lasting indirect effects in the sense that I now may become sensitive to that sort of situation more easily than I would have otherwise. Though it may seem unlikely for such a trivial thing as the phone ringing at dinnertime, more significant propensities to develop sensitivities could have been established, say, in one's youth.

A relatively temporary, localized shift in sensitivity due to the set of recent, repeated experiences is described in (rather than evoked by) Heinrich Böll's short story "Murke's Collected Silences." Murke works in radio production, and for the past two days he has been editing some tapes on the topic "The Nature of Art." Taking a break, Murke goes to the office coffee shop where he overhears other employees talking, and one shouts out, "Art! Art! Art!" "Murke felt a spasm, like the frog when Galvani discovered electricity. The last two days Murke had heard the word *art* too often; . . . it occurred exactly one hundred and thirty-four times in the two talks; and he had heard the talks three times, which meant he had· heard the word *art* four hundred and two times, too often to feel any desire to discuss it." Their discussion continued, however, and "each time one of them shouted 'art' Murke winced. It's like being whipped, he thought."[19]

---

18. In "The Paradox of Suspense" Carroll points out (p. 20) that concern about the outcome is a necessary condition for suspense. I argue in Chapter 5 that temporal factors can also influence one's cares and concerns: they can *make* us care when there are no independent grounds for doing so.
19. Böll, "Murke's Collected Silences," p. 130.

In the telephone example, the phone ringing occurred on only two occasions during the last several years, yet it was sufficient to establish a sensitivity to the situation-type "just about to sit down to dinner" in spite of its infrequency. This sensitivity manifests itself by my feeling a little apprehensive. Emotions are widely thought to have cognitive components—beliefs or thoughts that serve both to distinguish one emotion from another and to explain why each manifests itself in certain kinds of behaviors. Apprehensiveness is an emotion state whose cognitive component is something like, "something bad or untoward is about to happen." My two experiences of the phone ringing just at dinnertime the previous two evenings certainly do not justify a belief that something bad will happen that third evening—either that the phone will ring or that I will be interrupted yet again. But is it necessary to attribute to me the belief that something bad will happen in order to explain why I have the emotion? The explanation for the emotion offered above, that it's due to "good old-fashioned conditioning," suggests that a belief that something bad will happen is not in fact involved. Explanations in terms of conditioning are applicable to organisms that are not cognitively sophisticated enough to form beliefs and are applicable to humans with respect to those processes that take place independently of the beliefs they do form.

For my response to be an *emotion*, however, rather than merely an affect (such as a feeling of tension or uneasiness), my mental state must have a cognitive component. The emotion's cognitive component may take the form of an unasserted thought rather than a belief.[20] An unasserted thought is a propositional content of mind that is not believed but simply "in mind." An idea, by contrast, is a non-propositional content of mind that is also, of course, not believed ("of course," because it is non-propositional). Both unasserted thoughts and ideas may be occurrent—actively entertained or brought to mind, or "conscious"—or dispositional—"recorded" in mind and

20. This is Roger Scruton's term. See *Art and Imagination: A Study in the Philosophy of Mind* (London: Methuen, 1974), pp. 88–89. Among those who have defended the view that the cognitive component of emotions may be thoughts rather than beliefs are Peter Lamarque, "How Can We Fear and Pity Fictions?" *British Journal of Aesthetics* 21 (1981); Patricia S. Greenspan, *Emotions and Reasons: An Inquiry into Emotional Justification* (New York: Routledge, 1988), chap. 2, sec. (i); Noël Carroll, *The Philosophy of Horror or Paradoxes of the Heart* (New York: Routledge, 1990); and Richard Moran, "The Expression of Feeling in Imagination," *Philosophical Review* 103 (1994): 75–106. David Pugmire has recently argued against this view. See "Real Emotion," *Philosophy and Phenomenological Research* 54 (1994), p. 116, "Real emotion demands actual belief." See also Chapter 4, sec. II, and Chapter 5, sec. III.

thereby affect what one does and thinks of next, but not be an object of present awareness. Ideas, as well as thoughts, may generate affective responses, though not emotions.

I may think of a situation as being a given way without believing that it is that way. I may see a huge bank of gray clouds as a locomotive descending from the sky and think of the repeatedly rejected paper sitting in my desk drawer as an unappreciated masterpiece and the most important thing written in philosophy in the twentieth century. I may perceive and think of things as being in ways that are not, and that I well know are not, accurate or veridical. So in the telephone example, we can explain why I have the emotion "apprehensiveness" by referring to the fact that I think of the situation as one where something bad is about to happen. Why I think of it as being that way is most plausibly explained by my recent experiences of the past two evenings—the conditioning effected by the recent juxtaposition of events. In this case, what those recent experiences condition is my current thought and the attendant emotion.

It is possible to have an affective rather than an emotional response to the telephone's ringing that third evening. For example, I might become tense or uneasy. These are both affects; neither has a cognitive component that (in part) identifies it as the affect it is. Indeed, my uneasiness may generate the thought that something bad or unpleasant is going to happen ("Why do I feel uneasy? Maybe something bad is about to happen"), which thought then helps to sustain the feeling. In this way, affective responses can lead to evaluative thoughts and hence emotions.

It is not necessary to attribute an (irrational) belief to me, for example, that my dinner will be interrupted once again, in order to explain my emotional response.[21] A pattern of recent past experiences can establish a *cognitive association* (developed through "good old-fashioned conditioning") between a given type of situation (where I am at home, just about to sit down to dinner) and a certain thought (that something bad is about to happen), so that when (I realize) I am in that situation I tend to have that thought. At least one sort of connectionist model of mind has a very neat way of accounting for this conditioning. Neural pathways between nodes representing different ideas and thoughts (the idea of the situation type and the thought that something bad is about to happen) can be both created and

21. The argument in this paragraph is adapted from Greenspan, *Emotions and Reasons*, chap. 2, sec. (i), "Evaluation Minus Judgment," pp. 17–22.

reinforced by a particular pattern of experience. Hence, when I realize that I am in a situation of that type, there is increased likelihood
that the node representing the thought that something bad is about to
happen will be excited (because of the strengthening of the relevant
pathway), along with any connections or pathways that exist between
it and other thoughts, ideas, or feelings. Yet this explanatory apparatus makes no appeal to beliefs.

It is not at all clear, however, how to distinguish the psychological
state of believing something from the state of just thinking of it,
especially when merely thinking of it has cognitive and affective effects. To complicate things further, one may have an (occurrent)
unasserted thought of something one does believe, when the fact that
one believes it is not part of the psychological explanation for why the
ideas or emotions were generated. They might arise simply because
one thought of it—they would have occurred even if one didn't believe it. That is, in this latter sort of case, it is not the fact that one
believes it that explains why one engaged in the mental train of
thought or why one felt what one did, even though one does believe
it. It is simply the fact that one thought of it that does the explaining.
James Mill, John Stuart's father, in his zeal to reduce all mental contents to what can be accounted for by associationist psychology, held
that the extent to which one entertained a thought was the extent to
which one believed it. Such a crude analysis of the nature of belief is
surely incorrect. Believing something involves some kind of endorsement of or assent to what is believed, an endorsement or assent that
does not exist when one merely thinks of something or "unassertedly"
entertains the thought—even if one thinks of it semi-obsessively.
Since it is not at all clear what endorsement or assent consists in, it is
difficult to describe the crucial differences between believing something and merely unassertedly entertaining the thought of it. One
thing should, however, be clear: a thought's generating other
thoughts, emotions, or affects is not sufficient to show one has as-
sented to or endorsed the truth of what one thought of; it is not
sufficient to show one believes it.

One might argue that belief—the particular attitude one can take
toward a proposition—is in fact analyzable in terms of the functional
role of its mental content in one's "cognitive economy," that is, in
terms of some complicated set of relationships among sensory
"input," behavioral "output," and other mental states. Such a view has
a certain plausibility, and I do not wish to argue against it here. In
fact, I believe that my claims are consistent with at least some versions

of this view, depending on how one defines the functional roles that fix belief. What I object to—and hence the confusion I wish to avoid —is a particular rather simple-minded construal of the view that a propositional attitude such as belief is constituted by the role the propositional content plays in one's mental and behavioral economy. This simple-minded construal is the view that if a propositional thought has the psychological effect of inducing affective or emotion states, or other cognitive states, this effect is sufficient to show one believes it. This version of a functionalist analysis of the propositional attitude of belief is surely incorrect. Most outrageously, it denies that one can engage in hypothetical thought, that is, thinking through the consequences of a position even though one doesn't believe it (and perhaps even because one doesn't believe it). Less outrageously, it denies that one can engage in mental shifts and slides that produce different affective responses. It is possible to think of something one doesn't believe, and an affect or emotion may in turn be generated by that thought.

This discussion, of course, does not settle what functional role of a thought is sufficient to establish that one believes it. I have no general account of this, either for belief or other attitudes. Fortunately, such an account is not necessary for the purposes of this book. All I must do is establish that certain kinds of functional roles, such as where thoughts induce other thoughts, ideas, affects, and emotions, are not sufficient to establish that one believes that such-and-so is true.

One's psychological state or condition partially determines whether one will respond affectively or emotionally to a given verbal array and what kind of response one will have. The determining features of one's state or condition for whether and how one responds are not merely the ideas, memories, beliefs, desires, and so on, one has— not merely a matter of what mental contents are stored. Neither is it merely a function of what attitudes (such as beliefs) one has toward those contents. Another sort of determining feature is what role one's mental contents are "programmed" to play in generating new ideas, emotions, or whatever at any given time. The "programs" can be affected by patterns of past experience in a way that operates relatively independently of belief, as explained in the telephone example above. The fact that one can shift psychologically between two read- ings of the same piece of text, as in the Angela Carter example given at the beginning of section I, shows that it is not simply *what* mental contents are in one's mind but what psychological "gear" one is in that affects one's response. To recall another metaphor introduced previously, if you run one program you have one set of responses, and if another, another set.

My objective in this chapter has been to elucidate the nature of a mental shift or slide and to describe what features of the human mind it is necessary to posit to explain the capacity to engage in these shifts and slides. When a mental shift takes place in response to fictional literature, something changes in the way a linguistic string is processed. The shift occupies a point on a continuum between (a) a shift in perspective on a specifically describable array and (b) a more global shift in attitude, frame of mind, or point of view. Mental shifts are not always dramatic: they may comprise slow and subtle changes in sensitivities to what is read. With respect to both shifts and slides, we may not be aware that we have made a change or how we have changed. Nevertheless, we can, at least sometimes, voluntarily initiate some of these shifts and slides ourselves. It takes practice both to expand our capacity for making mental shifts and to initiate them. Furthermore, mental shifts and slides do not have to be initiated by changes in beliefs. One can retain all the same beliefs but experience something in a very different way precisely because one has shifted into a different "mental gear," similar to the way a car handles the same stretch of road differently when it is in a different gear and to the way a perceptual system handles a Necker cube in different ways.

In the following chapter I use the notion of a mental shift to explicate what is commonly known as empathy. When one starts to empathize with someone, one shifts into a different mental condition, so that one's pattern of thoughts and experiences *simulates* the (relevant) mental activities of that other person. I then use the notion of simulation to explain what it is to empathize with a fictional character.

Chapter Four

Simulation and Empathy

To make a mental shift or slide is to come to be in a different psychological condition, so that one's sensory "input"—experiences, ideas, or thoughts—will be processed differently, so that they will generate different experiences, ideas, or thoughts from what they would have if one were in some other psychological "gear." Sometimes one shifts psychological gears and then *simulates* what is going on in another person's mind. In doing so one empathizes with that other person. In the first three sections of this chapter I develop an account of psychological simulation. The first section distinguishes simulations from other types of imitations, the second section describes the sorts of psychological processes that constitute simulating, and the third section distinguishes *simulating* another's mental activity from having a belief or theory about another's mental activity. These three sections do not deal with fiction directly but constitute the philosophical foundation for an analysis of what it is to empathize with fictional characters. In section IV, I use the account of simulation to understand empathy with a fictional character. One empathizes with a fictional character, whom I shall call the protagonist, when one "shares" an emotion, feeling, desire, or mood of that character. The "sharing," on my account, is done through a simulation, which explains not only what emotion or affect one has but also how one can come to be in the phenomenological state identified with that affect. Section V explains how the similarity of experience between the empathizer and protagonist can be explained by this account, and section VI describes how this similarity of experience can be defended as knowledge of what it's like to be a certain sort of person or in a certain sort of situation.

I: What Is a Simulation?

Objects can be imitated. There are wooden nickels, imitation leathers, and fake Vermeers. Synthetics are a special kind of imitation. A synthetic has a great number of the internal structural properties of a specific naturally occurring substance, except that it is produced not by the usual, natural means but by alternative means, often a technologically sophisticated manufacturing process. Synthetic rubber is a manufactured version of the substance that comes from rubber trees. Many substances found originally in plants and animals can be produced synthetically in a laboratory. Some synthetics actually replicate the exact structure of the synthesized substance and hence are no longer imitations but realizations of that substance, albeit ones produced by alternative means and perhaps with certain different (accidental, not essential) properties.

However, not all imitations are synthetics. Artifacts—tables and chairs, cups and saucers, as well as Picassos and Vermeers—can be imitated but not synthesized. Furthermore, there can be imitations of natural kinds that are not synthetics. Imitations of natural kinds that are not synthetics merely give the appearance of being that sort of substance without having its essential structural properties, so that the imitation doesn't *behave* (except, to a certain extent, to the eye) like that substance. Imitation wood grain, naugahyde, faux granite, and marbleized finishes are examples. I will call such things "surface imitations." Imitations and synthetics are made for many purposes, including appearance, economy, and fraud.

I am not primarily concerned here with imitations or synthetics as just described but with simulations. Objects, kinds of objects, and the appearances of objects are imitated, but activities or processes are simulated. A process, procedure, or sequence can be simulated by another process, procedure, or sequence. An important category of imitation for Plato and Aristotle—one I would call a simulation—involves using the movements of one's own body to do the imitating. When a simulation is effected via overt human actions, we call it "pretending," "acting," "mimicking," "miming," or, in certain cases, "impersonating." Whereas imitations of objects have a greater or lesser number of properties of the object imitated (including structural and visual properties), a simulation has the same basic relationships among subprocesses as what it simulates. Thus, simulations instantiate some of the structurally significant features of the processes they simulate.[1]

Ordinary English does not always recognize the distinction between the ontological types—objects on the one hand and activities or processes on the other—that, respectively, are imitated or simulated. We speak of simulated leather and imitations of actions. As I use the term, however, only activities or processes are simulated. This limitation is important for understanding the nature of empathy (and sympathy), which I take essentially to involve processes, things we do, rather than merely states or conditions. We must be in a certain sort of state or condition to do the empathizing, but the empathizing itself is a process or activity.[2] Having a feeling of a certain sort is naturally thought of as a state or condition, but I argue in section V that the character of this feeling is explicable instead by the nature of the psychological processes going on.

I also occasionally make use of the concept of a model. Models, the objects, can be used to model activities or processes. A model of a bridge (the object) can be used to model (to simulate) how a real bridge will behave under certain conditions.[3] One can shift or slide into a psychological "gear" wherein one uses one's own mind to model what another person does psychologically (the mental activity that person engages in) under certain conditions.[4] This activity is crucial

---

1. See, e.g., Alvin I. Goldman, "In Defense of the Simulation Theory," *Mind and Language* 7 (1992): 108, "By 'mental simulation,' let us mean a mental process that is, or is intended to be, *isomorphic* in some relevant respects to the target process it is intended to mimic."

2. Adam Morton, *Frames of Mind: Constraints on the Common-Sense Conception of the Mental* (New York: Oxford University Press, 1980), first turned my thinking in this direction. More detailed analysis along somewhat the same lines is contained in Robert M. Gordon, *The Structure of Emotions: Investigations in Cognitive Philosophy* (New York: Cambridge University Press, 1987), chap. 7. His "Folk Psychology as Simulation," *Mind and Language* 1 (1986): 158–171, develops the same idea. My large debt to the work of Gordon should be apparent in this chapter, though his simulation account is used to explain belief attribution, and I use it to account for activities of imagination. Arthur Ripstein, "Explanation and Empathy," *Review of Metaphysics* 40 (1987): 465–482, has also been very helpful.

3. Arthur Ripstein uses this example in "Explanation and Empathy," pp. 475–476.

4. Not all simulation accounts are alike. See Robert Gordon, "The Simulation Theory: Objections and Misconceptions," *Mind and Language* 7 (1992): 30–32, where he contrasts his version of the simulation theory with the model model. The major difference

to empathizing with actual people, and a similar phenomenon figures importantly in those emotional and affective responses to fiction known as empathizing with a fictional character.

There is a difference between simulations and dissimulations. A dissimulation is a process or activity that does not have the same basic internal structural relationships among subprocesses as occur in what is allegedly simulated but only an external appearance of similarity.[5] They are analogous to surface imitations. Computer simulations of mental processes, for example, must not only produce the right kinds of "outputs" (e.g., utterances) when provided with relevant "inputs" (e.g., sensory stimulation), but they must do so in a way that is structurally analogous to the way humans produce them. Indeed, the "inputs" may be quite different but still serve the appropriate purpose of simulation if the ways they are processed are structurally analogous. The deeper the structural similarities among processes and subprocesses that occur during the subsequent manipulation of "inputs," the more thorough the simulation. Simulations, like synthetics, may become structurally *so* like what they simulate, in the most essential respects, that a given process or activity is realized or instantiated, rather than merely simulated. (This fact clearly has implications for whether our responses to fiction are really emotions or not. Whether they are will depend in part on how "deep" a simulation must go to cease being a simulation and start being a realization or instance of an emotion, a topic I address in section V.)

One famous example of a *dis*simulation is Weizenbaum's computer program ELIZA, designed to mimic psychiatric therapeutic discourse.[6] ELIZA keys in on certain words, such as "mother," and plugs them into

---

hinges on the self-referentiality of the first person indexical during the simulation. I side with Gordon that "I" need not be used self-referentially: one may not be modeling how *I* would respond in those circumstances but how *someone else* would respond. But I argue that one is still using one's own mind as a model. (See Richard Wollheim's defense of the possibility of centrally imagining someone other than oneself in *The Thread of Life* [Cambridge: Harvard University Press, 1984], pp. 75–76; and Richard Moran's arguments against Walton's self-referring requirement for imagining, "The Expression of Feeling in Imagination," *Philosophical Review* 103 [1994]: 87–88.) For opposing arguments see Kendall L. Walton, *Mimesis as Make-Believe: On the Foundations of the Representational Arts* (Cambridge: Harvard University Press, 1990), pp. 28-35; and Robert Nozick, *Philosophical Explanations* (Cambridge: Harvard University Press, 1981), pp. 636–638.

5. For this distinction, see Philip N. Johnson-Laird, *Mental Models: Towards a Cognitive Science of Language, Inference, and Consciousness,* (Cambridge: Harvard University Press, 1983), chap. 2 and passim.

6. Cf. Johnson-Laird, *Mental Models,* p. xii.

predetermined sentence forms, including questions, to generate a series of words that can be read as responses to a "patient's" comments. The computer program may generate "outputs" such as "How long have you felt this way about your mother?" or "Why don't you tell me more about your mother?" However, one wouldn't want to say the computer program simulates the underlying thought processes or mental activity engaged in by psychiatrists—provided one is not too cynical about how psychiatrists' minds work—even if psychiatrists (typically, or in individual cases) end up saying exactly the sorts of things the computer generates as responses. Simply generating the appropriate "output" does not constitute a simulation; it must be done by sufficiently similar means or processes.

There is an analogy between synthetics and simulations, on the one hand, and surface imitations and dissimulations, on the other. With regard to the latter pair, they have in common the fact that similarities between the imitation (or simulation) and what is imitated (or what is simulated) are only superficial. The surface imitation exists by virtue of the similarity of appearance; the dissimulation occurs by virtue of similarity of "output" of the process, even though the processes by virtue of which the output is produced are entirely different.

II: What Is Required for a Simulation?

Suppose I want to know what I would do and how I would react under a given set of hypothetical circumstances. To predict how I would act under that set of circumstances, I might (try to) imagine or simulate being in those circumstances: I conjure ideas and thoughts of what I would see and hear in that situation, to see what kind of thoughts, feelings or behavior they generate. (Throughout I use "thought" and "unasserted thought" for propositional contents of mind that are not believed and "idea" for nonpropositional contents.) My mind would go "off line" from my present sensory input, thoughts, and beliefs, and use these other ideas and thoughts as inputs instead. The ideas and thoughts of what I would there encounter would then play roughly the same roles in the hierarchy of mental processes that the actual sensations would have played in that situation (i.e., similar enough for what I'm doing to be called a simulation). My ideas or unasserted thoughts would play roughly the same roles as the beliefs and thoughts that I would have brought to, and employed when dealing with, the situation. Engaging in this simulation requires the ability to shift psychological "gears," to go "off line" from many (though not all) of one's current sensations and beliefs, so that ideas and thoughts of what one *would* encounter can then be recruited to play a role in a simulation.

Similarly, I might want to predict what someone else would do or how she would react in a given situation. I can attempt to simulate how *she* would "process" or "use" the sensations that would be available to her, in light of her beliefs and past experiences. This task is probably more difficult, since her beliefs, character traits, and patterns of past experience may affect how her sensory "input" is processed in ways that are alien to me. There's no formula for how to get one's mind to do one of these simulations, either for knowing what to do or how to get your mind to do it.[7] I have absolutely no idea how in general to describe how the relevant changes get made either in the brain's "wetware" or in its "programming" when I make one of these psychological shifts. But if anything should be clear it is that one doesn't *have* to know these things in order to make such a shift, any more than one has to know what the innards of a car do to shift gears or how a TV works to change channels.

Kendall Walton argues that "all imagining involves a kind of self-imagining (imagining *de se*), of which imagining from the inside is the most common variety."[8] On the contrary, there is no sense in which imagining that takes the form of a simulation has oneself as its object. It may draw on characteristics one has, and of course the imagining is engaged in by *me*, but neither of these makes the imaginer even part of the object of the imagining. I argue below that the kind of imagination employed in empathy involves simulation. The extent to which one empathizes is the extent to which one's own mental functioning simulates that of another person, and the empathizing is no more about the empathizer than the *protagonist's* mental activity is about the empathizer. (In the special case where the protagonist is thinking about the empathizer, simulating the thoughts and feelings of the protagonist would involve having thoughts and feelings about oneself.)

It may be the case that none of the ideas or thoughts I employ to

7. There is more to be said, however, about techniques for doing the simulating. In particular, see the discussion in section V.
8. Walton, *Mimesis*, p. 29.

trigger or carry out the simulation are new. They may have been stored in memory for some time and accessed on this occasion for the purpose of engaging in the psychological simulation. When I engage in a simulation it is not necessarily the case that I use ideas or thoughts I've never had before, nor is it necessary that I employ or end up with new beliefs. I might acquire new ideas, thoughts, or beliefs—especially as a result of engaging in the simulation. It will be necessary, however, to get my ideas and thoughts to play different sorts of psychological roles from the ones they would play when not engaging in a simulation.

"Simulation" is a success-term, as is "appreciating," and there are two obvious ways an attempted simulation may go awry. First, my imagination may just not be up to the task. I may not be able to conjure the relevant or sufficient numbers of relevant ideas or thoughts corresponding to the "input" an individual would receive, and that would be salient in that person's attention and experience. This deficiency may be exacerbated by a small storehouse of past experiences to draw from in conjuring the relevant ideas and thoughts. Furthermore, I may not be able to do the simulating; I may not be able to get the ideas and thoughts to play the sorts of roles that would be played by the actual sensations and beliefs. The remedy for these deficiencies, like the remedy for other lapses in ability, is experimentation and practice. Practice helps one conjure the relevant ideas and thoughts, and practice helps one to get them to play different roles.

The other obvious way an attempted simulation may go awry has more to do with deficiencies in beliefs than it does with incapacities of imagination. If I'm trying to figure out how I would respond in a given situation, I may simply be mistaken about what I'd see or which beliefs or desires of mine would be psychologically most effective in that situation. Similarly, if I'm trying to figure out how someone else would respond in that situation, I may simply be mistaken about how what she hears and sees would be processed psychologically. A certain caution is necessary here, however. It is not the case that I conjure every idea and thought I do because I in fact believe that is what I (or the other person) would see or because I believe that is what would be psychologically effective. It is not necessary to appeal to beliefs to explain why I conjure particular ideas and thoughts or to explain the roles they play in the simulation. The appeal to beliefs is not necessary here for the same reason it is not necessary to appeal to preconscious beliefs about what perceptual role a given aspect of a visual array will play in order to explain how one can effect a perceptual shift on something like a Necker cube: whatever explains why one had those beliefs could explain why one conjured those particular ideas and thoughts, which then play a given psychological role, without going through the intermediary of forming a belief about what role they will or could play.[9]

We do not have to determine in advance all the different adjustments we need to make, such as what sets of beliefs, desires, and attitudes need to be attributed to a person whose mental processes or activities we desire to simulate. We can first do the imagining (which, if successful, will be a simulation) and then make inferences about what we more or less spontaneously did to determine whether we are justified in concluding anything, on the basis of that experience, about what that person feels, believes, or wants. Of course, we must be able to monitor or make reasonably reliable inferences about our own states and activities in order to identify what is being simulated. But there is no requirement that we form (second-order) beliefs about others' beliefs, desires, or other aspects of their psychological condition in order to simulate being in the affective state that other person is in. Psychologists recognize the existence of a process called "cognitive trial and error." This process involves imagining (as opposed to believing) how a solution to a problem would work before exploring that solution physically by actually carrying out the proposal.[10] We can certainly bring ideas to mind and construct hypotheses without actually believing that they are true: we wait for the results of the experiment to form our beliefs. And we can also simulate mental activities without accepting the view beforehand that anyone (else), actual or fictional, is engaging in such activity.

9. I argued for this in Chap. 3, sec. II.
10. See, for example, James L. Gould and Peter Marler, "Learning by Instinct," *Scientific American,* January 1987, p. 83. They argue that organisms are specialized for learning tasks they are likely to encounter. Thus organisms have innate or instinctual abilities to select out meaningful units of, for example, speech, while ignoring irrelevant auditory stimuli. Given the variety of aspects of a work of literature that can function aesthetically as well as the variety of symbol systems that may be employed in artworks, the significance of the instinctual is likely to be virtually, if not actually, nil (especially since conditioned responses can create such pronounced effects). A mark of the greater cognitive capacity of human beings is that, rather than being "hard-wired" to select out certain units as meaningful, we are mentally flexible, so that a variety of different kinds of units can be taken as meaningful, at least in imagination.

III: Simulations Contrasted with Theories

Modeling or simulating, as described above, is a particular kind of exercise of imagination, which has its own benefits. In this section I describe in a bit more detail how simulation or modeling contrasts with more cognitive or theoretical exercises of the mind. The reason I am insistent on simulation's providing a model for imagining which does not involve beliefs about the psychological states of the person whose mental processes are being simulated is that this model is crucial to the understanding of what does (and doesn't) go on with empathy and to the distinction between empathy and sympathy.[11]

Simulating and theorizing are two different ways of reaching conclusions about how something is behaving, or how it will behave, under given conditions.[12] I have already explained what a simulation is. A theory, for these purposes, is just a systematic set of beliefs, specifically, beliefs about the nature of the phenomenon to be understood that help to explain why it is as it is, how it will behave, and why it behaves as it does, including beliefs about laws or lawlike generalizations about its behavior. Making a model, such as a model of a bridge, that simulates the way a given bridge (or a given sort of bridge) behaves under certain conditions is very different from constructing a theory or set of beliefs about how the bridge will behave under those conditions. Models are often constructed precisely because one doesn't have those beliefs (or even a set of hypotheses)—one doesn't know what laws or generalizations govern the object's behavior.[13] Models are a way of finding out how something will behave when one lacks the relevant parts of the theory, and models can prove helpful in coming to discover them. Mental models can be constructed without the theory just as physical models can.

11. This account of empathy is a departure from what I argued in "Imagining Emotions and Appreciating Fiction," *Canadian Journal of Philosophy* 18 (1988): 485–500. There I argued that to empathize with another person one must have second-order beliefs about what that person believes; in essence, one must develop, to that extent, a theory about that person's mental condition. Chap. 7 of Robert Gordon's *The Structure of Emotions* provides a very plausible alternative way of understanding the process of empathy that does *not* require attributing second-order beliefs to the empathizer.

12. See Simon Blackburn, "Theory, Observation, and Drama," *Mind and Language* 7 (1992): 187–203, for a discussion of real and apparent differences between simulation accounts of how we go about attributing beliefs to other people, dubbed the "model model," where one uses one's own mind to model another person's, and the "theory theory," where one forms a theory or set of beliefs about another person's mental states and draws conclusions on the basis of those beliefs.

13. Ripstein, "Explanation and Sympathy," makes this point, pp. 475–476.

Models may be structurally similar to what is modeled in unknown respects; indeed, we often count on that being the case when we construct a model. I can construct a model of a keystone arch without knowing anything about its weight-distributing properties, even though it behaves, in these respects, just like the arch in southern France that I modeled. I can then use the model—by taking away parts, subjecting it to different forces, and so on—to discover how it distributes the weight. Likewise, mental activity may be simulated in many respects and at fairly deep levels in ways one doesn't even realize.

It is clear that you have to know or at least be in a position to hypothesize something about whatever you construct a model of. But you don't need anything like a theory about how it will behave or beliefs about what the relevant laws or generalizations are. The point is not a trivial one. If a systematic set of (conscious or preconscious) beliefs were necessary for making models or engaging in simulations, the simulation would not provide an *alternate* means for finding out how something, or some kind of thing, will behave: it would not have this practical value. One of the great things about models is that you can actually show things you don't have any theoretical explanation for.[14] In the mental realm, you try things out "in your imagination," as we say, to see what happens.[15] In the case of psychological simulations, I make my own mind into a model of the other person's, shifting psychological "gears" so that ideas and thoughts are processed in a different way from the way I would process them under my own current circumstances (as long as the other person is different from me in these respects).

Modeling explains what it is to "get into it"—your personal psychological involvement is required for simulating in a way it isn't for theorizing. A simulation is made by having an unasserted thought of *p* play a certain role during the simulation process, rather than by using a second-order belief that "*S* would believe *p* under those circumstances" during the attempted simulation. In a simulation, I get a thought, *p* (which I don't believe), to play some of the roles it would play in someone else, *S*, who does believe it. But a second-order belief that "*S* would believe *p* under those circumstances" could not play that role. The second-order belief (*S* believes that *p*) plays a role

14. Ripstein, "Explanation and Sympathy," p. 476.
15. Gordon describes this as a kind of "pretend-play" or "make-believe" in "Folk Psychology as Simulation," p. 160.

in theoretical reasoning; the first-order thought (p) plays a role in simulation. Moreover, one doesn't *have* to have that second-order belief to get the unasserted thought of p to play the appropriate role in the simulation: one can engage in a kind of "trial and error" and see how it turns out.[16]

Because "simulation" is a success term, the usefulness of attempted simulations depends in part on one's ability to recognize what, if anything, one has successfully done. That is, there is a *reflective* component of the process. For example, one may ask oneself, does the thought of p yield, in my psychological process, anything like the emotions or behaviors exhibited by S? What happens in an attempted simulation may turn out to be sufficiently bizarre or implausible that one concludes one has failed. One decides whether a model models what it's supposed to—whether it does simulate how that thing is behaving or would behave under those conditions—partly by seeing if its effects accord with all or most of the relevant data, in this case, the other things one knows about the thing being modeled.[17] These beliefs, however, are also subject to revision.

I have concentrated above on *practical* simulation—simulations engaged in for a purpose. But it is possible to make psychological shifts and slides for no (further) purpose. A psychological shift or slide might just happen; one might just find oneself engaging in this imaginal activity—something quite common during reading. Or one might simply be "playing" or trying to see whether it's even possible to get one's mind to work in a given way. So, for example, I might (try to) sensitize myself to words that begin with the letter "r," so that I become conscious of the fact that a word, whether written or spoken, begins with "r." I may even sensitize myself so that I become amused whenever I hear such a word. Or I could sensitize myself in a different way, say, so that I become annoyed whenever I hear such a word and increasingly annoyed the more I hear. ("Art! Art! Art!") I might develop sufficient control over my mind that I can switch at will into an "amusement mode" or "annoyance mode," as easily as some people

16. Moran recognizes the phenomenon—that certain kinds of imagining do more than generate fictional truths—though he does not explain the mechanism by which this happens. See his "The Expression of Feeling in Imagination," sec. 3, esp. p. 89.

17. Cf. Ripstein, p. 480. I believe that too much has been granted by simulation theorists to theory theorists on this point. Even if, as Gordon says ("Objections and Misconceptions," p. 30), "theory" is needed to validate the simulation, simulation is a distinct psychological process from theorizing and carries its own benefits and affective charges. Goldman ("In Defense of the Simulation Theory," p. 118) recognizes that an even clearer case can be made for the lack of theory when one responds to fiction.

switch perspectives on the Necker cube. I can think of no earthly
reason to do this, except to show that it can be done. But who knows,
it may have some use after all—clever people can find a use for almost
anything.

In fact, some sorts of sensitivities we come to have when reading
fiction seem to me no less peculiar than the example just given. I
mean, why on earth should you put yourself in a state such that when
you hear or read "La libelula vaga de una vaga ilusión," the lilting
rhythm and pattern of "l's" and "v's" generate in you what I would
describe as a floating feeling? But this, I would argue, is precisely one
sort of sensitivity we have when appreciating the poem in which that
line appears. And whatever psychological shift or slide needs to be
made to put ourselves in such a state and to have such a sensitivity is
exactly what we should do (*one* of the things we should do) to appreciate the poem. Similarly, one of the things we do in appreciating
Henry James's "The Turn of the Screw" is to be sensitive to the
resonances of both the irony and what Brian Rosebury calls the "naive
precision" of the "Jane Austen-like formula, 'An unknown man in a
lonely place is a permitted object of fear to a young woman privately
bred'."[18] I propose in Chapter 11 that one advantage of developing
appreciative abilities is the kind of mental flexibility and scope that it
encourages and rewards. We don't always know in advance whether
a certain sensitivity will enable us to appreciate a work. Experimentation and "trying things out," letting the imagination wander, letting
the mind shift and slide into different "gears," is an essential part of
the appreciative process. This mental flexibility and experimentality
may also have benefits in terms of the way they enhance the power of
our mind, though this is not to suggest that every specific shift and
simulation is itself a beneficial activity.

IV: Empathizing with People and with Fictional Characters

It is possible to put oneself into, or shift or slide into, a psychological
condition such that one simulates or models the mental processes or
activities engaged in by a particular person during a given period of
time. I propose that what it is to *empathize* with another person involves simulation of this sort. Empathizing is an activity; if one wants

18. Brian Rosebury, *Art and Desire: A Study in the Aesthetics of Fiction* (New York:
St. Martin's, 1988), p. 129.

to empathize one has to learn how to engage in that activity, which involves a simulation of the mental processes and activities of a particular person during a particular period of time. Empathizing is also an ability, and like other abilities it can be exercised or neglected, honed by practice or left to rot.

I begin by examining two conditions for empathizing with other people. Neither condition is met when empathizing with fictional characters, though analogous conditions take their places. One is met by a reflective component of appreciation, and the other, discussed in section V, is met by reflection combined with a hypothesis concerning what accounts for the qualitative aspects of experience.

Empathy with another person requires that one "share" another's feelings, one "feel" things as that person does or did. Another condition necessary for empathy, one that brings out the asymmetrical character of the relationship, is that one engages in a simulation out of a desire to empathize with or understand a particular individual, the person with whom one empathizes.[19] As Richard Wollheim puts it, one must choose or select another person as one's "protagonist" in advance of the empathizing.[20] This additional condition for empathy eliminates certain counterexamples that could be produced if simulation were taken to be sufficient for empathy: for example, two people might happen to respond in the same way to the same situation, independently of each other, and neither would be empathizing with the other.

Having a protagonist, to use Wollheim's term, seems to be an essential condition for empathizing with an existing person, but I have reservations about requiring it as a condition for empathizing with a fictional character. Empathizing with a fictional character is not a relationship holding between two persons. Anna Karenina, Tristram Shandy, and Qfwfq do not now, and never did, exist. Nevertheless, one can empathize with them. Odysseus and Achilles may have existed, but to empathize with them does not involve simulating the psychological processes those people actually engaged in in response to the situations the *Odyssey* and the *Iliad* describe them as encountering, if indeed they did encounter any such situations. It rather requires responding in the ways Odysseus and Achilles are represented as responding.

19. Barry Smith and Newton Garver provided especially helpful discussion on this point when I read parts of this chapter at the State University of New York at Buffalo.
20. Richard Wollheim, *The Thread of Life* (Cambridge: Harvard University Press, 1984), chap. 3, esp. p. 68.

One may want to amend the second condition for empathy to state that one must select or identify, in advance of the empathizing, a *fictional character* as one's protagonist—as the individual one wants to understand.[21] Nevertheless, I am uncomfortable introducing even this requirement for empathizing with fictional characters, for though I am in general inclined to be psychologically realistic about the mental states of human beings, I am reluctant to say there is some psychological fact of the matter with respect to fictional characters. With human beings, the character of our neurology and perhaps our relationships to entities and events in our environments make it true that we are in the psychological states we are and that we engage in the psychological processing we do. There is no neurology to examine or even speculate about with respect to fictional characters (though there may be descriptions of their neurology) and no environment whose effects on that individual we can measure. Indeed, I am reluctant to reify fictional entities in general and am suspicious of attempts to use them in explaining and justifying both interpretations of and emotional responses to fiction.[22] The explanation and justification of both interpretations and responses to fictional literature depend on relationships between readers and what they read, not on relationships between readers and fictional entities.

Another reason I am loath to require the prior selection of a fictional character as a protagonist for empathy is that some examples of empathizing with fictional characters clearly do not satisfy this condition. Hence, they are counterexamples to the suggestion that prior selection of a fictional protagonist is a necessary condition for empathizing with a fictional character. For example, consider the response I had to a particular passage the first time I read *To the Lighthouse* by Virginia Woolf, described in Chapter 1: "[Mr. Ramsay, stumbling along a passage one dark morning, stretched his arms out, but Mrs. Ramsay having died rather suddenly the night before, his arms, though stretched out, remained empty.]"[23] I read this passage with surprise and incredulity. In thinking about this passage, I realized that it was reasonable to conclude that Mr. Ramsay also re-

---

21. As Kendall Walton points out, one can empathize with narrators, also, when they are "fallibly human," and one can have responses to narrators "in the various ways as we do to other human characters" (*Mimesis*, p. 361).

22. See my "Incompatible Interpretations of Art," *Philosophy and Literature* 6 (1982): 133–146, and "On Fictional Entities," *Philosophy and Literature* 7 (1983): 240–243.

23. Virginia Woolf, *To the Lighthouse* (New York: Harcourt, Brace & World, 1927), p. 194.

sponded with surprise and incredulity to his wife's death. My own responses to the passage are, in a sense, attributable to him—and they are one way I come to understand him (just as it is by examining the model of the arch that I come to understand the actual arch in southern France of which it is a model). I imagine stumbling down a dark hallway, stretching my arms out. Notice how much more effectively Woolf generates this feeling by writing "Mr. Ramsay stretched his arms out," rather than, "Mr. Ramsay stretched out his arms." In the former case, his arms are left, hanging *out,* for five phrases, before we're finally told they remained empty. I *feel* his vulnerability, his emptiness and loss, as it is evoked by this passage and hence also how important Mrs. Ramsay was as his source of security. Though Mr. Ramsay is not an especially sympathetic character in the novel, this passage enables me, if briefly, to empathize with him.

The passage from Harriet Doerr's novel, *Stones for Ibarra,* also discussed in Chapter 1, provides another example. The villagers' description of the "North Americans" as *"mediodesorientado"* evokes the very condition that it describes, *mediodesorientación.* In neither of these cases did I select, prior to having the feelings, these individuals as my protagonists, as individuals I am trying to empathize with or understand. I did not empathize with those characters intentionally or deliberately, but I did find myself empathizing with them. That is, I discovered that what was going on in me, psychologically, was something that could reasonably be attributed to them.

Affects, experiences, and various activities engaged in during the process of reading are among the constituents of appreciation: they are included within the experiential component of appreciation. But not all affects, experiences, and activities one has or engages in while reading are relevant or appropriate: *reflection* is necessary to identify and explain the relevance or irrelevance, appropriateness or inappropriateness, of any given affect or activity. Lack of reflection doesn't keep the experience from being relevant or appropriate; it just keeps one from knowing it is.[24] One's own responses are a starting point for reflection, and for developing interpretations. Emotional and affective responses can be considered affective "trials and error," that are then examined to determine if they do reveal anything we should know about the characters and the work.

With respect to Mr. Ramsay, it does make interpretive sense of the

---

24. Some qualifications need to be made on this claim; see Chapter 7. See Part Two for a fuller discussion of the role of reflective components of appreciation.

novel to attribute the same sort of mental condition to him that I
found in myself. Reflecting on my own psychological activity, I realized that it was important both for understanding Mr. Ramsay and
for understanding the novel that I identify what I was doing as empathizing with him. Similarly, in the case of the Evertons, I come to
realize that the psychological dislocation I feel is attributable to them
and, to a certain extent, to some of the Mexican villagers. The phenomenon is a large part of what the novel is about, and it enriches
and deepens my understanding of it if I actually experience the phenomenon myself. Thus, the requirement that one choose a protagonist in advance is replaced with a compound reflection requirement:
one must identify what affect or emotion one is either experiencing
or simulating, and reasonably conclude that that affect or emotion is
attributable to a fictional character. A conclusion is reasonable when
it is reached on the basis of the ways attributing the affect or emotion
to the character makes interpretive sense of the fictional work.

The Woolf and Doerr examples also show that, when the reader
empathizes with fictional characters, the initial stage of the simulation
does not have to consist of mental states having the same content as
the protagonist's. When reading the *Lighthouse* passage, I do not initially have the same thoughts as Mr. Ramsay, yet the passage generates feelings I can reasonably attribute to him. My feelings are
generated by qualities of the prose—the separation of the sentence
by square brackets, the ending of a clause with "out," and a long
verbal delay until it is resolved. I can use the feelings generated to
understand how Mr. Ramsay felt, supplementing them, as it were,
with the relevant content.

Alvin Goldman argues that empathy involves simulation, the first
stage of which is to take the perspective of the other person. This
stage consists in "imaginatively assuming one or more of the other
person's mental states."[25] Presumably Goldman means by "mental
state" something like a state having the same content, but not necessarily taking the same attitude towards that content. For example, if
my protagonist believes that p, in empathizing with her I unassertedly
entertain the thought that p. However, to imaginatively assume the
belief that p—that is, to imaginatively take the same attitude towards
that content—involves not simply putting oneself in a certain initial
mental state but making the thought that p (or perhaps some idea

25. Alvin I. Goldman, *Philosophical Applications of Cognitive Science* (Boulder, Colo.:
Westview Press, 1993), p. 141.

contained within that thought) play certain cognitive and affective and perhaps also behavioral roles. This second stage constitutes the simulating. Goldman also describes a simulation in terms of the generation of similar or homologous states, rather than in terms of the structure of the process that generates them. Too much emphasis is placed on the character of the state involved—what is analogous either to statically conceived states along the way, or to "output"—and insufficient emphasis on the character of the processes that produce those states.

This disposes of another challenge that might be launched against my proposed account of empathizing with fictional characters. If I am responding to the work, but a character is responding to the loss of a loved one or an alien cultural milieu, how can my mental activity possibly simulate that of the fictional character? The "input" side is obviously completely different. Noël Carroll raises this sort of concern in his discussion of horror fiction when he argues that there's a "telling disanalogy" between what a character experiences and what a reader experiences. "The character responds to a belief in a monster and the audience to entertaining a thought of a monster."[26] The reader, I would say, is actually responding to passages in the text, the elicitor; the thought helps to generate the response. But this discrepancy does not affect Carroll's point. He argues that because (what he calls) the *object* of the response is different in the two cases, then the responses must also be qualitatively different.

But, as we have seen, this conclusion does not follow. Even though the "inputs" are different—the emotions are not elicited by the same sort of phenomena—the psychological activity or processing of those "inputs" may still be structurally analogous. Computer simulations of human mental activities, for example, typically do not use the same sorts of inputs: human beings receive "input" from their sensory receptors in the eyes, ears, skin, and so on, but the inputs to computers are often produced digitally and "keyed in" through a keyboard. One need not have a model of human sensory receptors to model how that "input" is processed once it is received. So also a thought, stimulated by what I read, may initiate a process similar to the one initiated by what a fictional work says or implies that fictional character experiences (sees, hears, smells) when encountering x. My thought of x, just

26. Nöel Carroll, *The Philosophy of Horror, or, Paradoxes of the Heart* (New York: Routledge, 1990), p. 93. It should be pointed out that in this section of the book Carroll is talking about character identification rather than empathy, but, if his point holds, it would count against my account of empathy as well.

like the character's encounter with *x,* may initiate a process that yields apprehensiveness or anxiety, eager anticipation or delight. Or a text might say something contrary to one's expectations—just as a person might encounter something contrary to his or her expectations—so that the conflict between what one expects or assumes and what is actually said produces surprise. In the following section I develop a hypothesis to explain why responses can be qualitatively similar when there is sufficient structural similarity in the mental processes involved, even if the "inputs" or initial stages are different.

What determines whether I am empathizing is not what sensitivities I would have, for example, to the loss of a loved one or an alien cultural environment were I actually to encounter them, but rather what sensitivities I have to what I read, to the work or the text. My reading the novel and empathizing with a character in it may or may not reflect or change how I would respond to the actual situation were I to encounter it. Even if the thought of *x* affects you in a given way, *x* would not necessarily affect you in that way. Actually encountering a situation of a given type is a lot different from thinking of it. In the face of the actual situation, for example, you may concentrate your energies on what needs to be done (when you get flustered just thinking about it), or completely lose control (when you are calm, cool, and collected when thinking about it). The world certainly contains its share of selfish sentimentalists—those who weep for Little Nell but remain unmoved by the plight of America's homeless, Ethiopia's starving millions, and Rwanda's disease-stricken refugees. And it also contains its share of those who care and work for the extremely unfortunate among us but cannot get worked up over a piece of fiction. What conditions our responses to different elicitors —a work of fiction or an actual event or situation—may be quite different, and hence those responses may be quite different. The different responses simply manifest different sensitivities. Developing the ability to appreciate fiction is no guarantee of either ethical enlightenment or moral dissolution.

V: Simulation and Qualia

The other condition for empathy is that the phenomenological quality of experience is the same for the empathizer and the protagonist. It is important for any analysis of empathy that it be able to account for this similarity of experience. Though it is not sufficient for empathy that the empathizer and protagonist have similar experiences, it is commonly thought that some similarity of experience is necessary for empathy. To empathize with someone is to know what it's like for them, to experience things as they do. That is, the *phenomenology* of the experience is supposed to be at least somewhat similar, and the more similar the experience, the greater the empathy. In this section I develop my hypothesis about what accounts for the similarity of experience. When empathizing with fictional characters, however, there is no other existing being whose psychological processes one simulates. Instead, appreciation requires recognizing what psychological processes you are simulating—identifying your own affective or emotional condition—and also determining whether that condition is attributable to a fictional character with whom you are allegedly empathizing.

One exceedingly troublesome task in the philosophy of mind is to account for the nature of "qualia" and the phenomenology of conscious experience.[27] Most discussion has concentrated on the qualitative character of sensory experiences or quasi-sensory states such as physical pain. My concern in this book is rather with the affective or qualitative character of emotions, moods, feelings, desires, attitudes, and so on. I cannot hope to give anything near a full account of qualia. Under a fairly plausible hypothesis, however, the simulation account can provide some account of why feelings and emotions have the qualia they do and hence some rationale for the similarities in phenomenological quality of experience between empathizer and protagonist. If this hypothesis is correct, then the simulation account can accommodate at least one factor of explanatory significance when dealing with qualia. As a bonus, it also explains how empathy admits of degrees—how one can empathize more or less deeply with a person or fictional character.

My hypothesis is that the qualitative character of affective or emotional experience will be at least partly a function of the structure of the process out of which it arises. There are two different ways of thinking about emotions, moods, and feelings which accommodate this hypothesis. First, emotions and so on might be defined as states that are identified in part by their phenomenology, that is, a certain

27. The literature on this topic is extensive. Highlights include Thomas Nagel, "What Is It Like to Be a Bat?" *Philosophical Review* 83 (1974): 435–450; Sidney Shoemaker, "Functionalism and Qualia," *Philosophical Studies* 27 (1975): 291–315; P. M. and P. S. Churchland, "Functionalism, Qualia, and Intentionality," *Philosophical Topics* 12 (1981); and Daniel C. Dennett, *Consciousness Explained* (Boston: Little, Brown, 1991), chap. 12.

qualitative character of experience. According to this view, they have the phenomenology they do because the emotion states are the effects of certain sorts of processes. That is, the emotion one has requires that a given phenomenological state arises in a given way, as a result of a given sort of process. Alternatively, an emotion may be constituted in part by a process having a given structure. This account does not identify an emotion with a state or experience but with a process of such a nature or structure that it (characteristically, though not necessarily, since it may be interfered with or overridden) gives rise to an experience of a given character. On either account, the nature of the process is crucial, and the phenomenology of the experience is due to it. Either view is able to account for the phenomenology of experience in the way suggested by the hypothesis and for how experiences of the empathizer and protagonist can be similar.

In different mental processes, ideas, beliefs, thoughts, and so on take on different roles: one's ideas or thoughts function differently in relation to new sensory stimuli, thoughts, or whatever. To shift or slide into a different psychological gear is to run a different "program," and the qualitative character of experience depends on what program is being run.[28] The phenomenological quality of experience depends on the nature of the "program" being run because the affective quality of one's experience reflects the tugs, the dissonances, and other contortions that arise during the process or the ease with which something new is assimilated, its reaffirmation or collusion with one's other mental states.

In other words, not merely mental contents—what you're thinking of, what you're thinking of it as, or what you desire—account for the affective character of experience, but so too does the *role* your various psychological qualities play vis-à-vis your other beliefs, desires, and thoughts. For example, puzzlement (or in some cases, a kind of "intellectual fear") is produced by the tension between new information and something else you believe; relief, when that tension is resolved. What emotion or affect you have will depend on the relative strength of some desires over others, the dominance of certain thoughts in your mind, or the persistence of a thought despite your recognition that you do not have sufficiently good reasons to believe it. The antici-

---

28. I think talk about programs is a useful metaphor for capturing the differences between the kinds of psychological processes that may take place. Programs, however, are sets of rules, and I do not mean to imply that the mental or psychological processes I am discussing are governed by explicit representations of rules (though they may be describable by rules).

pation of pleasure (if not the pleasure of anticipation) would be produced by information leading you to believe your desires will be fulfilled. The nature of the processes responsible for affects without cognitive components are more difficult to describe, precisely because it's not the cognitive relationships among the contents of various beliefs and desires that are at issue. Nevertheless, it is not difficult to figure out in at least a vague way what's going on psychologically when you are tense, disturbed, or contented. Since a simulation preserves the structurally significant aspects of the process, if the character of experience depends on the structure of that process—as it does during a simulation—it should be accompanied by a similar phenomenology. The more superficial the simulation, the less similar the phenomenology—unless, of course, something phenomenologically similar can be produced by other means.

Bijoy Boruah argues that one's evaluative belief (identifying an emotion as the kind of emotion it is) may be inhibited from gaining ascendancy because of competing or conflicting beliefs.[29] The belief that someone is suffering unjustly would be identificatory of pity. Another belief, for example, that this person needs immediate help, may forestall or prevent the pity because it overrides whatever role the belief that the person is suffering unjustly might play. Hence, an emotion may be weakened or even prevented from occurring. I agree, but I would also emphasize that what this fact serves to show is that it is not just *what* beliefs one has that determines one's emotional response, but how those beliefs function in relation to one's other mental states (beliefs, desires, etc.)—that is, whether these beliefs have a dominant or weak role in affecting how what one encounters is processed.[30]

Two people's experiences in the same situation may be structurally similar enough that they involve a similar phenomenology even if there is no empathy. Suppose, for example, you and I are walking together, and a dog is lurking ahead of us. You're afraid of dogs, and hence you're frightened. I'm not afraid of dogs, but I see foam at the dog's mouth and behavior indicating it is rabid. I'm also frightened. We have the same emotion in response to the same object, the dog, but in relation to different properties of the dog. Though neither of

---

29. Bijoy H. Boruah, *Fiction and Emotion: A Study in Aesthetics and the Philosophy of Mind* (Oxford: Clarendon Press, 1988), p. 115.
30. The importance of the "how" in addition to the "what" reinforces the distinction Richard Moran draws between the content imagined and the manner of imagining it ("The Expression of Feeling in Imagination," sec. 3, esp. pp. 90–92).

us is empathizing with the other (neither of us takes the other as a protagonist), each of us could use our experience to understand, affectively, how the other felt. I feel something like your fear. The similarity in phenomenology, according to my account, is explicable by the fact that the belief that the dog is dangerous plays a role in the mental processing wherein it conflicts with a desire for self-preservation. What I don't feel is your phobia; I don't feel what it's like to experience fear in response to things one has no good reason to believe are dangerous.

By contrast, someone, call her Rachel, recognizes the dog is rabid, but is not frightened by it. Rachel also has a desire for self-preservation and a belief that the dog is dangerous. Her lack of fear is not due to a misunderstanding of what it is to be rabid but to the fact that Rachel knows how to deal with rabid dogs. She is confident she can handle the situation. Although she may experience an adrenalin rush (knowing she may have to act fast), she is not afraid. She instead feels a welling confidence, pride (in the fact that she knows how to handle this dangerous situation), and pleasure (that an opportunity has presented itself for her to show off). Her belief in the dangerousness of the dog *is not* in conflict with her desire for self-preservation (as it is with the person who is frightened) because she also believes the danger is manageable. The potential for conflict is diffused by the presence of these other beliefs, so that the belief that the situation is dangerous doesn't play the same role vis-à-vis her desire as it does for the rest of us. If she realizes, say, that her ways of dealing with rabid dogs are inapplicable in this situation, she may then become frightened, since the belief that the dog is dangerous will then assume the same role it has with you and me.

It is important to note that in the example I presented we *all* believe that the dog is dangerous. But Rachel also has beliefs I don't have, about her knowing how to handle such situations, thus altering what role the belief that the dog is dangerous plays in her psyche: it does not generate fear. One may think that if she's not frightened (because she thinks she can handle the situation) then clearly she doesn't believe that the dog is dangerous. But this assessment relies on much too primitive an account of what it is to believe that something is dangerous. The fact that the situation does call for special knowledge and abilities to keep from suffering harm is precisely what justifies our calling it dangerous. The situation does not cease to be dangerous (for her) if she (justifiably and truly) believes she has these special abilities. It's still a dangerous situation, in that she will get hurt unless she does exercise her special skills. Rachel knows this—and that's why she experiences the adrenalin rush. Indeed, it might be that she likes the danger—it makes her feel energized, emboldened, "alive." Thus, her belief that the dog is dangerous could have a psychophysiological effect, but not the effect of generating fear.

Another phenomenon shows once again it is not so much the character of an elicitor, or of what generates an emotion or affect, but the character of the process undergone which accounts for the phenomenology of experience. Sometimes emotions and affects—and, hence, by my hypothesis, the structurally relevant psychological processes—are initiated in surprising ways. Paul Ekman and his co-researchers conducted experiments designed to show the roles of physiological and autonomic factors in emotion. They asked subjects to perform both a "directed facial action" task, to test autonomic changes associated with various facial muscular changes, and a "re-lived emotional experience task," to test autonomic changes associated with the emotion.[31] Certain facial expressions are characteristically associated with certain emotions, such as a tightening of certain eye muscles with anger. Subjects were directed to move the appropriate facial muscles, and the descriptions of how they were moved were carefully designed to avoid enabling the subjects to detect the emotion with which they are characteristically connected. Contrary to what one might expect, the "directed facial action" task produced a greater and more distinctive pattern of autonomic activity than the "re-living" of an emotional experience. One can think of the facial actions as "going through the motions," as a relatively superficial simulation of an emotional condition, yet one that tends to put one in that condition as one proceeds to "act it out." To borrow my analogy from above, the facial actions cause one's psyche to slip into the appropriate gear much more easily than a deliberate attempt to "re-live" an emotional experience, as it were, from the phenomenology side down (rather than from the physically associated activity up).

Time-honored advice to writers includes the exhortation, "Don't tell them; show them." In other words, don't describe what someone felt; describe what they did, how they acted and behaved, what they thought, and how they saw things. The simulation account explains

31. Paul Ekman, Robert W. Levenson, Wallace V. Friesen, "Autonomic Nervous System Activity Distinguishes among Emotions," *Science* 16 September 1983, p. 1210.

why. An author is more likely to induce a simulation of an emotion or other affect felt by a character by "showing" rather than "telling."[32] Adam Morton has suggested that what it's *like* to be a cat (one of the things it's like to be a cat) is to be forever hesitating in doorways. This description of a certain pattern of cat behavior lets us know what it's like to be a cat—we can feel it by simulating the mental activity of cats presented with open doors. What is "shown" may also be one's thoughts rather than feelings. In William Shakespeare's *The Life and Death of King Richard III,* when Buckingham finally catches on that Richard has been and will continue to use him as ruthlessly as he has everyone else, he is momentarily incredulous and deeply wounded. His mortification quickly turns to alarm and dread over what Richard might do to him in the future. We can tell this by what Buckingham says, not because he describes his feelings, but because he describes his thoughts.

> "And is it thus? repays he my deep service
> With such contempt? made I him king for this?
> O, let me think on Hastings, and be gone
> To Brecknock while my fearful head is on!"[33]

What would be going on in Buckingham's mind to say these things? We can, to a degree, simulate his mental processes through reading what he says.[34]

Philip Johnson-Laird has argued that consciousness is a *serial* process terminating in propositional knowledge (knowing *that* thus-and-such is true), but that unconscious processes are parallel, or distributed, and provide us with nonpropositional knowledge (knowing *how* to do something).[35] To attend to a parallel process and hence "bring it to consciousness" would be to engage in a serial process (sequentially accessing it and its implications, by hypothesis, the mode of under-

---

32. George Mandler nicely sums up this likelihood in "Emotion," *New Directions in Psychology* (New York: Holt, Rinehart & Winston, 1962), p. 312: "There is good reason to believe that the most powerful environment for the induction of certain kinds of behavior is to have that behavior exhibited by others."

33. William Shakespeare, *The Tragedy of Richard the Third,* 4.2.133–37. *A New Variorum Edition of Shakespeare,* ed. Horace Howard Furness, vol. 16 (Philadelphia: J. B. Lippincott, 1908), p. 303.

34. I thank Bruce Bubacz for the example. He pointed out how mediocre actors deliver these lines only in *anger,* rather than with a more subtle complex of emotions.

35. Johnson-Laird, *Mental Models,* p. 468.

standing consciousness takes) and to necessarily alter the nature of the processing we engage in. I find Johnson-Laird's claims tremendously suggestive, though I'm suspicious of any contention that parallel processes are entirely inaccessible to consciousness (and that the outcomes of serial processes are entirely accessible), and that the former make no difference in the qualitative character of one's experience. It is my hypothesis that it is precisely the underlying character of these processes—whether they be parallel or serial—that is at least partly responsible for the phenomenal or affective quality of experience.

On my account, preconscious processes, those that are "lower down" in the psychological hierarchy and that constitute the "running" of a given "program," are not necessarily totally unconscious, but they do not manifest themselves in mental states having (propositional) content either. They manifest themselves through an affective quality of experience. Although an experience does not have propositional content, it might be said to have nonpropositional content in that it represents the sort of mental process being simulated. Thus, what one knows when one knows what it's *like* to be some way may be captured only inadequately by propositions expressing the propositional content of a mental state. "What it's like" would likely be captured better by gestures, by acting something out, or by descriptions of gestures, actions, or patterns of actions—in short, by something that induces a simulation of the relevant mental processes or activity.

Excessive self-consciousness is one factor that can alter the character of a mental process and hence interfere with a simulation. Readers who are constantly stopping to analyze what they are feeling and reading are likely to make the feelings themselves dissolve. Deliberations and reflections on what one is doing often compete with doing it. It may not even be possible to attend to a process without distorting the intrinsic nature of the process itself. Christopher Isherwood observed that "you will not make a plant grow in the earth if you are always digging it up to look at the roots."[36] Deliberations and reflections on what one is doing do not always compete with the doing, however: sometimes they are necessary, for example, in cases where constant or intermittent vigilance is required. The acquisition of some

---

36. Christopher Isherwood, *All the Conspirators* (New York: New Directions, 1958), pp. 114–115.

kinds of skills involves developing the ability to attend, reflect, and deliberate without interrupting the process. But on other occasions reflection and deliberation interrupt "the flow," momentarily stopping the process, in order that one might figure out what to do next or urge oneself on to do it.

Spontaneous engagement in a psychological process can have a qualitative character that is either different from, or at least more vivid than, one inaugurated deliberately.[37] Gilbert Ryle made a related point about motivation: a person who is highly motivated does not have to keep telling herself, "now I am going to get down to work"; she gets down to work without having to tell herself that.[38] Macbeth recognized the phenomenon in himself:

> I have no spur
> To prick the sides of my intent, but only
> Vaulting ambition, which o'erleaps itself,
> And falls on the other[39]

It interrupts the process (and the simulation of a process) if one has to urge oneself on, and backtrack, reexamine, and stop and figure out whether one is doing the relevant thinking and acting. Kendall

37. Johnson-Laird has argued that John Searle's infamous "Chinese room" example fails as a counterexample to functionalism as a theory of mind because it fails to preserve the "real time" properties essential to "understanding Chinese." The point of the "Chinese room" example is to show that a room fitted out with people and books filled with "translation rules" and so on does not "understand Chinese." This is the case even if the room replicates the functional relationships purportedly identifying the mental state of "understanding Chinese," say, where slips of paper with Chinese characters on them constitute the "inputs," slips of paper with English words on them constitute the "outputs," and masses of volumes of "translation rules" are consulted to figure out when a given output should be produced in response to a given input. Johnson-Laird points out that the individuals in the room will not act quickly enough to maintain the "real-time" properties of the system as a whole, which are essential to the character of the mental condition "understanding Chinese" (*Mental Models*, p. 475). "Understanding Chinese" is a mental condition, the kind of condition we know as "having an ability," identified in part in terms of the "real-time properties" of the process of translating from Chinese to English. These real-time properties, in turn, are important to the phenomenology of the experience, and the failure of what goes on in the Chinese room to preserve these real time properties would explain why the Chinese room, when it allegedly exercises the ability to understand Chinese, does not generate the right (or any) phenomenology of experience.

38. Gilbert Ryle, *The Concept of Mind* (New York: Barnes & Noble, 1949), p. 133.

39. William Shakespeare, *Macbeth*, 1.2.25–28. *A New Variorum Edition of Shakespeare*, ed. Horace Howard Furness, 3d ed., vol. 2 (Philadelphia: J. B. Lippincott, 1873), p. 73.

Walton has suggested explaining the difficulty of *deliberately* imagining something to be true (even though one knows it isn't true) by the presence, and hence imposition on your consciousness, of evidence for the falsity of what one is imagining.[40] This may well be the case: the affective quality of the experience, the feel of it, can be affected by the drag induced by this information on one's imagining—that is, by its intervention in the appropriate mental processing or activity. But it is also the case that a deliberate inauguration of an imaginal project often takes a bit of doing before it gets off the ground. Many of us are just not very adept at getting a different "program" up and running which functions to simulate, or realize, the condition we are imagining being in. Furthermore, the deliberateness of our mental actions interferes with the "running" of the program—with our "getting into it"—and hence either prevents a simulation or makes it sufficiently superficial that the affective or phenomenological quality of experience is affected.

A particular human mind's operations during a period of time, comprising both serial and parallel processes and subprocesses, might be simulated more or less thoroughly, depending on how deep the structural similarities are between the simulator and the simulated with respect to those processes and subprocesses. Indeed, one might actually come to engage in the mental activities or processes that another person is engaging in if one's psychological shift or slide goes deeply enough to count as realizing that activity rather than simulating it. But how deep is deep enough? The question itself assumes that one is being psychologically realistic about states, conditions, processes, and activities of the mind and about emotions, affects, and experiences. An answer to this question depends on developing a psychology that identifies emotions, affects, and experiences at least in part in terms of the mental processes or subprocesses that take place. Clearly, without a specification of the exact preconscious activity essential for the identification of a psychological process, it is not possible to give a prescription for determining whether that process is really going on, or whether one is simulating engaging in it, or, indeed, what process it is that is being simulated. There is no a priori way to know what subprocesses are essential to an emotion or affect, and there will likely be no general answer to the preceding question.

40. Walton, *Mimesis*, p. 15.

VI: Simulation and Knowledge

There is one other fortunate (though not merely fortuitous) implication of the simulation account. Affective responses to fiction that are
part of appreciating a particular work are often lauded as a source of
knowledge or understanding.[41] Thus, whereas I claim one can imagine what it's like to be a certain sort of person, or to experience a
certain sort of situation, through developing various sensitivities and
an ability to simulate the relevant mental subprocesses of such people,
or how one might feel in such situations, others claim that one can
know these things. But despite the fact that numerous writers have
defended the utility of literature on the grounds that it provides
knowledge of "what it's like" to be certain people or in various situations, there is no account of when the affective experiences one has
when reading count as knowledge and when they do not. Certainly,
not all of the emotional and affective responses one has when reading
fictional literature count as coming to know what it's like to be or to
experience something or other. Not even all cases of genuine appreciation of a fictional work, it seems to me, will provide such knowledge.[42] But the simulation account at least provides the beginning of
a structure for distinguishing cases when one has such knowledge
and when one does not.

In traditional philosophical circles, the paradigm of knowledge is
propositional knowledge, where a person knows that some proposition or other is true; for example, Louise knows that the key to the
front door is in the ginger jar in the living room, and Dolores knows
that mice have been eating her husband's sheet music stored in the
basement. To have knowledge, rather than merely beliefs (even true
beliefs) that such things are true, Louise and Dolores must have sufficient evidence for the truth of these claims. What constitutes suffi-

---

41. There are many who advance this position. Dorothy Walsh, *Literature and Knowledge* (Middletown: Wesleyan University Press, 1969), chap. 9; R. W. Beardsmore,
"Learning From a Novel," and Julian Mitchell, "Truth and Fiction," both in *Philosophy
and the Arts*, Royal Institute of Philosophy Lectures, vol. 6, 1971–1972 (New York:
St. Martin's Press, 1973); Martha Nussbaum, " 'Finely Aware and Richly Responsible':
Moral Attention and the Moral Task of Literature," *Journal of Philosophy* 82 (1985):
516–529, and *The Fragility of Goodness: Luck and Ethics in Greek Tragedy and Philosophy*
(Cambridge: Cambridge University Press, 1986); David Novitz, *Knowledge, Fiction, and
Imagination* (Philadelphia: Temple University Press, 1987). Some writers have also argued that fictional literature is a source of propositional knowledge, but they are not
germane to the present discussion.
42. See Chapter 11, sec. III, for a defense of this claim.

cient evidence is, of course, a hotly contested subject of debate which need not detain us here, but at least we have a framework for debating what is and isn't knowledge: what is known must be true, and one must have sufficiently good evidence for its truth, and believe it on the basis of that evidence.

But when the knowledge is alleged to be knowledge of "what it's like" to be a certain sort of person or to live through a certain type of situation, there is no readily apparent model for analyzing the difference between knowledge and mere imagination, as there is for analyzing the difference between knowledge and mere belief (or even justified belief when the justification is not sufficient to provide knowledge). For the object of this alleged knowledge is not expressed by a proposition; it is experiential.[43] Experiences are not true or false, though they may qualitatively approximate other experiences. The fact that similarity in experiences admits of degrees handicaps the application of the concept of knowledge; how similar is similar enough to *be* what it is like? Given that the experience itself is supposed to constitute the knowledge (n.b.: not the *belief* that one's experience is what it is like), there is also a problem of how to account for the relevant sort of justification. When does imagining what it's like become knowing what it's like?

The simulation account, however, helps to show that imagination can serve epistemic purposes, precisely because it provides a bit of conceptual apparatus—the notion of simulation—for distinguishing imaginal activities that count as knowledge from those that do not. For there to be something "it is like" to be a certain kind of person or in a certain kind of situation, certain types of mental processes must account for the character of the experience or experiences the relevant individuals have. Thus, if when reading a fictional work one is in fact simulating certain mental activity, one can then have such knowledge. For example, Patrick Süskind's *Perfume* constantly bombards us with descriptions of smell, giving us a kind of contact with persons and places uncharacteristic of modern life. In doing this he enables us to know to some degree what it was like to live in eighteenth-century France: "The streets stank of manure, the courtyards of urine, the stairwells stank of moldering wood and rat droppings, the kitchens of spoiled cabbage and mutton fat; the unaired parlors stank of stale dust, the bedrooms of greasy sheets, damp featherbeds,

---

43. This term is used by Theodore W. Schick, Jr., "Can Fictional Literature Communicate Knowledge?" *Journal of Aesthetic Education* 16 (1982): 37.

and the pungently sweet aroma of chamber pots. . . . People stank of sweat and unwashed clothes; from their mouths came the stench of rotting teeth, from their bellies that of onions, and from their bodies, if they were no longer very young, came the stench of rancid cheese and sour milk and tumorous disease."[44] To imagine living and working while being bombarded with such stenches is to know, to a degree and in a certain respect, what it was like to live in eighteenth-century Paris. The simulation account thus accommodates the fact that experiential knowledge, unlike propositional knowledge, will be a matter of degree, depending on how closely one simulates the relevant mental processes. To the extent that one's experience is due to the character of the mental processes that do simulate what it is to be such a person or to be in a certain kind of situation, one has knowledge of what it is like.

In this chapter I have attempted to explain a simulation account of empathy. It explicates *A*'s empathizing with *B* as primarily a matter of *A*'s engaging in mental activity that bears significant structural similarities to what goes on in *B*. Simulations can be carried out even when the "inputs" for the simulator and protagonist are different, and they don't require developing a theory or set of beliefs about human psychology or any human in particular in order to occur. Such simulations can be used for various practical purposes, including appreciating fiction. We shift or slide into different psychological "gears" as we read; this movement changes our sensitivities and how we respond to what we read. Having these responses is an important part of appreciation, and, on at least some occasions, responding as we do counts as empathizing with a fictional character. On these occasions the compound reflection requirement is also satisfied: one identifies one's own emotion of affect and reasonably attributes it to a fictional character.

44. Patrick Süskind, *Perfume: The Story of a Murderer*, trans. John E. Woods (New York: Knopf, 1986), pp. 3–4.

Chapter Five

Sympathy and Other Responses

In Chapter 4 I developed a general model of what goes on, psychologically, when one empathizes with a fictional character: one is in a psychological condition such that one processes verbal "input" in a way that *simulates* the mental activity and processes of the one with whom one empathizes—the protagonist. What goes on in the reader's mind simulates a process that constitutes having a given sort of emotion, affect, or desire, or being in a given sort of mood. For this simulation to constitute empathy with a fictional character, one must engage in the reflective component of appreciation, that is, recognize that this emotion or affect is attributable to the character. But not all responses to fiction are empathic. In this chapter I explain the nature of sympathetic responses to fictional characters and how they differ from empathic responses. Sympathy turns out to be a cognitively much more complicated process. These complications, moreover, help to show why sympathy, as opposed to empathy, has traditionally been linked with *moral* knowledge and understanding.

Not all responses to fiction are either empathic or sympathetic. There are several other kinds of responses to fiction—where kinds are individuated according to the nature of the psychological processes involved in generating the responses rather than according to the nature of the emotion or affect itself. In the second half of this chapter I briefly describe some of these other kinds of processes.

I: Sympathy

Empathy involves simulating the mental activity and processes of the person with whom one empathizes, the protagonist. The degree to which one empathizes depends on the depth of the simulation. A sympathetic response, however, does *not* involve simulating the mental activity and processes of a protagonist; it instead requires having feelings or emotions that are in concert with the interests or desires the sympathizer (justifiably) attributes to the protagonist. "In concert with" needs filling out, specifically, in a way that recognizes that quite a variety of responses may be in concert with an individual's interests or desires. For example, if George wins the lottery, I may feel sympathetic excitement, pleasure, anxiety (over his new responsibilities), or distress (since it's going to change his life so much).[1]

A response is sympathetic when and because an attribution of interests and desires to the protagonist, along with information relevant to those interests and desires plays a (certain sort of) role in generating the response. The sort of role it must play is one that makes one's responses "in concert with" the protagonist's interests or desires. The sympathizer treats them and the person who has them, in Richard Wollheim's phrase, "with favor."[2] I argue below that this treatment can be explicated as the sympathizer's having a desire that the specific interests or desires of the protagonist in question be satisfied. It is in this sense that when we are sympathetic, we take on another's interests as our own. Interestingly, protagonists may not even be aware of the information relevant to their interests or desires that is partially generative of the sympathizer's response.[3] This fact is illustrated by my response to Carlos Fuentes's short story, "The Cost of Living." Ana Rentería has been in bed for two weeks, growing thinner and weaker. Her husband rises early to see if he can find some extra work,

---

1. This account is consistent with Jonathan Bennett's use of "sympathy" in "The Conscience of Huckleberry Finn," *Philosophy* 49 (1974): 124, where it covers any sort of fellow-feeling. Bennett's article is especially instructive in exploring when, and whether, sympathy ought to part company with moral judgments—a recurring theme in the literature on sympathy. Kant's reference to "satisfaction in spreading joy" and "rejoice in the contentment of others" as sympathy (*Foundations of the Metaphysics of Morals*, trans. Lewis White Beck [New York: Bobbs-Merrill, 1969], p. 17) is also consistent with this usage.
2. Richard Wollheim, *The Thread of Life* (Cambridge: Harvard University Press, 1984), pp. 67–68.
3. Daniel Putman is explicit about this possibility for sympathy in "Sympathy and Ethical Judgments: A Reconsideration," *American Philosophical Quarterly* 24 (1987): 262.

but he is distracted by a girl. He buys her an ice cream; they rent a boat at the lake; he meets friends at a cafe. I feel sympathy for Ana in the form of consternation and exasperation. I have these feelings because I realize Salvador's behavior is contrary to her interests and desires, even though she does not know that he is not only not looking seriously for work but also spending what little money they have on someone else. Later, when Salvador is killed, I realize the implications it has for her—sick and unable to work, with no income and even unable to fix food for herself. I am distressed and pained for her, sympathetically, before she knows what has befallen her husband.

I also may respond sympathetically even when I don't share the beliefs of the protagonist, such as Antigone's belief that a person's soul will suffer eternal torture if a handful of earth is not thrown on the body at death. Furthermore, I may respond sympathetically to someone because of something *I* believe is important but which is unacknowledged by the character, thus *I* attribute certain interests to the character that the character doesn't recognize. I worry that Doro- thea will give into Casaubon's demands, and I want her to resist them, even though she herself is simply trying to decide what is morally the most admirable thing to do. I don't think the considerations that she herself takes to be overriding are the most important ones in the situation. Indeed, her excessive piety is often annoying. It takes spe- cial skills on the part of an author to retain readers' sympathy for characters who do not share our values.

A response is a "feeling *with*" a person, then, not in the sense that it is necessarily the same sort of response the person has (as with empa- thy), but because it arises out of a concern for that person.[4] This concern is reflected by the fact that attributing certain interests and desires to the protagonist helps to generate a response that is in con- cert with those interests and desires.

One can be sympathetic and still make mistakes. Sympathizers don't have to be right about the interests or desires they attribute to the protagonist. The sincere, reasonably intelligent effort to understand another's interests and desires, even if it misfires, may lead to sympa- thy. Responding in concert with a reasonable set of beliefs about the protagonist's situation and interests shows a person to be sympathetic to the protagonist. With empathy, by contrast, the extent to which

4. Douglas Chismar argues that one of the things that distinguishes empathy and sympathy is that empathy does not require that one cares about the protagonist and sympathy does in "Empathy and Sympathy: The Important Difference," *Journal of Value Inquiry* 22 (1988): 257–258.

one fails to simulate what is in fact going on in the protagonist is the extent to which one fails to empathize.

Given that one must be *justified* in attributing certain interests or desires to the protagonist, whether one is sympathetic admits of degrees. Exactly how reasonable was it to attribute that desire to the person or to think such-and-such was in her best interests? There are times when the response may be more projection than sympathy and other times when the response is primarily sympathy. I mention this variability not just to point out moral ambiguity in the situation but as a reason to caution against all-or-nothing demands for whether any given response was sympathetic or not. Pure cases of sympathy will be hard to find, in real life as well as in response to fiction. (In the following section I explore a rather extended example of sympathizing with a fictional character in order to explain how various factors, though not themselves responsible for one's response being sympathetic, can contribute to the response.)

Sympathy, as I have defined it, is narrower in some respects, broader in others, and generally more well defined than much philosophical and common usage. There is a tendency, both in ordinary and philosophical usage, to use "sympathy" and "empathy" interchangeably.[5] One prominent philosophical example of this habit is the discussion of "extended sympathy" (which is more or less what I call "empathy") in the context of interpersonal utility comparisons.[6] However, the differences between the psychological processes involved in sympathy and in empathy show that the two should not be conflated. Common usage tends to employ "sympathy" only on those occasions when there is an expression of condolence over a misfortune or loss—the sorts of situations calling for "sympathy cards." But shared joys as well as sorrows can be sympathetic, that is, in concert with the interests and desires of a person or character. Finally, much

5. See Douglas Chismar, "Empathy and Sympathy: The Important Difference," for an interesting brief overview of the history of "sympathy" and the invention of the term "Einfühlung" ("empathy"), though his account is subject to dispute (see Katharine Everett Gilbert and Helmut Kuhn, *A History of Aesthetics* [1939, rev. 1953; repr. New York: Dover, 1972], p. 537). Interestingly, the category of phenomena Theodor Lipps wanted to capture by his use of the term—where one imaginatively attributes one's own feelings to inanimate objects—has obvious aesthetic relevance but does not capture its typical current use of *sharing* another (real) person's feelings.

6. R. M. Hare, *Moral Thinking: Its Levels, Method, and Point* (New York: Oxford University Press, 1981); John Harsanyi, *Essays on Ethics, Social Behavior, and Scientific Explanation* (Boston: Reidel, 1976). For a critique of the moral utility of such appeals to extended sympathy see Alfred F. MacKay, "Extended Sympathy and Interpersonal Utility Comparison," *Journal of Philosophy* 83 (1986): 305–322.

common usage is simply not attuned to some of the special situations that arise, for example, that one can be sympathetic yet mistaken (though not negligently) about the protagonist's interests or desires.

My account of sympathy is narrower than those that require a sympathizer to have a desire to *act* in a helpful way. William Charlton has defended an account of sympathy that requires such a desire.[7] Colin Radford, in attempting to refute this aspect of Charlton's view, objects that "one may be moved emotionally by a feeling of utter helplessness, by the impossibility of being able to help."[8] But this does not refute the claim that the emotion is produced in part by a desire to help; quite the contrary. It may be because one does desire to help that one is frustrated by the impossibility of doing so. However, I agree with Radford's conclusion: not all emotions (a fortiori, not all affects) are generated in part or accompanied by a desire to do something, or, in the case of sympathy, a desire to help. Some emotions may be accompanied by desires, but not desires to do. Disappointment is engendered by the failure to obtain what one desires, but the desire is not necessarily a desire to do something. I may desire that something be the case (such as a desire that you score an 800 on your SATs) and experience disappointment when it doesn't come to pass, rather than desire to do something myself.[9] Other sympathetic emotions may not involve desires at all, such as my sympathetic sadness over my friend's loss of her mother. I may wish that I could do something or that I could have done something, but this response is different from having a desire to do.[10]

7. William Charlton, "Feeling for the Fictitious," *British Journal of Aesthetics* 24 (1984): 209f. His view is criticized by Colin Radford, "Charlton's Feelings about the Fictitious: A Reply," *British Journal of Aesthetics* 25 (1985): 380–383; and by R. T. Allen, "The Reality of Responses to Fiction," *British Journal of Aesthetics* 26 (1986): 64–68.
8. Radford, "Charlton's Feelings about the Fictitious," p. 380.
9. Alex Neill makes this same point against Charlton, "Fiction and the Emotions," *American Philosophical Quarterly* 30 (1993): 10. I have embedded it in an account, developed in Chapter 2, of differences between desires that and desires to do. Gregory Currie (*The Nature of Fiction* [New York: Cambridge University Press, 1990], chap. 5) dubs the conative component "make-desires," which are to be understood comparably to "make-beliefs."
10. Aaron Ridley, in "Desire in the Experience of Fiction," *Philosophy and Literature* 16 (1992), refers to this as a desire at the "logically prepractical stage of wishing that things were not as they were, or are" (p. 284). Robert M. Gordon, on the other hand, (*The Structure of Emotions: Investigations in Cognitive Philosophy* [New York: Cambridge University Press, 1987], pp. 30–31) contrasts desires and wishes, pointing out that wishes, among other differences with desires, are "rationally blind to one another," an important fact when assessing emotions and affective responses. I support Gordon's distinction between desires and wishes.

According to Charlton, since we know that what we are reading is fiction, we don't have real desires (to help fictional characters), but we have hypothetical desires to help real people who might be in a situation such as that delineated in the novel. But it is dubious that in reading fiction we develop such hypothetical desires with respect to real people; to suppose so posits too intimate a connection between fiction and real life. There are the selfish sentimentalists mentioned in Chapter 4, section IV, who get worked up over fiction but are uninterested in lifting a finger to help out actual people. Further, it is not at all clear in Charlton's account what mental role *hypothetical desires* could play, given that they are hypothetical. That is, an appeal to hypothetical desires doesn't make the generation of responses any less mysterious, since it's not clear what their psychological status is, as hypothetical, or how they can explain our having the responses we have. Finally, if sympathy covers any kind of "feeling with" a person, including sharing joys (and not merely sadness), clearly no desire to help is implicated and rarely any desire to do something. The only desire might be the desire *that* the current situation persists.

Patricia Greenspan includes sympathy under the rubric of *identificatory* emotions. Identification "standardly involves the assumption of practical responsibility for others."[11] In her view, emotional responses to fiction are exceptions to the standard case. However, as identificatory emotions, they involve a concern for self, desires for one's own safety and well-being because one is "in the same boat" as the person with whom one sympathizes.[12] In my account of sympathy, however, a response is not, qua sympathetic response, tied up with concerns for oneself; quite the contrary. Sympathy is "identificatory" only in the sense that one responds in concert with another person's interests and desires, but it must be because (one believes) the other's desires are what they are and not because one is concerned about one's own situation or how the plight of the other reflects on oneself. I discuss subsequently how difficult it will be to find "pure" cases of sympathy —cases unmixed with concern for self. Nevertheless, to the extent that an emotion or affect is due to a concern for self it will not be sympathetic.

According to Richard Wollheim, sympathy is involved not only when the person with whom one sympathizes is, as he puts it, in one's

11. Patricia S. Greenspan, *Emotions and Reasons: An Inquiry into Emotional Justification* (New York: Routledge, 1988), p. 74.
12. Greenspan, *Emotions and Reasons*, pp. 72, 73.

good favor but also when that person is in disfavor or when one feels a certain indifference to the person. That is, sympathy can involve looking on a character with favor—what I have called a response in concert with the character's interests and desires—or with disfavor— a response in opposition to a character's interests and desires—or with indifference, as long as the indifference generates a response and is not simply affective detachment. Thus, sympathy would encompass not only pity for Gloucester but also pleasure in his misfortune (what generally goes under the rubric of *Schadenfreude*), as well as feelings of apathy, indifference, or mere curiosity.[13]

Wollheim's model for various types of audiences, and hence various types of responses, includes only three possibilities. They are the detached audience, in which there is no affective response (though there may well be cognitive judgment), the empathic audience (roughly similar to my own account of empathy, as discussed in Chapter 4), and everything else, which has to fall into the category of the sympathetic audience. A typology of categories of responses requires more categories than these. I would narrow down the category of sympathy to accord with something closer to common usage, restricting it to only those responses in concert with the interests and desires of the character with whom one sympathizes, whether it leads to pleasant or painful affects. Unfortunately, we don't have ready-made categories for the remaining responses. *Schadenfreude* includes only pleasure from others' misfortunes. But there are other ways one can respond in opposition to a person's or character's interests or desires, most notably those cases where I experience some variety of displeasure at another's success. I may be angry that Alice wins an award (I hate Alice, and can't stand to see her succeed), disgusted with Joseph's laziness (though he's very happy being that way), and annoyed by Mark's neurotic behavior (though he's learned to live with it). In some cases, such responses as these will constitute sympathy with another fictional character in the work. I may be angry that Alice won because I sympathize with Karen, who is at least as deserving as Alice and is constantly being upstaged by her. I am disgusted with Joseph because I sympathize with Jane, his long-suffering wife. In these cases, the response is engendered not merely by how I think about Alice and

13. Wollheim, *Thread*, p. 67. This position is slightly different from what he defended in "Imagination and Identification," *On Art and the Mind* (Cambridge: Harvard University Press, 1974), pp. 66–67. In the earlier essay, he corrects his denomination of this sort of audience as sympathetic by saying, "or perhaps we should say, more generally, the reactive audience" (p. 67).

Joseph but because of the way they interfere with Karen's and Jane's interests. When that recognition partially informs a response in concert with their interests, the response is sympathetic. I discuss *Schaden-freude* and other *antipathetic* responses in section III.

It will not always be the case that my responses are informed by an attribution of interests and desires to other characters. It may simply be that, for example, Joseph's laziness disgusts me alone. That is, his behavior is at odds with something *I* hold to be of value, such as initiative and industry. My response is not sympathetic because it is not due to a concern over whether his interests and desires are satisfied or thwarted. It has to do with what *I* think about laziness. The psychological process for generating the response is different from sympathetic responses, and it will also be discussed in section III.

In this section I have emphasized the importance, for a sympathetic response, of attributing a desire or interest to a protagonist. Sympathy differs markedly from empathy in this respect, since the latter but not the former involves simulating the psychological role of a person's various thoughts, beliefs, and perceptions, rather than responding in ways informed by a reasonable attribution of certain interests and/or desires to them. Sympathy requires more than attributing interests or desires to a protagonist, however; it also requires a belief about what is, was, or might be in store for the protagonist and a desire that the protagonist's interests and desires be satisfied. Put formally, if S has a response generated by the following three conditions, then that response is sympathetic: (a) S believes A is in P's interest or that P desires I (or that not-I is opposed to P's interests or desires), (b) S believes something is, was, or might be in store for P that either promotes or conflicts with A or I, and (c) S desires that P's interest or desire in A or I is satisfied. Given that the cognitive component of emotion can be satisfied by unasserted thoughts and not just beliefs, the belief requirements in (a) might be satisfied by S's thinking of A as being in P's interest or thinking of P as desiring I. A comparable move can be made for (b). In this section I have discussed (a); in the following section I explore (b) and (c).

II: The Mechanisms of Sympathy

Desiderio is the narrator of *The Infernal Desire Machines of Doctor Hoffman*.[14] He was a protegé of the Minister, "the most rational man in the world" (p. 24), whose job was to combat the incursions of Dr. Hoffman's "massive campaign against human reason itself" (p. 11). Desiderio became a hero and saved the world from Hoffman's war against reason; the book is allegedly his memoirs written in old age.

The novel has a picaresque structure rather than a novelistic unity. Readers are carried along by the sheer power of Carter's writing and imagination, as well as by a mounting curiosity about how in the world, given the nature of his adventures and especially his attitude, Desiderio will ever emerge as a hero. In the chapter entitled, "Lost in Nebulous Time," he and Albertina are captured by the centaurs, and it gradually becomes clear that they have an ugly fate in store for him. One feels an increasing sense of foreboding in reading through the chapter. One day the bay mare says to Desiderio, "I shall come for both of you after prayers and you will go to the Holy Hill with me" (p. 188). Given what has been said about the Holy Hill as a place of ritual sacrifice, it is clear that Desiderio is in imminent danger. Upon reading this passage, my rather indefinite sense of foreboding was replaced by a specific fear: fear for what they will do to Desiderio on that hill. This response was not empathy, for it was a fear he himself did not feel. In retrospect, writing his memoirs, he remembers that there were signs of what was to come, but "we did not have the least idea what would happen to us on the Holy Hill for we were in Nebulous Time" (p. 189).

I experience fear; it appears to be sympathetic fear for Desiderio. What accounts for this fear? Sympathetic fear involves either the belief or thought of someone in danger (condition [b]), along with the desire that the person not be harmed (condition [c]). The sentence quoted earlier (from p. 188) elicits the belief that Desiderio will be brutally treated—probably tortured and possibly killed. This belief may produce fear *that* Desiderio will be brutally tortured, but it is not sufficient to ensure that I fear *for* him. In reflecting honestly on what induced my own emotional response, I must say that my fear was induced as much by my reluctance to subject myself to another of

14. Angela Carter, *The Infernal Desire Machines of Doctor Hoffman* (1972; repr., *The War of Dreams* [New York: Penguin, 1982]). The novel also raises questions about names and personal identity, questions I will have to ignore in order to concentrate on just a few responses to explicate their psychological mechanisms.

Carter's descriptions of sadism, which occur with increasing fre-
quency and violence in the book, than it was something I'd call sympathetic concern for Desiderio. If my desire is, as in this case, a perfectly
reasonable garden-variety desire to avoid being subjected to something seriously unpleasant, then my fear is for myself rather than for
Desiderio. The belief, then, that is responsible for my fear is the belief
that there will be a vivid description of Desiderio's torture, rather
than simply the belief that he will be tortured.

Yet this might be too simple a story. Why don't I want to be subjected to another description of cruel treatment to human beings?
Explicit descriptions of torture to any human being (or higher-order
animal) tend to be disturbing. The very thought of such cruel treatment is disturbing—a fact that probably plays a role in generating my
fear, even if my fear doesn't have anything to do with any special
properties of Desiderio in particular. (There is some evidence for this
explanation, since I had a similar response earlier in the book to the
treatment of the Count, who was boiled to death, even though the
Count was an even less sympathetic character than Desiderio.)
Thoughts of Desiderio tortured are thoughts of a human being tortured (though, as with a large number of Carter's characters, there is
something more or less not human about him). It is in reading about
him that I develop the fear, so there is at least this sense in which my
response is sympathetic specifically with him, given the situation he's
in. The thought of someone being tortured is disturbing in combination with my genuine, garden-variety desire for the well-being of
human beings in general. This is not a "hypothetical desire" of the
sort that Charlton posits, but an ordinary desire that I have that
people in general not suffer harm. The conflict between the desire
and the thought generates the fear.

Such thoughts are not always disturbing, and they certainly do
not always generate fear. Indeed, in reading "people are sometimes
tortured," one is likely not to experience fear or emotional distur-
bance.[15] Why does that thought generate (sympathetic) fear when I
think it in response to reading Carter's novel? My belief that Desiderio is about to be subjected to a brutal torture that I will have to
read about in excruciating detail plays an important role. Thinking
of particular tortures—needles under the fingernails, chopping off

15. R. M. J. Dammann uses this fact to develop his account of affective responses to
fiction in "Emotion and Fiction," *British Journal of Aesthetics* 32 (1992): see esp.
pp. 18–20.

fingers one at a time with an axe, hot pokers in the eyeballs—is disturbing. Having already read several of Carter's descriptions of brutality, including one of a marathon gang rape, one can understand why the thought of Desiderio's torture being imminent does not just lie dormant as a simple thought but anticipates explicit descriptions of the brutality he will suffer. The anticipated vividness and specificity of the description contributes to my experiencing fear on this occasion. It serves not only to threaten me personally, but it also brings my desire that people not be tortured to mind, or *affectively* "on line." I fear for myself, in being afraid that I will have to suffer through some gory passages. But I am also to a degree sympathetic with Desiderio.

The fact that thoughts such as "people are sometimes tortured" are typically not sufficient in themselves to generate affective responses shows why it is necessary to appeal to the particular way the work generates those thoughts, and how one's psychological state is conditioned by other factors, to get an adequate explanation of the response.[16] Otherwise, simply having thoughts appears to be affectively unmoving. This unfortunate impression is left, for example, by Ralph Clark's suggestion that responses are to be explained by one's "entertaining certain counterfactual suppositions."[17] Clark's resistance to appealing to some notion such as suspended disbelief, or provisional belief, to explain affective responses is on the right track, but what one needs to know is why entertaining certain thoughts, especially when they are counterfactuals, will at least sometimes generate feelings or emotions. The fact that one can think up situations in conflict with one's desires and even deeply held values should bring neither surprise nor chagrin. Of course one can think of such things. Important to explaining affective responses to fiction is the way the novel or short story brings one's desires or interests "on line," how it gets readers into a psychological condition so that they are sensitive to certain thoughts or ideas.

Condition (b) for sympathy states that *S* (the sympathizer) believes something is, was, or might be in store for *P* (the protagonist) that

---

16. In Chapter 10 I argue for the relevance of temporal factors in warranting a response to fiction. The way in which descriptions of brutality in the novel produce increasing sensitivities to the prospect of one of the character's being ill-treated provides an example of how the *sequencing* of passages in a novel provides temporal warrant.

17. Ralph W. Clark, "Fictional Entities: Talking about Them and Having Feelings about Them," *Philosophical Studies* 38 (1980): 347.

either promotes or conflicts with *A* (something in *P*'s interest or that *P* desires). As I have just argued, however, responses to fiction can be engendered by factors having more to do with one's own interests or desires than with those attributed to P. Those interests or desires can be brought "on line" by the content of what one reads and by the sequencing of passages in the text. Yet the waters are muddied by the role played by desires I have with respect to other people, desires that in this case explain *why* I desire to avoid more descriptions of brutality. I argued above that one may be sympathetic with Desiderio when one's response is partially explained by one's concern for the well-being of people in general. But this is clearly a pretty anemic version of sympathy and hardly sufficient to constitute having sympathy for Desiderio in particular. The latter requires treating Desiderio not simply as a member of a group germane to my having certain feelings and emotions (i.e., the group of human beings) but as someone whose particular qualities as an individual generate those emotions, or generate them in a way other than the way they would be generated by just any member of the group.

To have sympathy for a fictional character, one will attribute certain interests and desires to the character, such as, "It is in Desiderio's interest that he not be harmed." This attribution (along with the belief that he is likely to be harmed) will play a role in generating the response. It is difficult to sympathize with Desiderio partly because he doesn't appear to *have* any desires for his own well-being; hence, an attribution of those desires to him is unwarranted, and the attribution cannot play a role in generating a response. Thus, sympathy with him needs to be predicated on, if anything, a recognition of his interests rather than his desires. My own response to the ominous pronouncement that they would be going to the Holy Hill that day was only marginally influenced by a recognition of what was in his interests but more prominently by a desire to preserve myself from having to read through a description of what might happen.

Genuine concern for specific, individual human beings is characteristically implicated by broader concerns, as for human welfare in general. Certainly we don't want to complain that when mixed with these broader concerns a response is not genuine sympathy for an individual. However, sympathy for an individual goes further. It requires attributing desires and interests to that individual, perhaps merely reaffirming as desires of that person what one is inclined to attribute to people in general (e.g., desires for health and happiness), but paradigmatically more specific instances of these desires (e.g., not merely a desire to avoid pain but a desire for relief from her chronic aching back; not merely a desire to succeed but a desire that his garden will flourish after all that hard work).

Responses generated by attributing an interest to the protagonist and having beliefs about what will or may happen to him in relation to that interest are not necessarily sympathetic: the thought of Desiderio's escaping may produce disappointment, and thoughts or ideas of his pain may produce pleasure. It's possible to want someone to suffer; this is commonplace enough when one is motivated by revenge or hatred rather than care or concern. Sympathetic responses must be "in concert with" the protagonist's interest, not opposed to it. One way to assure fulfillment of this condition is if I not only attribute an interest or desire to the protagonist, but if I also desire that his interests or desires, because they are his interests or desires, are satisfied. The need for this desire is the source of (c) as a condition for sympathy. When there is an opposition between his interests or desires and my beliefs about what will or may happen to him, this desire will explain why I feel some variety of distress. When what I believe will or may happen to him supports or satisfies his interests or desires, I feel some variety of pleasure or satisfaction. (There may be several desires involved, of course, leading to "mixed feelings." I may be joyful over an opportunity, but anxious over the possibility of failure.) When I have sympathy for someone, then, the sense in which I adopt the protagonist's interests and desires as my own is that I desire that the protagonist's desires be satisfied.

The simplest way to understand the role of this desire in generating emotions and affects is to see it as a propositional attitude: the mental representation of the proposition (or relevantly similar proposition), "Desiderio will not be harmed," plays a certain role in my "mental economy." What kind of role will the proposition have to play for my attitude to be properly described as desiring it? Part of what characterizes my attitude towards the proposition as a desire rather than, say, an aversion, is that the role it plays vis-à-vis my belief that Desiderio is likely to be harmed is to generate such emotions as fear, distress, or anxiety. It is not only what I think or imagine that is implicated by my responses but also the role these thoughts play vis-à-vis other mental states. It is possible mentally to shift into a sympathetic mode so that beliefs about the protagonist's desires and about what will happen to him play an affective role such that one's responses are in concert with the interests and desires of the protagonist.

Is there something else that could constitute having a desire with respect to a fictional character other than being in a psychological state such that one would have such feelings? I can think of only one possibility. Sometimes the desire that someone else's interests or desires be satisfied is manifested not by how one feels but by efforts to figure out how to solve the protagonist's problem. This is a possibility even for fictional characters; in fact, appreciating a work sometimes requires contemplating various options a character has (at times simply to recognize he or she has no viable options; the consequent feelings of powerlessness and frustration are sympathetic responses). One might argue that this approach "objectifies" the situation into an abstract problem to be solved rather than shows a concern for the person. One can of course treat a person's dilemmas simply as so many abstract problems to be solved, but not all efforts to think up possible solutions objectify the situation in a way divorced from the desire. For example, it may be that one doesn't even bother to think up solutions unless one does desire the protagonist's interests and desires be satisfied. Spending the mental effort to think about the situation may be precisely how some people manifest this desire.

Such mental efforts may not constitute sympathy. Ralph might think up solutions just to show how stupid the protagonist and the plot are. No sympathy here. He might think of solutions to show off how smart and clever he is. No sympathy here, either. He might just enjoy the challenge. Still no sympathy. But he might, as we say, genuinely care about the protagonist. What constitutes caring about a character when one has cognitive responses to fiction? The cognitive responses occur because one desires that the protagonist's interests and desires be satisfied. What happens when one has such a desire? The mental representation of what the sympathizer desires with respect to the fictional character plays a psychological role such that the conflict between what one believes will or might befall the character and interests or desires one attributes to that character serves to generate additional cognitive activity in the form of thinking up possible solutions to the character's dilemma.

With real people, at least, there is always the possibility of some kind of action, which often allows us to tell whether we "really care" or not. Of course, some people are also good at just going through the motions—doing their duty, without caring for the individual being helped. Nevertheless, for practical purposes, that is the sort of thing we'd look to. When it comes to caring about fictional characters and about what happens to them, we clearly don't have the option of looking to whether the reader is willing to engage in action to benefit the protagonist. Thus, some sort of response—cognitive or affective —appears to be necessary to have the desire that appears in condition (c) of the analysis. If the propositional representation of the character's interests or desires is psychologically inert, one could hardly be described as having the desire.

It is possible to desire that an actual person's particular interest or desire be satisfied without caring about that person. The latter involves not merely desires with respect to a particular interest or desire of that person but for that person's interests or desires generally. "Caring about" someone licenses all sorts of counterfactuals; for example, if you were to find out she wanted such-and-such, you would want her to get it (with the usual caveat that it did not interfere with some more important interest). These aspects of caring apply also to caring about fictional characters. However, with real people, caring also manifests itself by thinking about them unprompted—wondering what and how they are doing and wanting to be with them. Parallels of these aspects of caring also arise with respect to fictional characters. I may think about Ana lying in her sickbed as her husband, Salvador, spends money on a boat ride with a girl he just met. I don't really wonder what she is doing, but I may picture her, lying there helpless, and pity her.

With real people, one might pretend to care. Pretending to care is a temporary condition, where one is able to put that person's interests and desires "on line" emotionally, at least for a brief period of time. One's ability to do this depends in large part on one's powers of imagination. As I argued in Chapter 4, one can learn to shift affective gears empathically or sympathetically. One's pretenses may be extended and thorough enough that one does become emotionally involved. Therefore, it may be difficult for such people (and others) to tell whether they really do care about someone. Emotional facility can have this disorienting effect. However, it is a matter of degree: we all do this to some extent. We allow ourselves to get swept up in another's plight, or we make ourselves care, at least for a while.

But what more is there to caring about a fictional character than being sympathetically affectively moved—even if the desire that the protagonist's desires or interests be satisfied is fleeting or momentary? Though I think it's reasonable to draw a distinction between momentarily putting a real person's cares and desires "on line" so that one has an affective response and really caring about that person, the distinction is less viable when it comes to caring about fictional charac-

ters. With respect to fictional characters, a failure to respond constitutes a failure to care. This is not necessarily the case with respect to
real people: we may indeed care, but we're temporarily distracted or
simply out of sorts. And there is a point to recognizing this—a moral
point. It recognizes that one may have a serious and deep attachment
to someone, in spite of the fact that one is left emotionless on a
particular occasion. The failure to respond doesn't entail that one
ceases to care. But there is no point to recognizing the existence of
caring about a fictional character when one doesn't respond; it does
not raise the same kind of moral issue. Emotional and affective responses to fiction are manifestations of abilities to appreciate. If one
fails to respond on a given occasion it is the appreciational ability that
is not being exercised on that particular occasion, not a failure of
one's moral sensitivities.

In Chapter 4 I argued for a kind of de facto empathy: I may
discover that I am empathizing with a fictional character in the sense
that I discover that what I am experiencing as a reader is a state
similar to one it is reasonable to attribute to a fictional character. I use
my own emotions and affective responses in a manner more in line
with Theodor Lipps's original concept of *Einfühlung:* I imaginatively
attribute my own feelings to an inanimate object (though here it is
extended to fictional persons, rather than to the literary work as an
object). De facto empathy is possible because having the emotions or
affects constitutive of empathy doesn't require attributing psychological or other properties to a protagonist in advance of (and as a generator of) a response, so it is possible to identify a protagonist for the
empathy "after the fact." But sympathy does require attributing desires or interests to a character, having a desire of one's own for the
well-being of that character, and having beliefs about what may or will
befall that character. A protagonist for sympathy cannot be identified
"after the fact."

In the case of certain kinds of responses (such as fear, anxiety,
pleasure, contentment, and disappointment), I may realize after the
fact that my response is in concert with an interest or desire it is
reasonable to attribute to a fictional character. If such a realization
helps to sustain the response (showing that I care about the character), even if it didn't help initiate it, the response clearly counts as at
least partially sympathetic. In the case of other responses, however,
such as surprise, there is no opportunity for such a realization to
sustain the response. It may still be useful to reflect on the possibility
of whether such a response, induced sympathetically, would further

appreciation of the work. I argued above that there is a value in recognizing my response to the passage from *To the Lighthouse* as de facto empathy. Comparably, there may be a value to be gotten out of the work from a sympathetically induced response rather than a self-interested one, something it is important to recognize even if one's response does not become de facto sympathy.

III: Other Responses

The preceding discussion is predicated on empathy and sympathy not being types of emotions or feelings—on a par with fear, pity, anxiety, contentment, amusement—but rather more generic ways of grouping types of responses. Any of the above—pity, amusement, and so on—could be empathic or sympathetic, and some responses, such as pride or grief, are highly unlikely if not impossible in relation to fiction (barring circumstances or beliefs that are very unusual) *except* as empathy or sympathy.[18] I have explicated two different processes of imagination that account for empathic and sympathetic responses. The imaginative mechanisms are very different in the two cases, requiring attributions of beliefs or desires to a character in the case of sympathy but not in the case of empathy.

But not all responses to fiction are empathic or sympathetic. What other generic categories of responses are there, and what psychological mechanisms explain them? I outline five different categories of responses below, and though it would be ideal to have an exhaustive list, I have no delusion that I provide one here. One caveat I have been emphasizing all along is worth repeating: responses will often be mixed, and the same response can have mixed sources (as in the example of sympathy with Desiderio).

First, antipathetic responses comprise *Schadenfreude*, enjoyment of a character's pain or misfortune, as well as its opposite, displeasure in response to a character's joy or success. There is a pleasure when Pip's sister is literally beaten out of her shrewishness in Charles Dickens's *Great Expectations*, and when Compeyson, who is out to destroy Pip, drowns. There is displeasure when Rosamond wins over Lyd-

18. Alex Neill argues for this in "Fiction and the Emotions," p. 4. I also endorse his conclusion that "our affective responses to fiction cannot usefully be treated monolithically, or as though they formed a homogeneous class" (p. 12). As I indicate in this section, different mechanisms may be at work in generating the same type of emotion or affect.

gate. Wollheim groups all of these responses under the rubric of "sympathy," and there is a rationale for this, for the psychological mechanism explaining the responses is the same. A particular passage either produces or activates the requisite set of beliefs and desires about the protagonist's interests and desires, circumstances relevant to the satisfaction or hindrance of those interests and desires, and the reader's own desires with respect to whether those interests and desires be fulfilled. But whereas sympathy requires desiring that the protagonist's desires and interests be satisfied, antipathy requires desiring that the protagonist's desires and interests *not* be satisfied. One's responses, then, will be informed by this desire, creating unpleasant responses when the protagonist's interests are satisfied and pleasurable ones when they are not.

A second category of response, metaresponses, are my responses to my responses to a work. I was surprised and disturbed by my desire to read another Angela Carter novel after determinedly finishing *The Infernal Desire Machines*, whose sadomasochism put me in such a dark mood. The power of her imagination and of her prose are addicting, and I was surprised and disturbed that I was so absorbed by it. Moreover, I wouldn't be at all surprised to find that evoking this sort of metaresponse was part of her aspiration, and the fact that we surprise ourselves with respect to the nature of our desires (as did Desiderio in the novel) advances one of the themes of the novel.

I was embarrassed at being sympathetic for so long to the unreliable narrator of Molly Keane's *Time after Time*. Maintaining that such responses are not part of appreciating a work is like thinking we're not supposed to be embarrassed when taken in by a practical joke or when duped by a forgery. This embarassment does not constitute a deep-seated form of self-assessment, of course, but a fairly fleeting and even entertaining diversion. Being taken in is part of the point (part of the work it is supposed to do), and the metaresponse is not simply an accidental accompaniment of being taken in.

Metaresponses are not very difficult to explain. They are ordinary responses to phenomena that we believe are real, that is, to one's own first-order responses. It is a fact about me that I discovered myself desiring to read another Angela Carter novel. I was surprised to discover this desire for the reasons I'd be surprised by anything (expectations were at odds with reality). I was fascinated for the reasons I'd be fascinated by anything (when something piques curiosity and interest); embarrassed for the same reasons I'd be embarrassed by anything (when I display a substandard level of competence); disturbed for the reasons I'd be disturbed by anything (upon observing behavior at odds with what I would like to believe about myself).

I have argued previously that some of our pleasures in response to tragedies involve metaresponses, in particular, pleasures felt in response to the fact that we do sympathize with a tragic figure.[19] These pleasures are an integral part of appreciating at least some tragedies; they are a way of reinforcing our common humanity through recognizing the importance of feelings of sympathy. One could argue that such pleasures are appropriate in response to classical Greek tragedies, given their moral objectives. By contrast, Bertolt Brecht explicitly denied that his plays were supposed to evoke sympathetic responses from audiences and encouraged a formal, stylized form of acting to inhibit audience involvement with the emotional lives of the characters. The effect of watching a Brecht play is often a kind of emotional alienation, which could itself be seen as a sort of de facto empathy with the characters who are alienated from the means of control over their own lives. Pleasure at feeling the alienation would be unlikely to enhance the functioning of the work, though metaresponses of frustration and futility might.

Responses to an author's achievement or accomplishment, failure or inadequacy, constitute the third category. I was occasionally dazzled by Alexander Theroux's facility with language in *Darconville's Cat,* yet I fairly quickly became annoyed with his self-indulgence and conspicuous verbosity. I marvel at the detail and precision of Joseph Conrad's use of symbols in *Heart of Darkness;* I delight in Jane Austen's subtle wit and irony. Once again, the explanations for such responses are of the garden-variety sort. What dazzles me, annoys me, delights me is explained by structurally the same sorts of things that would dazzle or annoy me in real life, for, in this context, a fictional work functions just like a real thing. It is real in the sense of being a person's work and very often the intentionally produced product of a person's skilled efforts. Theroux's novel is an interesting case in point. His facility with language is truly amazing, but it also becomes annoying, because it becomes an end in itself without serving any more interesting function of the novel. In the end, the writing comes off as almost pure self-indulgence. It's like someone who insists on making puns while you're trying to communicate: amusing at first but increasingly irritating as you try to convey your thoughts. Jane Aus-

19. Susan L. Feagin, "The Pleasures of Tragedy," *American Philosophical Quarterly* 20 (1983): 95–104.

ten's justifiably well-known first sentence of *Pride and Prejudice* verita-
bly drips with irony ("It is a truth universally acknowledged, that a
single man in possession of a good fortune, must be in want of a
wife").[20] I don't merely respond to the language and to the thought,
I admire her achievement, and, by inference in this case, I also admire
her. If the irony was not intended (something that is hard to believe,
but conceivable, I suppose), my response is inappropriate but no
more mysterious than my admiration of anyone else whose qualities
and abilities I have misjudged.

It would be remiss not to recognize that a great deal of the pleasure
of reading has to do with an appreciation of the skills of authors:
their style, imagination, ingenuity, mastery of a genre, cleverness,
insight, and ability to fill out a point of view. I suspect that cults of the
death of the author that have been taken too seriously have deprived
many earnest and serious readers of these pleasures. These pleasures
are, psychologically speaking, of a piece with the pleasures of appreciating exercises of skill or ability in general, whether of a baseball
player making an extraordinary catch and throw to first, a mason
building a mortarless stone wall, a Chinese chef making "doilies" for
Mu Shu pork, a gymnast, or a plasterer. Significantly, the ability to
appreciate skills carries with it the ability to appreciate lack of skill—
the lopsided stone wall or uneven plaster, holes in the "doilies," or
sluggishness in the baseball player. Most of us don't generally enjoy
seeing people fail, but it is misguided to let this disposition hinder us
from developing our own perceptual and conceptual abilities, even
when what we have learned to see is the crack in the golden bowl.

Still another set of responses comprises what I call responses to
verbal features of a work. Verbal features encompass diction, narrative voice, style, sentence structure—in short, anything about the way
language is used in the work.

An extended passage from Henry James's *The Golden Bowl* illustrates the sorts of phenomena I have in mind. In chapter six of Book
First, Part First, Charlotte and the Prince go to a shop in Bloomsbury
seeking a wedding gift for Maggie Verver. James describes some of
what they see: "Of decent old gold, old silver, old bronze, of old
chased and jewelled artistry, were the objects that, successively produced, had ended by numerously dotting the counter, where the
shopman's slim, light fingers, with neat nails, touched them at mo-

---

20. *The Novels of Jane Austen*, ed. R. W. Chapman, vol. 2, *Pride and Prejudice* (London:
Oxford University Press, 1932), p. 1.

ments, briefly, nervously, tenderly, as those of a chess-player rest, a few seconds, over the board, on a figure he thinks he may move and then may not: small florid ancientries, ornaments, pendants, lockets, brooches, buckles."[21]

There is a kind of "antique store" now, as well as then, crammed with little things and big things, bibelots and ornaments, so that one's eye darts from object to object, never resting, with no central focus, just "dotting" its way over the visual field. James's prose encourages the jumpiness, the hastiness, the urge to find something one desires while constantly backing off (just as James describes the shopman's fingers, "briefly, nervously, tenderly, as those of a chess-player rest, a few seconds, over the board"), by the way he describes the scene, with a list of names or short descriptions, choppy and abrupt. This choppiness encourages a sense of heightened curiosity and anticipation but also of being somewhat overwhelmed by an array that is ultimately rather shabby.

Shortly thereafter the shopman brings out his "golden bowl." "Charlotte, with care, immediately took it up, while the Prince, who had after a minute shifted his position again, regarded it from a distance."[22] Linguistically, the reactions of Charlotte and the Prince are contrasted. Charlotte's response is immediate but "with care." The description is simple and quickly makes the point. The Prince, by contrast, literally and figuratively distances himself from the object, though obliquely and after an interval of time. James's description is equally oblique and lengthened, not "immediately," but, "who had after a minute shifted his position again."

An exchange between Charlotte and the Prince after she has resisted purchasing the bowl provides a final illustration. In this passage, the effect is also, of course, due in part to content, but it is heightened by word choice and the rhythms of the dialogue. Charlotte speaks first.

"His price is so moderate." She waited but a moment. "Five pounds. Really so little."

He continued to look at her. "Five pounds?"

"Five pounds."

He might have been doubting her word, but he was only, it appeared, gathering emphasis. "It would be dear—to make a gift of

21. Henry James, *The Golden Bowl* (1904; Penguin Classics, 1966), p. 100.
22. James, *The Golden Bowl*, p. 104.

—at five shillings. If it had cost you even but five pence I wouldn't take it from you."

"Then," she asked, "what *is* the matter?"

"Why, it has a crack."

It sounded, on his lips, so sharp, it had such an authority, that she almost started, while her colour, at the word, rose. It was as if he had been right, though his assurance was wonderful. "You answer for it without having looked?"

"I did look. I saw the object itself. It told its story. No wonder it's cheap."

"But it's exquisite," Charlotte, as if with an interest in it now made even tenderer and stranger, found herself moved to insist.

"Of course it's exquisite. That's the danger."[23]

James calls our attention to the onomatopoeic quality of "crack" ("It sounded, on his lips, so sharp"). If we failed to respond to it when reading the word, his reminder comes so quickly that its potential for effect is not lost. The Prince is no longer oblique: he is curt, wastes no words, direct to the point of being abrupt, and maligns the very quality of the object Charlotte adores. Their contrasting judgments are emphasized by his repeating her phrase, and following it by his opposing conclusion. He does this twice—with her recounting of the price and her observation that it is exquisite. For the Prince, the look of the object tells "its story," and he concludes, "No wonder it's cheap" (not "inexpensive," but crassly being "cheap"). In Charlotte, its defect inspires something like compassion rather than disdain, and she defends the object by pointing out "it's exquisite," having found herself moved to do so. The Prince's words, however, "had such an authority." The Prince is not the type to find himself doing anything: he's not susceptible to mere belief or feeling, he *knows*, and he uses his knowledge to reaffirm his authority.

There's another fleeting reference in this passage that deserves mention: "He might have been doubting her word." Charlotte did lie about the price; the shopman had asked fifteen pounds, not merely five. This reference subtly attunes the reader to Charlotte's point of view, and perhaps a puzzlement over her motives. She was perhaps a little embarrassed about being so enamored of the bowl even at the higher price and self-conscious about it in her misrepresentation of

23. James, *The Golden Bowl*, p. 108 (original emphasis).

the price in order to make the bowl seem worth buying. But these emotions are of no concern to the Prince, who, after all, is the man who depends on Mrs. Assingham as his indicator of moral right and wrong.[24] We are reminded of Charlotte's little lie and feel a momentary cringe, but the Prince quickly moves on to something more important to him: pointing out that a bowl with a crack, even an exquisite golden bowl, is worthless. Its aesthetic flaw commands much more attention than Charlotte's little lie.

That we can and do respond to "verbal features" provides impetus for the view that there are special sorts of "aesthetic experiences" whose qualitatively distinctive character is unlike ordinary, everyday experiences. The experiences are alleged to be different because what elicits them are (allegedly) different from the sorts of things we generally respond to emotionally or affectively. But we have seen in Chapter 4, section IV, that the same emotions, or simulations of emotions, can be elicited by very different kinds of factors. In addition, the account of sensitivities developed in Chapter 3 can handle these sorts of responses nicely. The sensitivities account has the advantage of being able to accommodate affects as well as emotions, affective responses without cognitive components as well as those with. Salient features of the account are (a) the psychological state or condition of the reader and (b) features of the elicitor to which one is sensitive in virtue of being in that psychological state or condition. Whereas emotions require one's having a belief or thought (either elicited by what one reads, or preexisting and rendered psychologically active by what one reads), affects do not. Affects are more difficult to distinguish from one another because they can't be distinguished by their cognitive components. But this fact doesn't make them a categorically distinct type of emotion, such as an aesthetic emotion.

People are sensitive to auto alarms and barking dogs, and the longer or more frequently the alarms or dogs make noise, the more likely these sensitivities will increase. Some people are especially sensitive to subtle linguistic faults ("less" for "fewer," "different than" for "different from"), tone ("cheap" for "inexpensive," "loquacious" instead of merely "talkative"), or linguistic ticks ("as it were," "you know"). Though what one is sensitive *to* may vary, depending on whether one is listening, looking, reading (alleged) fact or fiction, the principle involved is the same. Formal or verbal features of language

24. See James, *The Golden Bowl*, p. 48.

commonly elicit affective responses, so there is nothing unique in principle about having sensitivities to these features of language used in fiction.

A final category of responses involve real-life values. Sometimes a reader likes or dislikes specific characters or what they do. These responses should not be confused with sympathy, empathy, or antipathy: in admiring Roger and being amused by Mark I don't necessarily sympathize with them; in being disgusted with Roger and impatient with Mark I'm not necessarily being antipathetic towards them (in the technical sense of "antipathetic" just explained). They are not metaresponses; they are not (merely) responses depending on sensitivities to formal qualities of a work or responses to the author or the author's skilled production.

Dot, in Louis B. Jones's early novel, *Particles and Luck,* drives a white Corvette but claims not to have enough money to feed her two young children.[25] She slaps her ex-husband, Roger, with a restraining order yet imposes on him to baby-sit. I don't like Dot. I don't wish her harm, I just don't like her. Roger, using an insurance settlement on his failed business, buys a truck (custom model, with all the extras), places a huge downpayment on a condominium ("super deluxe package," again, with all the extras), without any thought to how he will pay the monthly mortgage. Roger inspires pity and pathos. His behavior is exasperating. But his eventual homelessness is due not only to his character traits but also to his bad fortune ("particles *and* luck"). Yet, basically, I like him: he's good-humored, energetic, personable, reasonably intelligent, and hard-working, even if not in an entirely well-directed fashion. There are even times when I admire him. His neighbor Mark, meanwhile, is a whiz-kid physicist, awarded a chaired professorship at Berkeley at the age of 27. He's self-absorbed, neurotic, antisocial, and incapable of carrying on a casual conversation. He has a little tick that is at first amusing—he does things in multiples of fours, like tapping each leg of a chair four times before sitting down —but then becomes simply annoying. He hums the same tune all the time. He disconnects the battery cables from the car when he parks. He can't even fix his own toast because he gets lost in ruminations about what happens to the surface molecules of a stream of water. His wife has to leave post-it notes on the stove to remind him to turn

25. Louis B. Jones, *Particles and Luck* (New York: Random House, Vintage Contemporaries, 1993).

it off when she is out of town. And when he locks himself out of his condo for the second time in one evening, you just want to slap him.

I am faintly disgusted when Roger displays his kidney stones on the mantle and amused when Mark engages in a characteristic rumination about their chemical composition. I am appalled by Roger's children's flippant behavior and equally appalled by Mark's ineffectual attempt to take care of them by tucking them into a plastic tarp in a vacant apartment when he finds them wandering outside at 3 A.M. (one of the occasions he's locked himself out of his own apartment). Such responses as those named here—dislike, aversion, admiration, pity, annoyance, disgust, amusement, being appalled—may arise, of course, as empathy, sympathy, or antipathy, but they are clearly none of those in the examples just given. My dislike of Dot doesn't manifest itself in pleasure in her misfortune or a desire for her harm, nor is it sympathy with anyone whom she mistreats. Likewise, my annoyance with Mark is a response engendered by (descriptions of) his behavior, not sympathy with his wife or antipathy towards him.

A familiar strategy for explaining such cases as these is to appeal to how we would respond to actual such people and events were we to encounter them. The explanation for my annoyance with Mark would be that since I would be annoyed by someone with Mark's habits, I am annoyed when reading about these habits of Mark's; my dislike of Dot would be explained by that fact that since I would dislike someone who spends money on an expensive car when her children don't have adequate food to eat, I dislike Dot when I read that she behaved this way.

There is something to these sorts of explanations, though as stated, they are singularly unhelpful. What is it about me, psychologically, that makes it the case that I would respond in such a way to the actual persons or events? Since we are looking for psychological models to explain responses, just saying the same mechanism is at work does not elucidate what that mechanism is. Presumably, it has something to do with the *values* I hold. Psychologically, having a value is pretty similar to having a desire, though they are desires of a particular sort (not momentary impulses or short-term desires, but more general and basic and considered). I value people acting responsibly; an aversive response when perceiving, thinking of, or reading about someone who does not behave responsibly may manifest the fact that I hold that to be valuable. My having the value is partially constitutive of the psychological state or condition that ensures that when I read about Dot's irresponsible behavior I respond by disliking her. However, the fact that I hold a certain thing to be valuable does not in itself *ensure* that I will respond with pleasure every time I perceive, think of, or read about its being furthered, or with aversion when I perceive, think of, or read about its being contravened.

Other factors relevant to appreciation come into play when reading, such as sensitivities to verbal features of the language, as discussed with respect to Henry James. Indeed, sensitivities to language can lead us to respond to descriptions of persons, events, or situations contrary to ways we would ordinarily respond to them in "real life." I am delighted by Sir Henry Wotton's pungent witticisms in *The Picture of Dorian Gray*, but I would most likely be appalled and offended to hear someone spouting such remarks in earnest ("I like persons better than principles, and I like persons with no principles better than anything else in the world").[26] Oscar Wilde writes with style, and part of appreciating his work is to be caught up in that style, responding as if you, the reader, didn't disdain what in fact you do. You put some of your own values "off line" in order to appreciate what he's done.

Prose can be persuasive and not merely through the force of argument; it can change the ways we think and feel about things. Eugene O'Neill explodes in *The Iceman Cometh*, "To hell with the truth! As the history of the world proves, the truth has no bearing on anything. It's irrelevant and immaterial, as the lawyers say. The lie of a pipe dream is what gives life to the whole misbegotten mad lot of us, drunk or sober."[27] Philosophers reading this passage will probably recognize a sentiment with which they disagree, given how we are devoted to the search for truth and all that. But the passage is powerful and moving, creating a feeling in harmony with those who disbelieve in the power, value, and efficacy of reason and truth. That our responses may be generated in ways that contrast with our ordinary desires or values is explicable by the fact that those values may be put "off line," as responses are elicited by verbal features of the text that twist the way we think of things *as* being. Nevertheless, our existing values and commitments can and often do affect responses.

What is most controversial about appeals to values to explain such responses is the following. In real life, we have beliefs that a particular person or circumstance exists (call it an existential belief) and that this

26. Oscar Wilde, *The Picture of Dorian Gray* (New York: Nottingham Society, 1909), p. 11.
27. Quoted by Jerome Neu, "Life-Lies and Pipe Dreams: Self-Deception in Ibsen's *The Wild Duck* and O'Neill's *The Iceman Cometh*," *Philosophical Forum* 19 (1988): 254.

reality clashes with a value we hold dear. However, when reading fiction, we have no such belief—at least, I am not appealing to any such existential belief to explain the response. Instead of believing that there is such a phenomenon, we merely think of such a phenomenon. Doesn't this show that a different psychological mechanism is involved in generating the response?

There are two replies to this query. First, a thought can function the same way the belief ordinarily does, so that there is no different kind of psychological process involved but the same process where either thoughts or beliefs can play a certain role. Does anyone seriously deny that simply thinking of things, running over a scenario in one's imagination, can be affectively moving? Some, like Colin Radford, may have doubts about the rationality of being moved emotionally, but that doubt is quite different from denying that simply thinking or imagining something can ever produce emotional or affective responses. Indeed, to claim that such responses are irrational is to imply that they do indeed occur. Michael Weston, in his contribution to the Aristotelian Society symposium with Colin Radford, "How Can We Be Moved by the Fate of Anna Karenina?", makes this point about how to explain responses to fiction: "We can be moved, not merely by what has occurred or what is probable, but also by ideas."[28] Ideas have the power to evoke an affective response. For example, think of a vomit sandwich.[29] Any response? Think of a three-dimensional figure that is not a cube but which has six sides, all of which are squares and joined by right angles. Think of Anselm's claim that if that than which nothing greater can be conceived is conceived to exist in the understanding alone, then it is not that than which nothing greater can be conceived. These ideas are likely to generate different affective responses: disgust (and possibly amusement), puzzlement or bewilderment (since there is no such possible figure), fascination or curiosity (or, with a little luck, in the rare introductory philosophy student, awe and amazement).

I believe the inherent plausibility, indeed, the virtual certainty of the power of thoughts and ideas to evoke emotions and affects as a psychological fact has been undermined by its frequent coupling with a distinctively *philosophical* position about the *objects* of emotions. That an emotion has an object is a bit of philosophical theory; it is not part

28. Michael Weston, "How Can We Be Moved by the Fate of Anna Karenina?" *Proceedings of the Aristotelian Society*, supp. vol. 49 (1975): 85. See also the discussion in Chapter 3, sec. III, on thoughts as the cognitive contents of emotions.
29. An example kindly offered by Howard Niblock.

of ordinary, everyday "folk psychology." That all emotions have to have objects has become, in some circles, a bit of philosophical dogma (though the corresponding view that other affects have objects has thankfully not seen wide acceptance). Peter Lamarque has argued that the objects of our emotional responses are "thought-contents."[30] Thoughts and ideas certainly can be the objects of emotions: the idea of a vomit sandwich is the object of my disgust. But the situation is much less clear with other emotions, such as anger, fear, pity, pride, regret, relief, or guilt. Sometimes just thinking about someone doing something can generate anger, but that is not to say the idea or thought-content is the object of my anger. I'm not angry at or with the idea or thought.

Second, the fact that thoughts can generate responses in a way comparable to the way beliefs often do is not a phenomenon restricted to the reading of fiction. It is a fact of our everyday, real-life experiences as well. I feel distress when I think of a friend suffering a misfortune, pleasure in the idea of a profusely blooming garden (which, being realistic, I know I won't have). For this reason it is implausible to hold that when thoughts generate the experience it is some special kind of experience, an "aesthetic experience," even though it may be less (or sometimes more) vivid or intense. One of the contributions Kendall Walton has made in his discussion of emotions and fiction is that imagination—in his terms, "playing games of make-believe"—plays a role in many aspects of what we'd call an ordinary life.[31] David Novitz has also argued for the intimate interconnections between imagination and belief, knowledge, and skill.[32] Trying things out in imagination is a way of experimenting; imaginative play is a way of learning. These facts hold whether one is playing games, engaging in private ruminations, or responding to fiction. Emotions and affects occur as part of many everyday imaginative activities.

Once again I wish to emphasize the complexity of responses and the attendant complexity of explanations for them. Though a certain amount of simplification—to which I have repeatedly resorted myself

30. Peter Lamarque, "How Can We Fear and Pity Fictions?" *British Journal of Aesthetics* 21 (1981): 293.
31. Kendall L. Walton, *Mimesis as Make-Believe: On the Foundation of the Representational Arts* (Cambridge: Harvard University Press, 1990), esp. chap. 1.
32. This view pervades two of his books, *Knowledge, Fiction, and Imagination* (Philadelphia: Temple University Press, 1987), and *The Boundaries of Art* (Philadelphia: Temple University Press, 1992).

—is necessary in order to give an analysis, it is likely to obscure the nature (and value) of appreciation, and the role emotions and affective responses play within it. Several different sorts of explanations account for a single response, or for a fluctuating set of responses, such as those generated by a well-known passage in Samuel Butler's *Erewhon*. When the judge refuses to listen to the defendant's plea for leniency on the grounds that his breaking the law was due to his unfortunate upbringing, readers tend to respond with approval, a kind of pleasure in seeing that justice is going to be done and in knowing that cheap excuses will not be condoned. But in the fictional country Erewhon, contracting tuberculosis is against the law, and that is the crime of which the defendant has been convicted. In this case, his health may well have been undermined in childhood, making him more susceptible to disease, and exposure to the disease may be entirely against his will. It's not the defendant's fault; he genuinely couldn't help it. This scenario opens up the possibility of a whole range of responses: the righteous feeling that justice is being done (trading on my ordinary sense of values); a metaresponse of sheepishness over having had the righteous feeling, due to my realization that the law that was broken is itself unjust; surprise at the nature of the law; perturbation and anger with the author for putting one over on me; and a sympathetic response to the defendant (righteous indignation now on his behalf, rather than the feeling of righteousness with respect to the law). Several different factors play a role in generating responses in rapid succession, as both changes in judgment and different psychological factors acquire dominance.

In this chapter I have explored psychological mechanisms for a variety of kinds of responses, divided roughly according to the nature of the mechanism that explains them. Sympathy in its paradigm form requires attributing desires or interests to a protagonist, having beliefs about the circumstances of the protagonist relevant to these desires or interests, and having a desire that the protagonist's desires or interests be satisfied. More attenuated forms of sympathy can occur in which one or more of these three conditions is satisfied only after the initiation of the affective response. Antipathetic responses follow a similar model, except that the reader desires that the protagonist's desires or interests *not* be satisfied. In these cases, readers' responses will not be "in concert with" the interests and desires of the protagonist, but contrary to them.

Other responses have other explanations. Metaresponses are one step removed from the work and are responses to my responses to the work. As such, either the first-order response or a belief about it must play a role in generating the metaresponse. Such responses, in order to constitute part of appreciating a work, should also play a role in making the work "work," so that my having the metaresponse can be explicated as part of the functioning of the work. I may also respond to what I perceive to be accomplishments or failures of the author in writing the work. Thus, beliefs about or experiences of the author's achievements or failings, as such, will play a role in generating a response. Verbal features of a work may also be the salient factor in generating a response, including diction, style, and narrative techniques. Finally, real-life values can inform a response and constitute a significant factor in explaining why I responded to what I did, in the way I did.

PART TWO

WARRANT

Chapter Six

Justifying Beliefs about Emotions and Affects

So far I have been concerned with explaining affective responses to fiction. In recognition of certain psychological facts—that is, our ability to slip or slide into different psychological gears—I have developed a psychological model for explaining what goes on when a reader empathizes with a fictional character. In this simulation model, what goes on, psychologically, in the empathizer is structurally similar in significant ways to what goes on in the person with whom one empathizes. For readers of fiction, the simulation model entails that what goes on in the reader is structurally similar to what goes on when one has an emotion, mood, or affect—perhaps so similar that it counts as having that emotion, mood, or affect. Whether one has identified a protagonist in advance or whether one simply finds oneself empathizing with a character, the reflective component of appreciation is necessary to identify what one is experiencing as the emotion or affect it is and as empathy. Sympathetic and antipathetic responses are explained on a different model: rather than simulating having an emotion or affect, the response issues from attributing certain beliefs and desires to a protagonist. Other responses trade on one's ordinary beliefs and values and one's capacity to lose or develop sensitivities to various phenomena.

This discussion has proceeded in the interest of providing explanatory models for how emotional and affective responses can arise in response to fictional literature. It is now time to examine the normative aspects of appreciation. On what basis can responses be assessed as appropriate or relevant? How is it possible to assess an emotion or affect at all? Responsible readers will wonder about the relevance and appropriateness of their responses: am I reacting negatively because I'm in a bad mood? With pleasure because I like cats and there is a cat in the story? With fear because I break out in a sweat at the mere thought of spiders? Are these appropriate responses nevertheless? Do they have anything to do with appreciating the work as literature? How do they enrich, or conflict with, judgments I make about a work's meaning or significance?

Appreciation involves asking questions such as these. It thus includes a reflective component, that is, thoughts and beliefs about the appropriateness, relevance, or warrantedness of one's responses. These reflections may themselves alter one's mental state so that one then responds, or becomes inclined to respond, differently from the way one would have responded without engaging in the reflections. That is, reflection can lead us to shift or slide into a different psychological "gear." It is an important component of appreciation, an integral part of the process that enables one to get the value out of a work. Some of these reflections occur in the form of beliefs about the appropriateness of a response or whether it was warranted. What, then, is the epistemic basis for these beliefs?

I begin this chapter by describing a *teleological model* for appreciating artworks. According to this model, the evocation of emotions and affects is seen as the goal or purpose of a work of literature, and the character of these responses is, in principle, describable separately from the character of what elicits them. The ability to appreciate fiction is manifested by one's having the emotions or affects (as well as cognitive responses such as thoughts and ideas) that it is the goal of the work to produce. Deficiencies with this model as a framework for understanding appreciation, and hence for assessing emotional and affective responses to a work of fiction, are explored, and in the following section a *function model* is developed. It is subtly but importantly different from the teleological model in that it does not take the way the work is supposed to function as describable independently of the character of the work that is supposed to function that way. Readers' appreciative abilities are necessarily exercised in interactions with a text having the properties it has. The value of appreciation needs to be understood as a value inherent in being able to interact in appropriate ways rather than as being able to use the work as a means to the evocation of affective effects.

Since evoking affective responses is part of the function of a literary work, the function model for assessing artworks provides a structure for understanding how affective responses to a work can be assessed in the context of a whole set of beliefs about what a work is supposed to do and how it is supposed to do it. These beliefs require interpretive decisions about what a work means and says, what it symbolizes, expresses, presages, alludes to, and refers to. These decisions obviously include interpretive judgments, though what I say here about appropriateness and warrant is not derived from a commitment to the truth of any particular theory of interpretation. Instead, the claims in this chapter state conditions that any adequate theory of appreciation must satisfy. Thus, it is a philosophical analysis of the epistemology of appreciation, rather than a theory of interpretation. The major issue in the epistemology of appreciation, as I see it, is how it is possible to assess affective responses at all, as affects. Even if an interpretation of a work, or of a particular passage of it, is warranted, still more is needed to warrant a response of a given type to that work or to that particular passage. Appreciation involves not merely understanding but also responding.

Section III explains the different ways responses to fictional literature and beliefs about those responses can be assessed. I warn you, this section will be a little tedious. But it is important to understand the different types and levels of assessment that are possible, because many people make what I call "the simple answer fallacy" when it comes to assessing responses to fiction. The simple answer fallacy, in its general form, goes like this: if there's no simple answer, there's no answer. (How often have you heard a view dismissed simply on the grounds that it is too complicated?) The bottom line is that, if there's "no answer," then you can, with epistemic impunity, believe anything you like. The simple answer fallacy is tempting because it keeps us from having to work through the tedious details. But it also keeps us from understanding the truth that lies within those details.

Differences of opinion can often be resolved by showing that once you work through the details, two views are not actually in conflict but rather opinions about different things. Moreover, genuinely conflicting opinions may each be justified because the complexity of the issue leaves matters sufficiently inconclusive that there is equal justification for different beliefs. In neither case is it "all up to the individual." Whether a belief is justified and whether a response is warranted are not simply for the believer or responder to decide. And just because different beliefs may all be justifiable, it doesn't follow that one can simply believe whatever one likes. One must arrive at the conclusion contained in one of those options on the basis of whatever makes it a justifiable option. It may be very difficult to tell, in specific cases, whether readers are justified in believing or warranted in responding as they do. Even if the principles were clear, the application in specific cases often remains murky.

I: A Teleological Model of Assessment

When something is assessed teleologically there is an end, goal, or purpose of that thing (or things of that kind) in light of which the object is judged. This end, goal, or purpose must be describable independently of the means used to achieve it. This essential feature of the teleological model constitutes the most important respect in which it differs from the function account described and defended in the following section.

A teleological model for assessing a literary work of art takes having emotions or affects as at least part of its goal or purpose. The artwork, on this view, is seen as a *means* for generating certain kinds of emotions and affects. Having emotions or affective experiences would then be at least part of the point of appreciating and developing the ability to appreciate such works. This view is certainly at the foundation of many aesthetic experience theories, such as that of Monroe Beardsley (though some qualifications are needed if one considers him as holding this view), as well as earlier theories such as those of Clive Bell and John Dewey. Aesthetic experience theories typically include the claim that aesthetic experiences are themselves "intrinsically valuable." It is also sometimes claimed, by Clive Bell, for example (though notably not by Dewey), that such experiences cannot be produced except by works of art.

Aesthetic experience theories are not the only views about the value of art which lend themselves to teleological construal. Whenever the intrinsic qualities of the emotional or affective experiences themselves are highlighted as having a special value, the view becomes, to that extent, teleological. Thus, Jerrold Levinson, while arguing that many responses to music are valuable and enjoyable as responses to particular notes, also identifies some responses as enjoyable in themselves. As he puts it, we become "cognoscenti of feeling, savoring the qualitative aspect of emotional life for its own sake."[1] Malcolm Budd states suc-

---

1. Jerrold Levinson, "Music and Negative Emotions," *Pacific Philosophical Quarterly* 63 (1982): 327–346; repr. in *Music, Art, and Metaphysics: Essays in Philosophical Aesthetics* (Ithaca: Cornell University Press, 1990): 306–335.

cinctly that "the value of a work of art as a work of art is the intrinsic value of the experience that it offers."[2]

The common ingredient of teleological views, that the experiences artworks are supposed to produce are intrinsically valuable because of their phenomenology or qualitative character, explains why it is good to have (good) works of art around. Good works of art achieve the appropriate end or goal—they provide experiences that are (allegedly) intrinsically valuable—whereas bad works do not. Classic aesthetic experience theories, such as those of Beardsley, Stolnitz, Bell, and Dewey, describe and define aesthetic experience as an experience that carries with it a special sort of pleasure and feelings of fulfillment —an experience that is worthwhile in itself. But the implausibility of such a view has become glaring in recent years, and it is naive and short-sighted to think it is the purpose of works of fictional literature, and artworks in general, to provides these kinds of experiences.[3] Appropriate responses to (good) fiction include a great variety of emotions, feelings, moods, and imaginings, and not all of them are pleasurable, or prima facie bearers of intrinsic value.

A general characterization of intrinsically valuable experiences it is the goal or purpose of artworks to produce is unlikely to be forthcoming. Nevertheless, it may well be that at least some appropriate emotional and affective responses to fiction are intrinsically valuable. Notice, however, the occurrence of the word "appropriate." One thing the teleological model cannot do is account for which experiences are appropriate to have to a given work. That is, it cannot be used to assess whether a given emotion or affect is appropriate: it cannot explain which kinds of emotions are appropriate to have in response to which features of a work. This model rather assumes the appropriateness of the response and then provides a basis for determining what that response shows about whether the work is good or bad. But why are some responses—those that have intrinsic value—appropriate to have in response to some works, but others— those that lack such value—inappropriate? The aesthetic experience

---

2. Malcolm Budd, "Sincerity in Poetry," in Eva Schaper, ed., *Pleasure, Preference and Value,* (Cambridge: Cambridge University Press, 1983), p. 154.
3. E. D. Hirsch, Jr., who defends the importance of arts education and cultural literacy, is wary of terms such as "intrinsic value" and "for its own sake." See "Reflections on Cultural Literacy and Arts Education," in *Journal of Aesthetic Education* 24 (1990): 4. I don't conclude, as he does, that there is a group of artists and works that "should be known in common by all students" (p. 4), but I think his cautions about how unpersuasive it is to defend the value of the arts in terms of intrinsic value are very well taken.

view needs to be supplemented by another theoretical apparatus to explain why it is appropriate to have those experiences in response to certain works and not others. It would also need an additional apparatus to explain why certain emotions and responses are relevant to certain aspects of the work. Some theories, such as Beardsley's, do provide this additional apparatus.

It would be foolhardy to assert that it's never the case that fictional works of literature, considered as works of art, have as part of their purpose to evoke feelings of a given sort. In general, however, I am much persuaded by Collingwood's views on this subject: there is something wrong in thinking that writing fiction, or, producing art, is merely or even primarily a craft whose function is to elicit feelings of a given kind, such as horror, amusement, or romantic sentimentality.[4] There are numerous formulas and techniques for making sure a work is effective in these ways, and writers of mystery novels, screenwriters of popular films, and authors of "modern romances" have varying degrees of skill in putting them to work. According to the teleological view, it wouldn't matter whether the writer employed a shopworn formula or imaginative innovation: that is the point, after all, of separating the nature of the effect from the means by which it is produced, something that is essential to the teleological account. If the point is to get a certain sort of emotional effect, it won't matter how you do it.

The teleological model has a certain appeal, however, on other grounds. It is possible for people to read a given work because they want to experience certain emotions or other affects, when they believe reading the work will provide these experiences for them. I know several people, myself included, who reread the novels of Jane Austen for this very reason. But the point is not to have the experiences at any price; it is to have the experiences as they are elicited by relevant features of the work. Indeed, there is a kind of paradox if one's desire is only to have the feelings, for if one's desire in rereading *Pride and Prejudice* is simply to have the feelings one had the last time one read it, one may very well not have them. (I characterized this in Chapter 2 as a desire that I have certain feelings rather than a desire to do, i.e., to appreciate.) Having those feelings depends on being sensitive to Austen's prose style and irony. If one doesn't care about how she uses language and what she's trying to say and do in the

4. R. G. Collingwood, *The Principles of Art* (New York: Oxford University Press, 1938), chap. 2.

novel, and one only cares about the end product, having the feelings, the chances of one's *having* the appropriate feelings are virtually eliminated.

A teleological model for assessing artworks may hold that what makes it valuable to have emotions in response to a work is something other than intrinsic value or pleasure. It has been suggested that knowledge is the benefit accorded by the appropriate emotions or affects, not the pleasurable qualities of the experiences.[5] For example, emotions could be a means for obtaining knowledge about oneself.[6] They could trigger self-reflection, so that one comes to recognize that one has certain beliefs and desires one previously hadn't realized one had or of which one hadn't realized the significance. However, it's arguable whether engaging in and gaining knowledge from this process of self-reflection is part of what it is to appreciate the work of fictional literature, instead of one of the benefits that may accrue from reading or appreciating it. Nevertheless, the emotional response one has to a work may be judged as desirable or valuable according to whether having it leads to a further beneficial activity or condition. But this view will not help us understand the appreciation of literary fiction as works of art unless we can understand why works having the character they have warrant feelings of that sort.

We all know that the reasons why it is good to do something—even if we grant them—are not always sufficiently motivating, and it is not essential to the teleological model that we be motivated by or interested in the kind of thing it is actually the purpose of the work to produce. Furthermore, and I think even more important with respect to works of fiction, we most often don't even know what responses are appropriate to various parts of it before reading it. None of this is a problem for the teleological account. What is a problem, however, is that the purpose of the work is to produce a response of a given character, when this purpose can be separated from the means employed for evoking that response. Such a view treats the work as a mere *stimulus* for a response rather than as a *ground or warrant* for it. That is, the teleological model lacks an account of the character of

5. Martha Nussbaum, *The Fragility of Goodness: Luck and Ethics in Greek Tragedy and Philosophy* (New York: Cambridge University Press, 1986); David Novitz, *Knowledge, Fiction, and Imagination* (Philadelphia: Temple University Press, 1987), and *The Boundaries of Art* (Philadelphia: Temple University Press, 1992).
6. I thank members of my seminar at the University of Wisconsin, spring 1990, for impressing the importance of this point on me. See also Don Mannison, "On Being Moved by Fiction," *Philosophy* 60 (1985): 86.

the work that explains why a given response is relevant or appropriate and why we are warranted in responding to certain features in a given way. Therefore, we cannot justify our belief that a response is relevant, appropriate, or warranted, without an additional theoretical apparatus that explains the relevance, appropriateness, or warrant for responses.

The teleological view, as I have described it, might be attacked on the grounds that the way an experience or emotion is generated constitutes a relevant factor in identifying what kind of experience it is. This argument is tantamount to denying that the end or purpose of the work can be identified independently of the means for producing it. For example, if the end or purpose is conceived as being a pleasurable experience, Gilbert Ryle's arguments—that pleasure, as a mental state, cannot be identified independently of the (pleasurable) activity you're engaging in—are germane. According to Ryle, pleasure (or enjoyment) is not a feeling. Pleasure is either a propensity-fulfillment (doing "with your whole heart" and not wanting to do anything else), or the word "pleasure" is used to replace other words that are names of moods signifying agitations.[7] In the latter case, the real feelings—tickles, tingles, pangs, thrills, twitches, and flutters—may be enjoyed or not. One could say the same of emotions—one might enjoy feeling proud or even angry. But then these emotions and affective states are the real concern: are they relevant or appropriate, or am I warranted in responding in those ways?

The first point, that pleasure or enjoyment is a way of doing, finds its analogue in aesthetic theories that any experience is to be at least partially identified in terms of the qualities of the work that generated it. Beardsley and Stolnitz, for example, emphasize that the experience must arise out of direct attention to the work itself.[8] However, I don't think it is plausible to tie the identification of what kind of emotion or feeling one is having to the character of what is eliciting it. In Chapter 1 (section I) I proposed that we must in principle be able to say that different people have different emotions or affects (broadly speaking, different sorts of experiences) in response to the same qualities of a work. Different backgrounds or past experiences, or perhaps different psychological dispositions, would explain why people re-

7. Gilbert Ryle, *The Concept of Mind* (New York: Barnes & Noble, 1949), p. 108.
8. Monroe Beardsley, *Aesthetics: Problems in the Philosophy of Criticism* (New York: Harcourt, Brace & World, 1958); Jerome Stolnitz, *Aesthetics and Philosophy of Art Criticism: A Critical Introduction* (New York: Houghton Mifflin, 1960).

spond differently to the same things. At any rate, it can't be a defining feature of emotions and affects of given sorts that they arise in response to certain sorts of phenomena.[9] However, even though an emotion or affect has identity conditions that are independent of what elicits it, it doesn't follow that why it's *valuable* to have it can be described independently of the elicitors and conditioners that *warrant* one's having the response.

II: A Function Model of Assessment

On the teleological model, a work is a means to a separately describable end, an end that might conceivably be produced by some other means. Nelson Goodman's quip that "works of art are not race-horses, and picking a winner is not the primary goal," is appropriately lodged against a teleological account of the nature of the value of a work of art.[10] But it cannot be lodged against a function account. If one's primary goal were to "pick a winner," one would not be interested in a work's function, but in an end product or condition. By contrast, a function cannot be described independently of how various parts or aspects of a thing are supposed to function. A work has a function, or a variety of functions, and its parts have functions, which are described in relation to the functions of other parts and in relation to what kind of work it is.[11] This may seem like a small difference between the teleological and function models, but it has major implica-

9. I do not deny that the nature of the elicitor is ever relevant to identifying one's psychological state or condition. For example, hallucinations that are introspectively indistinguishable from perceptions are still not perceptions. The character of the process generating the experience is, in this case, a necessary part of the identification of the kind of experience it is, either a hallucination or a perception. There are, in addition, debates in the philosophy of mind over whether the nature of the elicitor affects the content of one's mental state—for example, debates about methodological solipsism and the relevance of "twin earth"-type counter-examples to it. Nevertheless, whether a given affect or emotion is of a given sort (e.g., fear) is independent of whether what elicits it is the perception of an actual enemy in the bushes, the perception of a friend whom one thinks to be an enemy, or the result of an optical illusion produced by a particular pattern of leaves and shadows.

10. Nelson Goodman, *Languages of Art: An Approach to a Theory of Symbols* (Indianapolis: Bobbs-Merrill, 1968), p. 262.

11. See James D. Wallace, *Virtues and Vices* (Ithaca: Cornell University Press, 1979), chap. 1, for a discussion of the interrelatedness of so-called factual and normative judgments, specifically, about what kind of thing something is, what is normal for that kind of thing, and how the parts of that thing are supposed to function.

tions for the nature and importance of appreciation and the emotional and affective responses we have to literature that are partially constitutive of that appreciation.

On a function analysis, objects are judged insofar as they are things of a given kind. It should be no surprise that different interpretive theories sanction different conclusions about what kind of a thing an individual work is and hence lead to different interpretations and evaluations of it: an object or entity can be several kinds of things at once and be interpreted and evaluated as an instance of any of these several different kinds. The kind of thing one takes an individual work of literature to be, moreover, will dictate to some extent what kinds of properties are aesthetically or artistically significant, either because they are definitive of works of that kind, or because they are an innovative treatment of something that is definitive, or perhaps because they tend to disqualify a work as member of that kind.[12]

"Function" is not used here in the sense in which "functionalism" is used in the philosophy of mind. At the core of functionalism, as a philosophy of mind, is the idea that a mental state is a function of physical states but also that many different physical states may instantiate the same mental state. Hence, it assumes that there is, in principle, a way of separating the mental, which is held to be a function of the physical, from the physical realization or instantiation of it.[13] As I shall use the term, a work's functions are essentially connected with the operations of its parts, which themselves figure in functional descriptions of it. A work may have multiple functions even if it cannot fulfill one when it is being used to fulfill another.

Appreciation—and the emotions and affective responses partly constitutive of it—is not an end product, a state or condition one might be left in. Appreciating a work is a process wherein one engages with a work. This book is concerned with the activity of appreciation, what a reader is to do—and hence with how a work is supposed to function in relation to what readers are supposed to do. The point is to make an object function as it is supposed to, to make the work

12. Kendall Walton has termed the first and third, respectively, as "standard" and "contra-standard" properties of works. See his "Categories of Art," *Philosophical Review* 79 (1970): sec. 2. Of special interest is Walton's discussion of the way one's perceiving a work to be a work of a certain kind or category depends on what properties one perceives as standard, variable, and contra-standard.

13. For this reason Hilary Putnam has characterized functionalism as a kind of dualism. See "Philosophy and Our Mental Life," in *Mind, Language, and Reality: Philosophical Papers of Hilary Putnam*, vol. 2 (New York: Cambridge University Press, 1975).

work, to make it do what it is supposed to do. "Making it work" is a process or activity, not an end product. "Making it work" requires making parts or aspects of it work as they are supposed to. To do this, as one reads one must make various kinds of psychological shifts and slides—in attitude, orientation, or disposition—so that what one reads affects how one responds to what one reads next. I discussed the importance of the temporally extended nature of the reading process in Chapter 1. Appreciation occurs in and through time and involves having a succession of thoughts, imaginings, desires, emotions, and other affective experiences. The character of what one reads should affect one's psychological states and conditions and alter what one responds to subsequently and how one responds.

Each work of fictional literature is like a new gadget with certain similarities to and differences from others we have known and used before but whose functions we are not quite sure of. If I have a gadget, and I don't know what it's supposed to do or how, it would not be at all bad, tactically, to start punching buttons and pulling levers to see what happens. The mental shifts and slides, the alterations in my sensitivities, are the literary analogues of pushing buttons and pulling levers on some gadget whose function I don't know. I see what I can make it do and use this to figure out what it is supposed to do. Sometimes we conclude that it won't work, or that it works only occasionally or partially, and that the design of this "gadget" is, to that extent, faulty. Conversely, one may discover many things it does —things one can make it do—that are not among its functions. A would-be tragedy that makes us laugh when we are supposed to feel pity and fear is to that extent a failure (though one may, for a while, think it is supposed to be a parody and hence that it is *supposed* to be funny). I may also enjoy reading such a work every now and then for its amusement value, even though that isn't even partially constitutive of its value as a work of art. Thus, what a work does may either constitute auxiliary attractions or exhibit its failings.

Many ideas go through our minds as we read, and we automatically allow many of them just to "float through," putting them "off line," without the least delusion that they are relevant or appropriate to, or warranted by, the work. I think of how I need to call the electrician or about what I will have for dinner. The same is true of emotions and affects: their mere occurrence does not ensure their relevance or appropriateness or that they are warranted. I might just be in a bad mood or unusually reactive to certain kinds of subject matter.

Which responses are relevant, appropriate, or warranted is ex-

plained by an account of the work's functions: what it is, what it is
supposed to do, and how it does (or fails to do) it. Appeals to such
an account justify our believing that certain responses are relevant,
appropriate, and warranted. As we read we acquire more and more
justification for beliefs about how to assess our responses, since we
acquire more and more material for building an account of the work.
The character of the account we have built at any given time affects
how we respond to what we read subsequently. Responses themselves
provide "data" for building an account. We use our own responses to
develop ideas about how the work works, how these experiences fit
into a more general idea of what the work is supposed to be doing,
and how the different parts of the work work together to do it. The
account and our responses have a reciprocal relationship—each both
affects and provides warrant for the other—and both are constituents
of appreciation.

I was initially attracted to Rosamond Vincy in George Eliot's *Middlemarch*, but that attraction eventually turned to suspicion and then
to loathing, so that every time she snuck around behind her husband's
back, undoing everything he was trying to accomplish, I wanted to
throttle her. These feelings reinforced my empathy with Lydgate, her
hapless husband, who was initially duped by the same qualities in her
that I was. But is this anything more than a happy coincidence? Why
does it matter that I empathize with Lydgate? Is this empathy simply
gratuitous, or does it play some further role in my appreciation of the
novel? It is important that I empathize or at least sympathize with
Lydgate because he is the sort of person who cares about members of
society whom the medical profession tended to victimize. My empathy
with Lydgate reinforces one of the "messages" of the novel, specifically, that sympathy, or "human fellow feeling," is at the foundation
of civilized society and moral behavior. Rosamond is incorrigibly ego-
tistical and therefore lacks the psychological prerequisites for being a
member of a human community.[14] It is not merely knowing this fact
that constitutes appreciating the novel. My disdain for her and empathy with Lydgate enable my heart to reinforce what my mind tells me
is George Eliot's point. I become like a member of civilized community insofar as I empathize with those who care about the victims of
society. Part of Eliot's point is that not only ideas are important;
feelings are important, too. What is required for appreciation is get-

14. See Suzanne Graver, *George Eliot and Community: A Study in Social Theory and Fictional Form* (Berkeley: University of California Press, 1984), pp. 200–224.

ting the value out of the work—using it to do what it is supposed to
do. The feelings I have about Rosamond Vincy in *Middlemarch* play
an important role in the way the work works. Their role is revealed
by a partial account of how they are to function in relation to the
overall purposes of the work.

In contrast, witness my responses to some early passages of William
Boyd's *Brazzaville Beach*. In this novel, Hope Clearwater tells how she
came to live in a small house on the African coast. Hope is English
and lives alone; she has a German boyfriend named Gunter. Her
neighbors are German and Syrian, and visitors to the beach tend to
be Europeans. So how does she begin her story?—"Let's start with
that day I was with Clovis. Just the two of us. . . . I never really
warmed to Clovis—he was far too stupid to inspire real affection—
but he always claimed a corner of my heart, largely, I suppose, because of the way he instinctively and unconsciously cupped his geni-
tals whenever he was alarmed or nervous." [15] What was my response
as I read this? Clovis sounds like the kind of guy you meet in bars
who makes you want to stay home Saturday night and watch a video
rather than go out and meet people. I was somewhat amused but also
a little puzzled at this description. Hope debated whether to stay with
Clovis a while or go back to Hauser and endure his cynical gossip. I
became even more puzzled, even a little startled, when I read later,
"A small ant seemed to have trapped itself under the strap of my
brassiere and I spent a few awkward minutes trying vainly to locate
it. Clovis impassively watched me remove first my shirt and then my
bra." [16] I thought this might be a foretaste of a little quirkiness in the
novel.

Readers who are quicker than I am will have figured out that Clovis
is a chimpanzee. When I discovered this, I was delighted by what I
took to be Boyd's cleverness, a little teaser inserted at the beginning
of the novel to amuse and loosen up the reader. These responses are
at odds, however, with everything else in the book; it's not a light,
teasing book but very deliberate, not amusing but reflective. I do
believe that my amusement was somewhat warranted and that Boyd
was toying with unsuspecting readers such as myself. But my responses don't play any role whatsoever in furthering the purposes of
the novel—unlike my hatred of Rosamond and empathy for Lydgate.
One misses nothing if one isn't amused, except for the temporary

15. William Boyd, *Brazzaville Beach* (New York: Avon, 1990), pp. xv–1.
16. Boyd, *Brazzaville Beach*, pp. 1–2.

diversion of the experience itself. The sensitivities it displays are not used or followed up in the novel and not instrumental to the work the novel is to do.

Making a work work is clearly different from justifying a belief (i.e., defending a claim) that what one does makes the work work. Responding appropriately to various features of a fictional work is like performing an action (like pressing a button) that is one step in the process of getting some gadget to work. Justifying a claim that one's response is part of appreciating a work is like justifying a claim that performing an action of such-and-such description (e.g., pressing that button) will get that gadget to work. If one is to justify a belief or claim that the work is deficient in that respect, one needs an account that explains what those features are supposed to do, and how it is that they don't do it.

What explains why I pressed the button, however, may well be factors that have nothing to do with the sorts of things that will justify a claim that pressing the button will get the gadget to work. What explains why I pressed the button may be described in terms of psychologically idiosyncratic beliefs or desires, the application of a "rule of thumb" or the product of some kind of randomizing mechanism. It is not necessarily the case that I do what I do because I believe it will work: a fortiori, because I have good reasons for believing it will work, that is, good reasons (or any reasons) for doing it.[17] I may have reasons for wanting to make it work, yet no reasons for doing the particular things, *x, y,* and *z,* which I do in making it work. That is, I may have no reasons, much less good reasons, for believing that that makes it work. This fact reflects the account of appreciation as involving "norep" desires presented in Chapter 2—that is, as involving desires to do where there is no (enactive) mental representation of what one desires to do. Yet, at least in some cases, what one does makes it work, and the claim that pressing the button will help get the

---

17. There are certain affinities between my approach here and Dennett's emphasis on the importance of "satisficing" when making moral or practical decisions "in real time." Engaging in good reasoning is not a matter of having one's mind process information according to the laws of logic but a matter of adopting procedures and techniques for reaching conclusions that sometimes sacrifice the goal of reaching the *best* answer in order to satisfy, to some degree, the goals one has. See Daniel C. Dennett, *Elbow Room: The Varieties of Free Will Worth Wanting* (Cambridge: MIT Press, 1984), esp. chap. 5. For critiques of the "mental logic" theories of reasoning see Philip N. Johnson-Laird, *Mental Models:* (Cambridge: Harvard University Press, 1983), esp. chaps. 2, 5, and 6. See also D. N. Perkins, *The Mind's Best Work* (Cambridge, MA: Harvard University Press, 1981), pp. 25–28, on experiments testing how people solve practical problems.

gadget to work can be justified by describing the role the button-pressing plays in relation to what the gadget is supposed to do, something I may clearly not know about when I do it.

Analogously, one may respond appropriately to features of a work of fictional literature without knowing that one is and without being able to defend the claim that one is. I don't always have beliefs about what kind of thing the work is or about what is good or desirable that provide *my* reasons for having this or that affective response. At least some of the reasons I have for believing empathizing with Lydgate is appropriate are not reasons why I empathize. And I don't have reasons for being amused at Boyd's description of Clovis. Many—though certainly not all—of the experiences we have as we read, look, and listen are well described as "reactions." I don't react in way *R* because I believe (much less, believe for good reasons) that *R* is an appropriate response to good-making, or even significant, features of the work: what explains why I have the response will not necessarily be beliefs or reasons that justify claims that responding that way is part of appreciating good-making features of the work. What explains why I have the response may involve features of the work whose function, in relation to other features of the work, is to produce just such a response. This fact doesn't justify my belief that my response is appropriate; my believing this fact, along with other parts of an account that explain what the work is, what it is to do, and how it goes about doing it, may, however, provide some justification for the belief that my response is appropriate.

What sorts of considerations will justify a claim that one's response is part of appreciating a work? Just as one needs good reasons for believing that pressing the button is part of making that gadget work (which reasons may be provided only after one presses it, or after one fails to press it, so they cannot serve to explain why one pressed it), one needs good reasons for believing that responding in this way to that situation is part of making the fictional work "work," part of getting it to do what it is supposed to do. What work you think the novel (or other work of art) is supposed to do is part of your interpretation of it. What justifies a belief or claim that a response is part of appreciating a work is not merely that it is the right sort of response to the right sort of thing but the fact that one can fit it into an account of what the work is, what it means, and what it is supposed to do. It is only in light of such an account that one can defend the claim—that is, justify the belief—that one responded in the right way to the right sort of thing, or in a way that was warranted. The account elevates a mere reaction into a response (just as having the appropriate justification can elevate a mere belief to knowledge). The elevation of the reaction to a response requires not merely that the reaction have the right etiology but that it is worked into an account of what the work is, what it means, and what it is supposed to do. Justifying beliefs or claims that a given experience is part of appreciating a work requires developing such an account, though simply having those experiences may not require developing such an account, or at least not as full an account as one can produce after the fact. However, some experiences will not be possible unless one develops at least a partial account of the work, since they will depend on one's having some of those beliefs.

The development of an account of what a work is, what it is supposed to do, and how it is supposed to do it (i.e., its function) constitutes the *theoretical* component of appreciation. Affective responses, meanwhile, are among the data for interpretation and evaluation. Normally, part of the process of building such an account involves judging whether one's own emotional and affective responses are warranted by aesthetically or artistically significant aspects of the work and whether they are the appropriate sorts of responses. This is the *reflective* component of appreciation as it is exercised on the *affective* component. Emotional responses may themselves depend on a preliminary comprehension of the work or on assumptions about its meaning or significance. But these preliminary assumptions need not amount to an interpretation in the sense of a theory or account. At any rate, the comprehension or attribution of meaning ("interpretation," if you will) that responses depend on is different from the interpretive conclusions or hypotheses that use those responses as data.[18]

The reflective component—accepting or rejecting a response as appropriate or relevant—can alter how one is mentally inclined to respond to what one reads next. Something like this occurred during my response to the passage from Virginia Woolf described in Chapter 1: my judgment that my surprise was appropriate led me to empathize with Mr. Ramsay. This kind of "double-checking" is characteristic of what we might call aesthetically responsible appreciators of works of literature, just as it is characteristic of morally and epistemically responsible persons. Believing that one's response was relevant or appropriate, and even having a belief about what one's response

18. I thank Robert Audi for helpful discussion on this issue.

to a particular feature of a work *should* have been, can serve to alter one's attitude or frame of mind so that one will respond differently (that is, differently from the way one otherwise would have) to at least some parts of the work one reads subsequently. It is important not to insist on a rigid psychological ordering of the three components of appreciation.

III: A Typology of Assessment

I have described how beliefs about a work (the theoretical component), responses to a work (the affective component), and assessments of those beliefs and responses (the reflective component) all contribute to appreciation, as understood according to a function analysis. The idea of a function of a work of fiction provides a rationale for an assessment of responses to it. It provides the framework within which the plethora of responses and the beliefs about the warrantedness, appropriateness, and relevance of those responses can be assessed.

We have models for assessing beliefs where their function—truth or rationality—provides the rationale for their assessment. Patricia Greenspan, Ronald de Sousa, Jenefer Robinson, and the neurologist Antonio Damasio have all argued that emotions and feelings also have something like functions and that they can be rationally evaluated in light of them.[19] Such views are of course controversial, and whether or not they can be made out, the role of responses to fictional literature cannot automatically be assimilated to such models. The function of affective responses in making a work work may or may not accord with the sorts of roles real-life emotions are expected to play. Indeed, I suggest in Chapter 11 that there is good reason not to expect the functions of responses to fiction, and hence the functions of fiction itself, to piggy-back on other types of values, and therefore that we should recognize a certain autonomy to the value of fictional literature and our responses to it.

Thus, I suggest that the framework for assessing responses to fiction is provided by a function analysis rather than any real-life role emotions and affects may be supposed to play. In this section I more

19. Patricia S. Greenspan, *Emotions and Reasons: An Inquiry into Emotional Justification* (New York: Routledge, 1988); Ronald de Sousa, *The Rationality of Emotion* (Cambridge: MIT Press, 1987); Jenefer Robinson, "Startle," *Journal of Philosophy* 92 (1995): 53–74; Antonio R. Damasio, *Descartes' Error: Emotion, Reason, and the Human Brain* (New York: Grosset/Putnam, 1994).

or less catalogue, while explaining more fully, the kinds of assessments that can be made both of affective responses and of our beliefs about the appropriateness, relevance, and warrantedness of those responses. Since a great deal of work on justification in general has been done with respect to the justification of beliefs, I will use some of the concepts and distinctions developed there to provide a structure for distinguishing assessments of emotions and affects, adapting it as necessary to the different subject matter. The affective realm turns out to have very interesting analogues to the sorts of assessments that are made of beliefs.

Assessment of beliefs depends on our notions of truth and rationality: it is with respect to truth (or falsehood) and rationality (or irrationality) that beliefs are ultimately assessed. A belief may be true or false, and it may be justified or unjustified. These represent two different kinds of assessments that can be made of belief; that is, with respect to their truth and with respect to their rationality. The two kinds of assessments may part company with respect to any given belief. Even if a belief is not true, one may nevertheless be justified in believing it. Reading about things in ordinarily reliable sources and being told things by ordinarily reliable informants standardly provide justification for believing what one reads or is told, even if they don't guarantee its truth. A belief may, however, be true, yet a person may not be justified in believing it. Interpretations of the states of crystal balls, ouija boards, tea leaves, and decks of cards do not justify beliefs, even if what we interpret them to mean turns out to be true. One can believe true things for absurd reasons.

Moving up to a new level, we can also form beliefs about whether our beliefs are justified. My belief may not be justified, but I may mistakenly believe that it is; my belief may be justified, and I may mistakenly believe that it isn't. Beliefs about the justifiedness of one's first-order beliefs are second-order beliefs. An example of a first-order belief is my current belief that it is snowing. A second-order belief is the belief that my belief that it is snowing is justified. Let us say my belief that it is snowing is justified because of what I see when I look out the window. In this case, the character of my perceptual experience along with some background knowledge about snow justify my belief. My second-order belief (that my belief that it is snowing is justified) is justified by my realizing the following: I believe it's snowing on the basis of what I see, and such visual experiences, under the present conditions, are generally reliable.

There are two assessments of responses that are analogous to the single assessment of the truth of a belief. I will refer to them as appropriateness and relevance. One way an emotion, mood, or feeling response can be assessed analogously to assessing a belief as true is with respect to whether it is a response of an appropriate kind or sort. By a kind or sort of response I mean the particular type of emotion, feeling, mood, desire, or whatever, such as horror, awe, amusement, anxiety, shock, or disgust. Though examples are bound to be controversial, the following should be illustrative.

At the end of Kate Chopin's *The Awakening*, Edna calmly kills herself by swimming out into the sea.[20] For readers to realize what she is doing takes about the length of time it takes to read a single page of text. We read of her thoughts while she is swimming, punctuated with a narrator's observations about her increasing fatigue and final exhaustion. Several different kinds of responses may be appropriate during this reading, including a small shock or mild anxiety ("Oh, no! She's not going to do *that!*"), fear, hope (that she will turn back before it's too late), regret, and maybe even frustration and anger that, once again, a troubled heroine ends up dead (and she dies by her own choice). But certain emotional responses to this passage seem pretty clearly inappropriate: hilarity, jealousy, guilt, and pride.

The case of pride illustrates how difficult it is to provide unequivocal examples of *in*appropriate emotional and affective responses. For if pride consists in part of a belief that something good has resulted from one's own efforts, how would it even be possible to feel pride in response to this passage? Yet, *sympathetic* pride would be possible if one believed that Edna's actions involve courage and if one were proud of her for taking this decisive step. I call it sympathetic pride because one is responding in sympathy with Edna, in the sense that concerns for her interests and desires are implicated in one's emotions and feelings. It is not empathic pride because one does not share the affective experience with her. There may always be some story to tell about how a given emotion or affect could be seen to appropriately arise. But this fact also shows how dependent an assessment of the emotion or affect is on explaining the *basis* or rationale for the response. There is a plausible alternative story to tell about what one thinks of in relation to the passage, how one experiences it, and how

20. Kate Chopin, *The Awakening* (New York: G. P. Putnam's Sons/Capricorn Books, 1964), pp. 301–303.

this relates to the rest of the novel. The "plausible alternative story" raises the issue of warrant as much as or more than appropriateness. I deal with warrant below.

Consider an alternative story that explains how guilt is possible in response to the passage from *The Awakening*. Some people have an inordinate capacity to experience guilt in relation to just about anything, and it is possible to conceive of someone reading the above passage and experiencing sympathetic guilt. Sympathetic guilt is characterized by a particular cognitive component, in this case, thinking of having been in a position to have done something but not having done it—for example, by not being a person who was good enough to rise to the occasion as needed. There is not anyone in particular in the story with whom one empathizes in feeling this way. Rather, the general idea of having been in a position to have done something and not done it gives rise to feelings of guilt. That general idea plays the role that the thought "I was in a position to help but I didn't" plays in ordinary guilt. A way in which actual, rather than sympathetic, guilt might arise is if one thinks of oneself as the sort of person who, if one had been in a position to help, wouldn't have done enough. Thus, reading the story makes one feel guilty for not being the sort of person who would have helped even if one had been in a position to do so. Again, once one understands how such emotions might arise, they begin to look appropriate. But they look appropriate because they begin to look warranted. Conceptually, we need to keep appropriateness and warrant distinct, but, psychologically, a defense of an emotion's appropriateness seems to depend on explaining what warrants that sort of response. This dependence along with our ability to fabricate what looks like warrant makes it difficult to cite clear examples of inappropriate responses.

Jerzy Kosinski begins *The Painted Bird* with a narrator's description of some background information about the boy who is the novel's protagonist before starting the boy's first-person narrative a few pages later. "In the first weeks of World War II" the boy's parents sent him "to the shelter of a distant village," believing "it was the best means of assuring his survival." But his "parents lost contact with the man who had placed their child in the village," his foster mother dies, "and the child was left alone to wander from one village to another."[21] One might appropriately respond to these passages with distress, sad-

21. Jerzy Kosinski, *The Painted Bird* (New York: Bantam, 1965), pp. 1–2.

ness, feelings of futility, and the omnipresent (empathic, with the parents) guilt. It would be inappropriate to be dazzled, puzzled, comforted, embarrassed, or satisfied.

One more example, with a somewhat different tone. Ivy Compton-Burnett's novels expose the psychological swamp that underlaid the veneer of propriety in Victorian life. Though very proper—even the children talk like Henry James—Compton-Burnett is merciless in exposing the hypocrisy of the upper classes. The first paragraph of *Brothers and Sisters* methodically flays the character of Mr. Andrew Stace, each sentence penetrating another layer of propriety to reveal the extent of his self-absorption and self-deception. For example, she writes, "Women he carefully did not despise, regarding the precaution as becoming to an Englishman and a gentleman, and not considering whether it implied a higher opinion of women or himself."[22] Compton-Burnett's insights are searing and her verbal skills are considerable; they appropriately evoke delight and admiration. Readers who identify with Stace may feel guilt or anger. But pity, fear, grief, and jealousy are hardly appropriate.

A response may also be assessed with respect to the appropriateness of its intensity or duration. Gentle amusement strikes me as an appropriate response to the passage from Ivy Compton-Burnett but not hilarity or gales of laughter. I would also argue that a cynical little laugh, expressing a cynical little amusement, would also be appropriate when reading the dénouement of *The Awakening*, as if to say, "here we go again." Empathic feelings of hopelessness and dejection may be appropriate responses to the Kosinski passage, but mere disappointment seems somehow inappropriate. For the purposes of assessing appropriateness, a typology of emotional and other affective responses is necessary, including criteria for identifying each response and for individuating responses from one another. In this particular case, one suspects that differences in intensity constitute differences in kind. Unfortunately, I do not think that our current psychological understanding of how to individuate emotions and affects is sufficiently precise to allow for a very clear determination on this issue. (I explore some difficulties in identifying and individuating affective responses to fiction in Chapter 8.) Let us simply acknowledge, for the purposes of this chapter, that there is both appropriate-

22. Ivy Compton-Burnett, *Brothers and Sisters* (1929; London: Allison & Busby, 1984), p. 5.

ness in relation to *kind* of response and in relation to *intensity*, and let's leave it an open question when and whether the latter ultimately collapses into the former.

The second way of assessing an emotion, mood, or feeling response that is analogous to assessing beliefs as true is with respect to whether it is a response *to the work*, and, specifically, to aesthetically or artistically significant features of the work. "Artistically significant" is here meant to include features that manifest talents of the writer, features having to do with the skill and control an author exercises in writing the work; and "aesthetically significant" is meant to include features of a work a writer may not have been aware of, or did not intend, or that did not arise out of the writer's knowledge base or talents. Responses that are responses to (aesthetically or artistically significant features of) a work are relevant, and those that aren't are irrelevant.

Certain examples of irrelevant responses are proverbial: the student's fantasizing about sex in the middle of reading *Crime and Punishment;* a reader's recollecting happy times and warm feelings about her grandmother when reading *The Grapes of Wrath.* These are the sorts of cases where one is tempted to say that readers are not responding to the work at all but daydreaming or fantasizing. Nevertheless, the responses are elicited by the work, though by features that are either artistically or aesthetically irrelevant, or not relevant in the ways the reader experiences them.

The notion of relevance and its attendants, "the aesthetic" and "work of art," are objects of controversy. Criticisms range from the (rather innocuous, though important) claim that they arise in specific cultural and historical contexts and do not identify cultural universals to the claim that the use of them has served to reinforce and perpetuate reactionary political purposes. Nevertheless, it is not possible even to talk about the nature and value of appreciating fiction without introducing a notion of the object that one is appreciating. As I argued in Chapter 1, the abilities one exercises when appreciating fiction require one to interact with an object, in this case a set of inscriptions. Various subsets of those inscriptions, as interpreted, elicit responses. The appropriateness, relevance, and justifiedness of those responses bears on whether one is exercising an ability to appreciate, and assessments of their appropriateness, and so on, signal the existence of a desire to appreciate, or, a desire to develop and exercise the ability.

A more literary and less political qualm also needs to be addressed.

It is clear that responding to a work requires imagination and an active involvement on the part of a reader, going beyond what is presented "in the work." This requirement limits the usefulness of the notion of relevance, and I readily acknowledge this limitation. Yet the notion of relevance is not entirely inapplicable. Quite the contrary: imaginings need *ultimately* to be elicited by a portion of text that constitutes part of the work. The abilities exercised in appreciation are of the sort, described in Chapter 1, that maintains a perceptual acquaintance with an external object. It is that work we are to read and appreciate. What constitutes the work is, of course, a disputed matter, one that goes beyond the concerns of this book.

Just as a great deal of epistemology has to do with the justification or rationality of belief, and not merely truth, so also assessing affective responses to fiction as part of appreciation may turn out to have a great deal to do with justification or warrant, as much or more than it has to do with appropriateness and relevance. We can assess whether a belief is true and also whether someone is justified in believing it. Similarly, we can assess whether a response is relevant or appropriate and also whether someone is warranted in responding to what they do, as they do.

According to Robert Audi, there is a distinction between "belief justification" and "situational justification."[23] The former refers to cases where one justifiably believes something: the adverbial construction indicates that justification characterizes the act or activity of believing, in that the justification one *has* is actually the basis on which one forms the belief. With "situational justification," by contrast, one may *have* justification for believing something when either one doesn't believe it, or when one believes not on the basis of the justification one has but on the basis of other, not-so-good reasons. I will be using the term "warrant" rather than "justification" (for reasons to be explained shortly), and my focus will be on the analogue of Audi's "belief justification." Thus, if we were to follow Audi's linguistic distinction, I will be examining what it is to "warrantedly respond." This locution is decidedly awkward, however, and I am doubtful that sufficient perspicuity is gained by using it. I shall instead use the phrase, "a person is warranted in responding" or "has warrant for responding," and it should be understood that, unless explicit excep-

23. Robert Audi, *Belief, Justification, and Knowledge* (Belmont, Calif.: Wadsworth, 1987), p. 2.

tion is made, this entails that a person responds "on the basis of," or because of, the warrant one has. That is, what warrants the response helps to generate it.[24]

"Warrant" is the most general term I use for assessments, and I will use it as a generic term to include both justification and grounds. *Epistemically* speaking, grounds are provided by the nonpropositional contents of experiences such as the experiential content of visual, auditory, gustatory, and other sensations. Some epistemologists hold that beliefs can be grounded in experience, for example, that the particular character of my current visual experience of a reddish roundish blob grounds—and therefore warrants—my belief that here is an apple. In addition, beliefs about the current position and movements of one's body may be grounded in proprioceptive and kinesthetic sensations. With respect to emotions, Patricia Greenspan has argued that some emotional responses to situations can also be grounded in the character of one's perceptual experiences (she calls this "perceptual warrant"). In my terminology, what grounds a response is what one is warranted in responding to by virtue of the character of what elicits the response. Note that it is not experience that grounds responses; properties or features of the work ground responses. The reason for this shift is explained in the following chapter, where the possibility for grounding responses is explored. Both one's responding to *that* feature of a work and one's responding to it in a given *way* might be grounded in the work.

"Justification" has a narrower range of application than "warrant." Only beliefs provide justification, and the only things that can be justified are beliefs. In section II I discussed how an account, or a set of beliefs about how a work is supposed to function, provides justification for believing a response is relevant, appropriate, or warranted. These are paradigm cases of justification: the justification of second-order beliefs (i.e., beliefs about the relevance, appropriateness, or warrantedness of one's responses). These are second-order beliefs because they are beliefs about the justifiedness of other mental states (the first-order mental states); that is, they are beliefs about what assessments the responses themselves should be given.

Because I am concerned with warrant not just for beliefs but also

---

24. Some readers may at this point be worried about so-called wayward causal chains, i.e., cases where what warrants the response does help generate it but in a way other than the way it is supposed to. I cannot address this concern here, but I reaffirm that the sorts of ways responses are generated are to be understood on the models developed in Chapters 4 and 5.

for responses, I will call it "personal warrant" instead of "belief warrant." The *personal* mode of assessment assesses the *person*, and in this
case, it assesses the person with respect to his or her behavior. In
assessing a person's behavior, one assesses that person's actions, taking into account that person's past experiences and current states (i.e.,
the various things that condition a response). These experiences and
states may be atypical and misleading with respect to the nature of
the world in general, yet they are all the person has to go on. That is,
a response might be inappropriate to the situation as it really is but
warranted in light of a person's past experiences with respect to those
sorts of situations.

Consider again the passage from Virginia Woolf's *To the Lighthouse*
where I respond with surprise and incredulity upon being informed,
parenthetically, of Mrs. Ramsay's death. Suppose on reading the passage in question I respond with surprise, but suppose also that in
reading the book up to this point I had been skipping chunks of text
here and there in an effort to get through it quickly. The surprise
elicited by the passage in question would have been appropriate, that
is, the response would still be of an appropriate *sort*. If some compan-
ions were talking about how surprised they were in reading this passage, I could honestly say that I was surprised, too. It would even be
relevant because it is elicited by an aesthetically or artistically significant feature of the work (the subordinate clause of the parenthetical
passage). However, as with a true but unjustified belief, I have
"lucked out," because my surprise is not conditioned by the appropriate past experiences with preceding portions of text and hence is
to that large extent unwarranted. Warrant is conferred not simply by
the fact, of which I am aware, that that passage mentions Mrs. Ramsay's death, but by the fact that this is the first time in the novel her
death has been mentioned. This is a fact of which I am unaware, and
which, given the irresponsible way I've been reading, I am in no
position to be aware of. My surprise, though appropriate, is unwarranted; that is, my surprise isn't generated by what warrants it.

I have so far been discussing the question, "What warrants one's
responding with *surprise?*" One can also ask what warrants having a
response, such as surprise, of a particular intensity—be it mild, medium, or strong. But there is another sort of question to ask about
warrant: "What warrants my responding to *that* particular passage?"
That is, what warrants its having a certain level of salience in my
attention which manifests itself in an affective way? Sometimes what
warrants its having a certain level of salience will include relational

features, which in this case are easy to identify, such as that there's nothing in the text prior to this point about Mrs. Ramsay's death. The possibility of there being *grounds* for responding to a particular passage is explored in Chapter 7.

One unfortunate part of our legacy from Kant is the view that one cannot be *argued* into or out of the experience of aesthetic pleasure, since it results from the exercise of taste and is not a "cognition." Though appreciation involves a broad range of responses, not merely pleasure, a belief in the irrelevance of reasons or argument has unfortunately persisted, abetted by convictions that affects and emotions are immune to assessment. The typology for assessment developed here shows the numerous ways responses to fiction can be assessed. In fact, they are so numerous that the possibilities may easily be felt to overwhelm. Nevertheless, the basic principles are few: just as beliefs are assessed with respect to what we might call their function— to be true, rational, or both—so also responses to fiction are assessed with respect to their function—to play a role in appreciation. It is a mistake, I contend, to think of appreciation as consisting of a set of affective or emotional experiences (even if in addition to whatever cognitive or theoretical components appreciation might have). Rather, appreciation is an activity that is the exercise of an ability. One can learn how to appreciate; one can develop the ability to appreciate, including the ability to have affective responses; and one can assess how well one has done in appreciating a work. Assessment is necessary both for developing the ability to appreciate and as a component of appreciation itself.

Chapter Seven

Passional Grounding

In the previous chapter I focused on what determines whether one is justified in believing or claiming that a given response is relevant, appropriate, or warranted. I there developed a function model to show how such beliefs could be defended, a model that can apply independently of the acceptance of any particular theory of interpretation. Justifying such beliefs requires developing a relatively detailed and systematic account of a work that involves, in part, recognizing a role for the sorts of phenomena warranting the response. The more elaborate the account, the more ammunition for justifying beliefs about the appropriateness of, relevance of, and warrant for a response.

The model proposes that beliefs about the appropriateness of a response are defended by describing the role the response plays in an overall appreciation of a work, in "making the work work." But this sort of defense may look irremediably circular, the same way a coherentist theory of belief justification, on which it is obviously built, looks circular. In a coherentist theory of belief justification, all beliefs are justified by other beliefs, leaving the system of beliefs—though consistent, coherent, and interrelated—unsupported by a foundation in "reality." Is there any way to ground responses in qualities of the work and thus to end a regress of justifications of beliefs about what responses are warranted?

In section I I explore features of the grounding for responses that warrant assessments of them as relevant. In section II I discuss the phenomenon of passional grounding; that is, when responding—not a particular kind or sort of response, but simply responding—is grounded. In section III I apply these ideas to aesthetic passional grounding, rejecting one and defending another application of passional grounding to the appreciation of fictional literature.

I: Grounding and Relevance

In Chapter 6 I explained that because I am interested in the process of appreciation, and hence in how warrant for responding to what one does, as one does, can change, I am especially interested in "personal warrant"—when a *person* is warranted in responding as one does, to what one does. In what follows, however, I speak of responses as being grounded rather than of a person's responding to what one does as one does as grounded. The peculiarity—indeed, ungrammaticalness—of the expression "a person's responding as one does is grounded in . . ." is revealing. People are not grounded (unless they are errant teenagers) any more than people are appropriate or relevant. The responses are appropriate, relevant, or grounded, whereas people may be warranted or unwarranted in responding to what they do, as they do.

The fact that responses (rather than a person's responding) are grounded tells us something about the nature of grounds: the ground is there whether one knows it or not. We need not worry about what the person does or doesn't know in relation to her or his changing circumstances. That's one point of appealing to grounds: it's a place of gravitational certainty in the face of psychological uncertainty. We generally think of "the ground" as being stable (unless, perhaps, you live in Los Angeles or San Francisco)—though with the possibility that in exceptional cases its status as terra firma can be overturned. Ground provides a place to stand and serves that function regardless of the person's cognitive or affective state.

To constitute part of appreciating a work, responses must be relevant; they must be responses *to the work*. Assessments of a response as relevant are peculiar in that a response may be relevant even if there is no warrant for responding in that particular way to the work. One gets credit simply for, as it were, making contact with the work. I call this epistemic grounding. This accomplishment seems minimal enough, but anyone who has read anything written in the last twenty years about literary criticism or reading and interpreting texts will recognize what a contested area epistemic grounding has become. Many theorists do not accept that "works" exist at all as independent objects of our attention and scrutiny. I am not going to enter into that debate here; I simply make explicit what my position is: one must appeal to a work, as an object in the external world, as something to which one responds. The necessity of this appeal follows from the account of appreciation as an ability involving a perceptual acquaintance with an external object, as described in Chapter 1. It is implicated by the function analysis, where using the work in the ways it is supposed to work is essential to appreciation. And it is essential to my defense of a certain value of developing and exercising abilities to appreciate, as described in Chapter 11.

Though I am using "grounds" in a normative sense to refer to a kind of warrant that can be provided for responses, the normative and etiological actually cross paths here. The assessment of a response as relevant follows from its having the right sort of etiology. Its causal source must be "the work." But then we are confronted with that problematic question, what is "the work"?

Traditionally, grounds for beliefs have been stripped of as much theoretical content as possible, so as not to bias the defense of a belief by employing a conceptual network that prejudices individuations of objects and attributions of properties to them. If we were to follow this practice for grounding responses to fiction, grounds would have to lie in characteristics of the marks on the page—their shapes, orientations, and relations. But these grounds are at best a text in need of interpretation, not a work of literature. Literature is composed of language, and what one reads—ultimately, what one responds to—is always interpreted as inscriptions of words in a particular language. Hence, familiarity with the language—a set of background beliefs and information—conditions responses to what one reads. The properties of the marks, simply as marks, will not warrant a response in a way that supports its relevance to the work.

If we consider a slightly looser notion of grounds, where the elicitor is conceived as a word, phrase, or sentence *in a language* (rather than as an uninterpreted set of marks), then responses might be relevant because grounded in these properties of the work. Furthermore, if one allows the reification of various structural properties of a work —such as sentence length and structure, in so far as these can be experienced as a unit—they could also serve as grounds. Both structural properties and "meaning" properties of individual units within a work are, of course, subject to interpretation. Think of these as "conditional grounds"; they are examples of a looser sense of "grounds," under which a response could be aesthetically grounded.

Responses to fiction are epistemically conditionally grounded in external facts about the world. We need to be able to make distinctions with respect to fictional literature that enable us to form plausible *beliefs* about the nature and existence of the world—in this case, that part of the world that is the fictional work. Making such distinctions involves the mundane perceptual ability to discriminate one letter from another in order to read the words, an ability anyone who can read takes for granted. But it is a learned ability—we learn to make the kinds of discriminations relevant to distinguishing and identifying different words in our language. The importance and difficulty of this task should not be underestimated: think about the difficulty English monolinguals have doing this (visually) with languages such as Persian or Arabic that do not use the Roman alphabet, and (auditorially) with virtually any foreign language with which one is unfamiliar.

Even if one takes a literary work to be a culturally constructed entity, appreciation still must be grounded in facts about the world (i.e., relevant distinctions among different marks) in light of which the literary artwork is constructed. In this case, the fact about the world will not be a linguistic structure but a set of marks. The psychological fact that a background of experience and beliefs is necessary in order for the reader to come to make the relevant discriminations and that different experiential backgrounds will lead to the construction of different works is no objection to the view that appreciation must be grounded in something in the external world. It only shows that it takes a bit of doing for one to come to be able to make the relevant discriminations of the relevant facts, and that the same facts may lead to the construction of different works.

There is, of course, a whole field of literary study, called textual criticism or textology, concerned with classifying and preserving the "data" for identifying a text.[1] I am eager to grant, moreover, that there may be parts of works where there is no fact of the matter with respect to what character or word is inscribed. This absence leaves an indeterminacy with respect to what actually constitutes the work in those passages. However, it doesn't follow that there will never be grounding for responses to and beliefs about the work in the properties of the work as a piece of literature.

---

1. See Graham Falconer's interesting observations on how textual scholars have clung to the notion of a single text for each work, in "Genetic Criticism," *Comparative Literature* 45 (1993): esp. p. 13.

There is a certain artificial purity to considering literary fiction as constructed purely of language. Mixed media cases of the sort mentioned in the introduction complicate the claim that linguistic inscriptions considered merely as marks do not ground responses. Even though appropriate responses will likely depend on one's having at least a fledgling account of the work and background knowledge of literary conventions, one may nevertheless respond to what are artistically relevant visual features of a text. The use of different colors in the text of Michael Ende's *The Neverending Story* is a device whose significance does not emerge from its visual properties alone but from the relationship it bears to the context of the novel (i.e., a character in the novel is reading a book whose text is in different colors). Nevertheless, one may respond to the use of different colored passages of text (a response likely conditioned by the fact that one hadn't encountered colored text in a work of fiction before). For another example, at one point in Patrick Süskind's *Perfume*, a conversation between Baldini and his assistant Chénier is written in the form of a dialogue within a play.[2] A feeling of a somewhat stiffened formality and slightly forced politeness suffuses this passage. Having this response depends on recognizing the convention being employed and understanding that this use of it indicates that the exchange is a kind of scripted politeness, in which each character knows (though neither knows the other knows) it is a ruse undertaken for the purpose of saving face. Yet even the fairly common convention within novels of indenting the contents of a letter or note being read by a protagonist has the effect of facilitating reading the note either in the voice of the character who wrote it or with the mindset of the character who reads it. Language, rather than the visual properties of inscriptions, is, however, the primary medium of literature.

Responses to a work must be epistemically grounded in facts about the work, or else those responses are not relevant to appreciation. Appreciation includes at least this, though it's clearly not just this. This grounding implies nothing about what, aesthetically, warrants a response or about what kinds of responses might be warranted. These grounds, because they take the form of external facts about the world, merely provide a way for people to be linked up with facts about the world, which in the case of literature are facts about the work. In what follows I will be assuming that the appreciative experience of

2. Patrick Süskind, *Perfume: The Story of a Murderer,* trans. John E. Woods (New York: Knopf, 1986), pp. 57–58.

the work is, as I described earlier (conditionally epistemically) grounded; that is, it reflects the relevant linguistic discriminations and identifications of words and phrases of the language in which the work is written. Given that this grounding is conditional, there may be disputes about what the properties of the work are and hence about whether a response is epistemically grounded.

II: Passional Grounding

There are at least two more ways a response might be grounded. The most obvious way that a response might be grounded is if certain facts about the work ground one's responding in the way one does. Such a response may not ultimately be aesthetically appropriate (because the grounds might be undermined or overridden), but it may nevertheless be grounded in the particular features of the work to which one responds. I call this "type grounding," as a shorthand way of indicating that a response of a particular kind or type may be grounded. Type grounding and other kinds of type warrant are discussed in Chapters 8 through 10.

Type grounding is different from passional grounding. A response is passionally grounded if and only if facts about the work ground one's emotionally or affectively responding, independently of whether they provide any grounds for one's responding in any particular way rather than another. If one's response is type grounded, it will also be passionally grounded, but it does not follow that if a response is passionally grounded then it is type grounded. Passional grounding concerns what I call the "affectivity" of a response, rather than its being the particular response it is.[3]

Passional grounding is a more obscure notion than type grounding, and I have lifted the basic concept from Patricia Greenspan's discussion in chapter four of *Emotions and Reasons*.[4] Greenspan is concerned with the *rationality* of emotions, not with aesthetic assessments of emo-

---

3. Jerome Shaffer attacks this dimension of emotion in "An Assessment of Emotion," *American Philosophical Quarterly* 20 (1983), concluding that "by and large there is little to be said in favor of emotions" (p. 161).

4. Patricia Greenspan, *Emotions and Reasons: An Inquiry into Emotional Justification* (New York: Routledge, 1988), chap. 4. Unfortunately, I have found it necessary to use different terminology from hers, which complicates the exposition of her view. I shall use my terminology in explaining her view. In particular, her notions of warrant and appropriateness are different from mine. Basically, for the purposes of this chapter, what I am calling passional warrant is what she calls appropriateness. (See note 7.)

tional responses to fiction.[5] It is an important part of her account that there is a basis for evaluating emotions which is independent of the rationality or justification one has for an emotion's cognitive component. This independence makes her account ideal for assessing not only emotions, but also other kinds of affective responses—those that do not have identificatory cognitive components—even though her discussion focuses only on emotions. In this section I discuss Greenspan's account and how I have built the notion of passional grounding from it. In the following section I apply the notion of passional grounding to responding to fictional literature.

On Greenspan's account, an emotion is a feeling of comfort or discomfort directed at a propositional thought. She also argues for a position I have already accepted that the cognitive components of emotions may be "unasserted thoughts" and do not have to be beliefs.[6] An emotion is warranted when it is "keyed to," or induced by, a significant subset of the perceptual evidence available. Warrant "amounts to 'fitness to significant perception' . . . rather than fitness to the facts or even to the total body of perceptual evidence."[7] For an emotion to be *grounded,* the thought, and hence the emotion, will be induced by "a significant subset of the perceptual evidence available." An example, adapted from Greenspan, illustrates what constitutes a significant subset of the perceptual evidence available: I visit a stockbroker to discuss investing my money. There is something about the way his eyes change in focus that evokes the thought of his being untrustworthy. I think of the stockbroker *as* being untrustworthy, and this thought gives rise to the emotion—in this case, suspicion.[8]

For the purposes of passional warrant, it is immaterial whether it is suspicion, some other emotion, or some other affect that is generated by the significant subset of perceptual evidence available. In other

---

5. Greenspan does make some claims about the irrationality of identifying with fictional characters, but those need not concern us here.
6. Greenspan, *Emotions and Reasons,* pp. 17–22.
7. Greenspan, *Emotions and Reasons,* p. 88, uses "appropriateness," not "warrant," as her term of assessment. I understand her to hold that appropriateness is a particular form of rationality. It is the specific sort of rationality an emotion has when it is keyed to a significant subset of the perceptual evidence available. In my discussion, however, I will simply use the terms "warranted" or "grounded" rather than "appropriate," since I have been using the notion of appropriateness in this book in a systematically different way from the way she uses it. Simply for the sake of clarity, throughout my exposition of her view I will use the terminology that I have developed in this book rather than the terminology that she uses.
8. Greenspan, *Emotions and Reasons,* p. 5. Also, I can't let this pass without offering my apologies to my own stockbroker, Rosemary Olshanski-Karp, for this example.

words, it is not type grounding—warrant for an emotion or affect of a given kind or type—that is provided by the perceptual experience. What the experience provides is, if anything, passional grounding. That is, one's response will be grounded if responding affectively to those features of the work is warranted.

In Greenspan's example, one has a visual experience, and the emotion or affect results from it. The perceptual experience induces a thought that in turn induces an emotion. Notice that she works with an internalist conception of grounds, where experiences, rather than facts about the world, ground emotions. On an externalist construal of grounds, such as the one I use, the refocusing eyes themselves ground the response. This position is theoretically cleaner in an important respect, since an affect may infuse or permeate an experience and not merely result from it. Especially with affects (rather than emotions), where there are not any intermediary identificatory thoughts, the perceptual or phenomenological quality of one's experience itself will likely be affectively laden. That is, to use Greenspan's example for illustration, one might perceive the eyes *with* suspicion. The affectively infused experience is probably more common in reading fiction: one reads *with* feeling. In such cases, the affective qualities of experiences arise contemporaneously with their perceptual/cognitive aspects, and the affect may even serve as a way of unifying disparate cognitive aspects into *an* experience. For example, when I view the stockbroker's eyes with suspicion, the various eye movements "make sense" in that they are experienced as symptomatic of some kind of unacceptable character trait. This is one reason I use an externalist sense of grounds: that is, affects are (conditionally) grounded in features of the external world (the work) rather than in the qualities of our own experiences. Our experiences must be elicited by features of or facts about the world; it is this connection with the world, rather than qualities of experience, that grounds responses.

It is a crucial part of Greenspan's example that I haven't had past experiences with people who had the particular feature—eyes that focus and refocus—that generates the response. But it makes one wonder: if there's no psychologically innate response mechanism to explain it, and it is unlearned, it looks like it is pure chance that one had this thought (i.e., the thought of the stockbroker being untrustworthy) in response to that perception. What led one to have that thought? Isn't it plausible to think that whatever led one to the thought, such as something in one's own past experiences, is what, if anything, provides the evidence for the belief that such people are not to be trusted? If so, wouldn't it be that past experience that warrants one's responding and not just the features of the world one is currently experiencing? Two issues arise. The first is to identify as grounds features of a work that can be defended as grounding responses without appealing to past experiences of readers to make it seem plausible to think they are grounds. I attack this issue in the following section. But there is a second issue, and that is how past experiences may explain one's responding to particular features without warranting responding. So let us suppose, for the sake of argument, that a past experience with someone whose eyes changed focus in this way, or an experience with someone having sufficiently similar qualities (leaving aside questions about what makes them sufficiently similar), is the *only* possible explanation for how the thought could come to you. It is still possible for that past experience to generate the thought, without the memory of it (or the fact that you've had such an experience before) providing any *justification* at all for the belief that this person is untrustworthy. That is, this story of the genesis of the thought and the response may be irrelevant to a passional assessment of the response.

What follows is an example of how that might happen. Suppose you have a very untrustworthy acquaintance, Paul, whose eyes behave in a way similar to those of the stockbroker. Paul has some kind of genetic astigmatism that makes his eyes behave this way; it has nothing to do with his untrustworthiness, and you know all this. You still might establish a cognitive association between seeing eyes change their focus and the idea of untrustworthiness, simply because of the concurrence of these two features in Paul, even though you have no reason to believe there is anything more than an accidental connection between the two. Another possible scenario is that you've seen a movie where the villain's eyes behaved this way (or read a novel where the villain's eyes are described as moving this way—and you visualized the event while reading the novel), thereby establishing a mental association between untrustworthiness and refocusing eyes. Clearly, reading about the eyes of an untrustworthy character in a novel or seeing them move in a particular way in a movie is no reason to believe that in the real world (as they say) people whose eyes move that way are untrustworthy. This situation is of course reminiscent of 2500-year-old worries about the power of theater, and more recent worries about the power of novels and films, to *distort* our thinking by using images and stereotypes that are morally harmful and epistemically short-sighted but that may nevertheless create cognitive associations in our minds and hence warp our thought processes—and thereby our emotions and sensitivities.

Nevertheless, it should be clear from these examples that it is possible to explain why one had a thought by appeals to what was experienced in the past, even though that past experience doesn't provide any grounds for the response to the stockbroker or any justification for a belief in an emotion's cognitive component. Similarly, many past experiences one has had might explain one's affective associations with what one reads without those past experiences' warranting the associated affects.[9]

Another aspect of Greenspan's analysis needs attention. It is not clear at this point what aspect or properties of what I perceive are responsible for my having the thought, "this person is untrustworthy." Could it be simply the fact that what I am attending to is the person's eyes? This can't be right, because there is no indication this person responds with suspicion (or in any other way) to a person's eyes when they are functioning completely normally. Rather, it is the specific fact that the stockbroker's eyes are changing their focus. My perception of the refocusing generates the thought of untrustworthiness, and then the emotion, suspicion. But why do the refocusing eyes capture my attention? Part of the reason I think and feel the way I do is because, in relation to my experience, this "eye behavior" is unusual. Notice that it is not the *fact* that this eye behavior is unusual or abnormal that explains my response, but rather the fact that it is unusual *in my experience*. The fact that it has been rare, or perhaps nonexistent, in my experience in the past may warrant a belief that it is unusual. But such beliefs and warrant for them do not provide *grounds* for responding, though they may provide warrant (i.e., non-grounds warrant) for my responding to what I do as I do. Grounds are provided by features of a work; my responding to those features is not, therefore, grounded in such past experiences and beliefs.

I may "key into" something under one description, when what war-

---

9. I discuss in Chapter 9 how, in a very general sense, past experiences do warrant a response. One is supposed to draw on one's past experiences when reading a work. That is, in drawing on past experience one is doing the right kind of thing. Though this is only a very small part of the story, it is an important part that is often overlooked. It also has tremendous implications for explaining how emotional and affective responses can be warranted *at all*.

rants my keying into it under that description is something else, such as the fact that what I key into satisfies another description. That is, what makes me key into it is one thing; what makes what I key into a significant subset of the perceptual evidence available, and hence makes keying into it generally adaptive (and hence why it gets to ground a response), may well be another. In this example, let us say I key into the refocusing eyes because of my past experiences with Paul; what makes keying into refocusing eyes generally adaptive is that refocusing eyes are abnormal and unusual. The fact of their abnormality establishes why the refocusing eyes ground my responding to them, though it doesn't explain why I respond to them.

It is clearly necessary to use the description of the specific aspects or properties that elicit the response to explain why the respondent did respond to it. There is no formula for discovering what this is or even for which kinds of descriptions may prove "warrantable." For responses induced by microlevel features may be warranted whereas responses induced by macrolevel features are not, and vice-versa. It would be a mistake to think that only the most finely-tuned, microlevel description of the features inducing the response could constitute a significant subset of the perceptual evidence available. For suppose there are several different ways one's eyes can change their focus—very subtly different movements—some of which are highly correlated with untrustworthiness and others not. "Connoisseurs" of eye movements might develop the ability to detect the difference, but it hardly seems appropriate to condemn the person who responds with insecurity to all cases of peoples' eyes changing focus—including the cases where there is no correlation—as inappropriate. As Jerry Fodor has pointed out, if one is going to err, it is generally better to err on the side of "false positives." We start our perceptual learning by making broad distinctions and then, with practice, become more finely discriminating. Some things it is "generally adaptive" to respond to might eventually be perceptually and conceptually shorn up into more rigorous categories with the passage of time.

Greenspan's example is especially persuasive in illustrating what I call "passional grounding" because some empirical findings lend support to the view that certain categories of phenomena, such as facial movements, do constitute significant subsets of the available perceptual evidence and that human beings do respond to them even without contextual factors necessary for perceiving them as significant. Paul Ekman has for a long time investigated facial muscle movements that he claims constitute species universal, and not merely culturally specific, expressions of emotions.[10] Different patterns of eyebrow movements, for example, are alleged to be expressive of fear, anger, and sadness. Research he did in culturally isolated tribes in New Guinea during the 1960s documented the existence of such "emotion-prototypic" facial movements. If indeed a certain downward and inward movement of the eyebrows *is* an emotion-prototypic expression of anger, as he alleges, then it would seem there would be "general adaptiveness" in "keying in" to that particular eye movement. It would be generally adaptive to "key in" to it because it (presumably) would be useful to be able to pick up on the fact that someone is angry. And it could be generally adaptive to "key in" to it even if you didn't know that it was *anger* that was being expressed and even if there isn't any set way or ways it is useful to act or feel in response to that anger. Furthermore, it might well be generally adaptive to "key in" to such a facial expression even if there are enough good "actors" around who can successfully mimic the eyebrow movements even when they are not angry.

In the example, the emotion is elicited by the refocusing eyes qua rapid changes in focus (i.e., dilation and contraction of the pupils). The emotion's being grounded in this perceptual experience would be ensured by its being generally adaptive to "key in" to someone's eyes behaving in this way; it is not dependent on the rapid refocusing of this person's eyes being indicative of his untrustworthiness. That is, my emotional response is not warranted because it is produced by some kind of "untrustworthiness indicator" but rather because it is "generally adaptive" for that particular kind of thing to capture our attention at some level. Keying in on something may be generally adaptive even when keying into it generates "false positives."

An affective response, as a response to a particular sort of feature of a work, thus manifests "attention," at some level, to this feature. However, why should this sort of thing ground affective responses rather than a cognitive response such as "this feature may signal something worth watching," or simply a greater perceptual interest or attention? We clearly have a "cognitivist" bias where issues of rationality and justification are concerned: we want to evaluate the propositional component of belief. When the belief is as attenuated as "this

10. See Paul Ekman, Robert W. Levenson, Wallace V. Friesen, "Autonomic Nervous System Activity Distinguishes among Emotions," *Science*, 16 September 1983, pp. 1208–1210. The title of this piece is unfortunate, for it does not at all describe what they claim to have shown. See Chapter 3 for additional discussion of this point.

feature may signal something worth watching," you have to wonder what the specific benefits of having a belief, something with a propositional content, are supposed to be. (Notice that the belief is not a comparative; i.e., it does not say, "this feature may signal something more worth watching than features x, y, and z.") When the belief is so attenuated, it would be reasonable for a cognitive system, S, to be constructed in such a way that it will be (at least marginally) more responsive to feature f, at any rate for a while, rather than in such a way that it forms a propositional thought about the possible significance of f that it may or may not believe. The former at least ensures that f does in fact make a little more of a difference to S, which simply having the belief doesn't. Of course, one could build cognitive systems in which beliefs, at least certain kinds of beliefs, have more influence over our actions, too. But this possibility is not to the point, because it is not our job to build an ideal cognitive system. Our job is to understand what good reasons there might be for being the sort of system we in fact are. And in fact there is a good reason for creatures to respond affectively and not merely cognitively to their environments. Affects have a rationale: they are a way of being responsive to certain features of the environment when those features are worthy of our attention.

Like it or not, we are affective creatures. Rather than debate whether it would be better if all of us learned to eliminate all feeling from our lives (all pleasure, desire, excitement, as well as all distress) —the prospect of which, I suspect, most of us would not view as desirable—we should ask what constructive roles feelings and emotions play in human lives. Greenspan argues persuasively that they have epistemic significance. Many writers have argued persuasively that they have moral significance. It's pretty obvious that they have aesthetic significance, in being a major part of our appreciation of literature and other arts. In all of these realms, of course, they may be appropriate or not, warranted or not (just as beliefs may also not be true or warranted). Neither affective nor cognitive systems are immune to error or dysfunction. In the following section I explain how the sort of grounding of affective responses rehearsed here can be adapted to explaining the grounding of affective responses to fictional literature.

III: Aesthetic Passional Grounding

There are several ways that Greenspan's notion of the general adaptiveness of responding to a significant subset of the perceptual evidence available might be used to explain how emotional responses to fictional literature are grounded. I consider two of them in this section, arguing against one and defending the other. Instead of being grounded in a strictly visual subset of the evidence available, however, responses to literature are grounded in a linguistic unit—a significant subset of a linguistic array. In Chapter 1 I provided some examples of the kinds of linguistic units that might elicit a response. They included whole sentences as well as single words and phrases. The question now is whether such passages ever provide aesthetic passional grounds for a response. I repeat that emotional and affective responses to literature will never be grounded in the strictest sense, that is, in uninterpreted strings of marks. The grounding will always be conditional upon understanding the unit of language as a unit of the language.

The first possible way of applying Greenspan's notion of "significant subset of perceptual evidence available" is one that is distinctly *revisionist*, as it uses the notion I have lifted from Greenspan to identify what is aesthetically and artistically significant. That is, the features of a work that are aesthetically and artistically significant would be precisely those features it is generally adaptive to "key in" to. This approach would make general adaptiveness in other respects—for epistemic, moral, political, perhaps also religious purposes—the criterion for identifying what is aesthetically or artistically significant. This revisionist view would eliminate any distinctive understanding of the nature of the aesthetic, since the aesthetic would be assimilated to what it is generally adaptive to "key in" to for epistemic, moral, prudential, or other reasons. If responses satisfying this criterion are to that extent rational or reasonable, and one uses it as a criterion of the aesthetic, it would be conceptually impossible for a relevant response to a work to be irrational or unreasonable (at least in this respect).

This sort of move may well prove appealing if one wishes to erase any independent or relatively autonomous conception of the aesthetic and to assimilate it to theories of interpretation which see art as playing only political, social, or moral roles. But one might also see it as holding the aesthetic hostage to these other interests. I see no reason to rule out the possibility of there being legitimate aesthetic concerns that provide their own kinds of rationale and values. Indeed, it is part of the project of this book to show that there are such things and how those values are achieved in appreciating fiction. Thus my objection to the revisionist view is precisely that it reduces aesthetic value, and hence any aesthetic grounding of emotional and affective responses to fiction, to other types of value, such as the epistemic and the moral. It begs the question, so to speak, on one of the crucial issues left to be explored.

An alternative way of employing the criterion is to say that a response is aesthetically grounded when one responds to a significant subset of the linguistic array, where that significance is not judged in terms of general adaptiveness for other purposes but for aesthetic purposes. That is, are there kinds of things—properties of writing—it is generally useful to "key in" to for the purposes of appreciation? Courses in "art appreciation" and "literature appreciation" virtually always assume that there are such features—at least to the extent of providing "rules of thumb" for what kinds of things to watch out for. Certain aspects of the medium can be manipulated and controlled by the artist, and they are the kinds of things that are likely to be of significance. In the case of fiction, such aspects include voice and shifts in voice (first-person narrative, third-person omniscient narrator, etc.), use of dialogue, diction, imagery, symbolism, syntactic characteristics of individual sentences, chapter and paragraph divisions, and overall structural properties of a work.[11] That is, "literature appreciation" courses are supposed to provide information that will draw one's attention to aesthetically and artistically significant aspects of a work. Ideally, criticism and instruction in appreciation will change readers in such a way that it is more likely that what they are warranted in responding to by virtue of what they have learned will be both relevant and appropriate.[12] If there are such things as grounds, however, one needn't be told about them in an educational setting to be warranted in responding to them: a response will be grounded in properties of the work independently of any past experiences or reasons one has been given for believing that they ground a response.

There's something to be said for this. It has to do with the very basic issue of what our general attitude or approach should be toward a work of literature. Should we be affectively so cautious that we

---

11. Monroe C. Beardsley has a useful discussion of these in *Aesthetics: Problems in the Philosophy of Criticism* (New York: Harcourt, Brace & World, 1958), chap. 5.
12. I thank Bill Tolhurst for making this point so succinctly.

never respond unless we have a set of beliefs, constituting a partial account of the work, so that a belief that that particular response is (passionally) warranted can be justified? Or should we affectively "go for it," recognizing that some responses will be inappropriate but willing to pay the price in order to get the benefits of having more responses, some of which will be appropriate and relevant even if insufficiently warranted? It seems to me that the arguments are totally on the side of the latter. Mistakes can be corrected (through the reflective component of appreciation); misdirections can be rectified. We get the benefits generally recognized to accrue from procedures that turn out to generate "false positives." "Getting into it," manifesting a desire to appreciate, virtually requires "letting ourselves go" in a way that, at least for short periods, is unchecked by obsessions about warrant and justification. What saves us is the ground, which is there whether we know it or not.

In Chapter 2 I argued that wanting to appreciate a work is structurally analogous to curiosity of an amalgamated type, where one wants not merely to know some particular thing but wants to find it out oneself. Similarly, with the desire to appreciate, one wants not merely to know what the value of a work is, but one wants to get the value out of it oneself. But doesn't the view that responses are grounded make them look more like fixated behavior patterns rather than exercises of genuine desires? To be exercises of desires to appreciate, responses must be embedded within a larger project of exercising and acquiring relevant skills of appreciation. Responses, though grounded, cannot be accepted uncritically by a reader as grounded. There are no foundations for responses from a psychological viewpoint—there is no foundation on which one may stand without fear of future contradiction—*if* one's desire is to appreciate. But there are foundations from an aesthetic standpoint: one's responses may be grounded in features of the work—but to be warranted in judging that they are, one's responses must be embedded within the wider project of appreciation. Somewhat paradoxically, this embedding occurs only if one is psychologically prepared to give up one's responses as grounded.

Different theories of interpretation and understanding will take different sets of grounds as providing warrant. Whether one's response is aesthetically passionally grounded depends on whether there is a theory that takes the sorts of things one is attuned to and sensitive to as grounding a response. That is, the grounding of the response depends on the existence of such a theory, not on one's awareness of the existence of such a theory.

Aesthetic grounding of responses differs from epistemic grounding of beliefs in this respect. Whether a belief that this pen is pink is grounded in my color experience of the pen is not dependent on the existence of a theory of any sort. If my belief is so grounded, it is so grounded independently of what epistemologists have proposed about warrant for beliefs. But in aesthetics we are not talking about knowledge of the world but about responses to works of art. Works of art play certain roles within the personal, social, and cultural lives of human beings, and those roles make the grounding for responses dependent on theory. No gadget's functions are dictated by nature; gadgets become gadgets in acquiring functions by virtue of their design, selection, use, and roles. There is a whole range of "gadgets" we call fictional literature, and membership in the group is partly defined in terms of how various aspects of a work are supposed to function. That is, when a piece of prose is a literary work of art, its effectiveness will be due to a significant degree to voice, diction, style, imagery, and so on. These aspects of a work constitute the artistic analogue of "significant subsets of perceptual evidence available." Sensitivities to these aspects of a work will help make the work work; they will be generally adaptive for the purposes of appreciation.

Why should the mere existence of a theory make it the case that a response is grounded in what the theory holds, even if one is unaware of the theory? Not everything we do as members of a culture or society is done with an awareness of what we are doing. If one takes a more global, reflective stance, it is often possible to see patterns that remain hidden to the participants.[13] Appreciating fiction is something we do not merely as individuals but as members of a community; the nature, function, and value of literature all have to do with social and cultural phenomena. Our behavior, vis-à-vis literature, has cultural implications. Sometimes our behavior partially constructs a paradigm of appreciation, as in the sensitivities we have to various parts of a work. Responses that result from those sensitivities are thus grounded because we function within a social and cultural network. And, of course, to pretend that an individual's responses will fail to be influ-

---

13. I have drawn out some consequences of this phenomenon in "Feminist Art History and *De Facto* Significance," in Peggy Zeglin Brand and Carolyn Korsmeyer, eds., *Feminism and Tradition in Aesthetics* (University Park: Penn State University Press, 1995).

enced by various aspects of a culture that reflect certain ways of doing, thinking, and responding presents an implausibly isolationist view of the nature of the individual. Cultural attitudes and practices are partially constructed by a whole range of phenomena, and individuals living and functioning within a culture will not remain immune to its influences. Thus, the individual's acquaintance with a particular literary theory is moot when the theory also constructs and reflects a set of cultural attitudes and beliefs.

Aesthetic grounding depends on theory because it is not part of "nature" but part of "culture." The grounding exists independently of the awareness of the particular individual who is responding to a work, because that individual lives and breathes as part of a human community, a community that not only has developed the relevant theories but that also contains multiple manifestations of attitudes and beliefs that give rise to the theory with which an individual will virtually inevitably come into contact. But a response may also be grounded independently of one's awareness of the theory to allow for the fact that a person can be "doing the right thing" with the work, even if unaware of that fact. Appreciation builds on this initial appropriate activity; the initial activity is necessary for a more fully developed appreciation. Though minimal, it is still "doing the right sort of thing" and constitutes a kind of "natural ability," as we sometimes call it, that can then be developed and refined. Without that development, of course, the ability will come to very little—just an occasional responsiveness to aesthetically or artistically relevant features of a work. It is an ability of a very minimal sort. Yet responding to such features of a work is relevant, and our assessments of responses should reflect that fact.

This chapter has led back into familiar material—traditional admonitions about how to attend to fictional literature to appreciate it—but in a new context. Responsiveness to these sorts of phenomena is grounded in its general utility for the purposes of appreciation. In this way responses may be aesthetically passionally grounded; that is, simply the fact of responding affectively to these sorts of things is warranted. Furthermore, the responses are grounded; it is not the person who is warranted in responding. Passional grounding is like gravity; it connects us with the world—in this case, the work. Grounding "defends" responses without putting the person on the defensive; it is simply the way things are supposed to be.

Type grounding and type warrant, however, present a more complicated situation. Responses are type warranted when one is warranted in responding in a particular way, with a response of a particular kind or sort. Preliminary to the question of type grounding or warrant is an investigation of how to identify and individuate types of responses: the subject of Chapter 8.

Chapter Eight

Identifying and Individuating Emotions and Affects

The previous chapter dealt with passional warrant, that is, with what warrants affectively responding to fiction at all. I sought a rationale for having some response, rather than no affective response at all, and argued that affectively responding is grounded by features of a work that are significant because of their general usefulness for appreciation. That is, learning to appreciate fiction requires one to develop certain kinds of sensitivities, so that one is responsive to precisely those sorts of features. In this chapter and the two next I address how responding in a particular *way* may be warranted. This is *type warrant,* and it addresses what kinds or types of emotions or affective responses are warranted.

Since I want to understand what warrants responding in one way rather than another (or what makes one emotion appropriate and another inappropriate), the first task, logically speaking, is to understand how to individuate and hence identify different types of emotions and affects. Real progress has been made in understanding the components and logical structure of some emotion types—fear, pity, anger, guilt, shame, and a few others. Unfortunately, this work does not get us very far toward understanding affective responses that figure in the appreciation of fictional literature. The level of our current understanding of emotions and affects in general is a major stumbling block when it comes to defending responses as appropriate or warranted. In this chapter I discuss some of the handicaps our current level of comprehension produces for understanding type warrant for affective responses.

I: The Need for a Typology of Emotions and Affects

Once upon a time many people thought feelings and emotions could be identified by the character of one's experiences, by the way it felt to be in the throes of, for instance, pity, fear, grief, or remorse.[1] This view of emotions conforms to an equally primitive view about experiences of art. Christened the "Immersion-Tingle theory" by Nelson Goodman, it holds that if you immerse yourself in an artwork properly and completely you will feel a unique and satisfying emotional tingle as a reward.[2] People used to call these emotions "aesthetic experiences," and producing them was held to be what was valuable about art.

Though this collection of views is a parody of what anyone has actually believed, it has a definite elegance, unfortunately at the expense of plausibility. An emotion is not identical with a certain kind of "felt quality" of experience. No internal sensation or experience enables one to distinguish emotions from other kinds of psychological phenomena or to distinguish one sort of emotion from another. Neither will a special feeling quality enable one to distinguish emotional responses *to fiction* from other emotions; it is not even the case that they are always less intense than emotional responses to objects and events in real life—even when the response is a simulation, as explained in Chapter 4.

It will be clear from what I have written above that I am generally sympathetic to cognitive theories of emotion, at least those that allow unasserted thoughts to constitute their cognitive components. Thus, fear, anger, and pity will be individuated from one another at least in part by different cognitive components, roughly, respectively, the belief or thought that one is in danger, the belief or thought that one has been done an injustice, and the belief or thought that the object of one's pity has suffered an undeserved misfortune. Thus, I accept one bit of psychological theory about relevant identifying and individuating characteristics of emotions. The fact that this is a theory rather than a bit of introspection is important. If emotions and other affects are psychological phenomena, the names of particular emotions and these other affects will refer to psychological states or processes whose

---

1. This view has a more sophisticated contemporary residue. For example, Stephen R. Leighton argues in "Feelings and Emotion," *Review of Metaphysics* 38 (1984): 303–320, that feelings are necessary to emotions and can determine what emotion is present.
2. Nelson Goodman, *Languages of Art: An Approach to a Theory of Symbols* (Indianapolis: Bobbs-Merrill, 1968), p. 112.

underlying nature is elucidated by whatever psychological theory turns out to be correct. That is, the defining features of emotions will be revealed by whatever psychological theory has the greatest explanatory and, where appropriate, predictive value.[3]

Despite the progress that has been made in individuating emotions, virtually nothing of the sort has been done for non-emotion affects— especially for what generally pass under the rubric of "feelings." Indeed, the term "feelings" has a decidedly unscientific air about it— the sorts of things people refer to when they can't give any good explanation for their behavior or beliefs. Are they even scientifically respectable entities, the sort of thing a science of psychology ought to investigate? Or should they be tossed into the dustbin of suspect entities, along with intuitions, karma, and energies? The fact that we don't have a very developed vocabulary for feelings accentuates their indescribability, implicating them as bogus rather than simply mysterious.

I suspect that much of the popular derision and even contempt heaped on fictional literature as works of art gather support from the generally suspect status of emotions and feelings in general. And though emotions have recently gained a more respectable status— how else? through the recognition that they have *cognitive* components—feelings and other affects still lag far behind. But without some creditable ways of identifying and individuating feelings, as well as other non-emotion affects such as moods and attitudes, it is impossible even to begin defending feelings as appropriate or warranted responses to fiction. Yet feelings are an important part of appreciation, perhaps more important than emotions, even though the latter have garnered the bulk of recent attention.

Understandably, most discussions of responses to fiction have concentrated on fairly easily identifiable emotional responses to well-known works—for instance, fear felt in response to horror movies, the pity we feel for Anna Karenina and sadness over her plight. As Alex Neill argues, progress in understanding responses to fiction will be made by considering individual emotions rather than by trying to generalize about them across the board.[4] Along these lines, Noël Car-

---

3. On the meaning of theoretical terms being theory dependent, see Hilary Putnam, "The Meaning of 'Meaning'," in *Mind, Language, and Reality: Philosophical Papers of Hilary Putnam,* vol. 2 (New York: Cambridge University Press, 1975); and Saul Kripke, "Naming and Necessity," in Donald Davidson and Gilbert Harmon, eds., *Semantics of Natural Language* (Dordrecht: Reidel, 1972).
4. Alex Neill, "Fiction and the Emotions," *American Philosophical Quarterly* 30 (1993): 12.

roll has made significant progress in distinguishing fear, horror, and disgust in a more finely tuned manner,[5] and David Pole explored similar affective terrain in "Disgust and Other Forms of Aversion."[6]

If we are to take this lesson seriously, there is an immense task ahead of us. First, the quantity of types or sorts of emotions and feelings is enormous. Various philosophers have attempted to develop overall categories for grouping types of emotions to get a grasp on the relevant conceptual groupings of this enormous lot. It is well known that Hobbes thought that all emotions fell into two categories (desires and aversions); Descartes thought there were six (an interesting grouping, really: love, hatred, joy, desire, wonder, and sadness); and Spinoza thought all emotions were a mixture of three kinds of phenomena (pleasure, pain, and desire).[7] Classifications such as these might establish a foothold for assessments of warrant, insofar as an emotion or affect would be warranted or appropriate qua emotion or affect of a given type. Indeed, I rely on a large-scale division in the following chapter to make some headway in the task of type assessment.

The second reason why pursuing the analysis of individual emotions and affects presents an immense task is that individual emotions, and especially affects, may have very different concatenations of non-cognitive identificatory components that do not sort out into a neat logical structure.[8] This problem is recognized by the view that an emotion consists simply of a cognitive component and a general arousal of the autonomic or central nervous systems (ANS and CNS).

5. Nöel Carroll, *The Philosophy of Horror, or, Paradoxes of the Heart* (New York: Routledge, 1990).
6. David Pole, "Disgust and Other Forms of Aversion," in *Aesthetics, Form, and Emotion* (London: Duckworth, 1983).
7. For an idea of how diverse psychological theories of emotion are, see Robert Plutchik and Henry Kellerman, eds., *Emotion: Theory, Research, and Experience*, vol. 1: *Theories of Emotion*, (New York: Academic Press, 1980). Also useful is K. T. Strongman, *The Psychology of Emotion* (London: John Wiley, 1973). For more philosophically oriented surveys see William Lyons, *Emotion* (Cambridge: Cambridge University Press, 1980), and the anthology edited by Cheshire Calhoun and Robert C. Solomon, *What Is an Emotion? Classic Readings in Philosophical Psychology* (New York: Oxford University Press, 1984).
8. Belief components of emotions have received more attention than desire components. Yet desires are crucial: e.g., one of the things distinguishing fear that p and hope that p is the desire that not-p in the case of the former and the desire that p in the case of the latter. ANS and CNS activity in emotions and affects will also likely find a role as components of desires implicated by those affective states. Recognizing the role of desires won't necessarily make assessments easier, however, since even the possibility of assessing the rationality of or warrant for desires is controversial.

Many emotions are typically accompanied by arousal of the ANS—
heart muscles, smooth muscles of the intestines, blood vessels, stom-
ach and genito-urinary tract, and various glands activated by the nervous system. But there are few receptors for ANS activity, so the
argument runs, indicating that there could be little *felt* difference
among emotions even if different emotions were accompanied by
different ANS activity. Furthermore, some emotions, such as contentment, are at least phenomenologically lacking in physiological
arousal, though it is still possible that they have physiological correlates. More importantly, it is also claimed, there appear to be virtually
no emotion-specific ANS or CNS arousals. ANS and CNS arousals
might be used as measures of emotional intensity, rather than as a
means for *differentiating* emotions from one another.[9]

Nevertheless, various researchers have investigated which physiological phenomena might be correlated with, and ultimately integrated into, a definition of various emotions. Probably best known to
philosophers is the research of Paul Ekman and colleagues reported
under the headline, "Autonomic Nervous System Activity Distinguishes among Emotions."[10] Though the headline is misleading,
Ekman did show that there was a correlation between certain ANS
activity and facial expressions we generally identify as expressive of
each member of a circumscribed set of six emotion types. For a couple
of lesser-known examples, William Frey has also attempted to identify
noncognitive correlates of emotions by comparing the chemical composition of tears generated during an emotional distress and tears
produced through an irritation to the eye.[11] Richard Davidson has
found that different patterns of hemispheric activity in the brain (as
well as different well-defined facial expressions) accompany happiness as opposed to disgust.[12]

These or other correlates may come to play a defining role in the

9. George Mandler is one of the better-known exponents of this view. See *Mind and Emotion* (New York: John Wiley, 1975), p. 66.

10. Paul Ekman, Robert W. Levenson, Wallace V. Friesen, "Autonomic Nervous System Activity Distinguishes among Emotions," *Science*, 16 September 1983, p. 1210.

11. William Frey, "Not-So-Idle Tears," *Psychology Today* 13 (1980): 91.

12. Richard J. Davidson, Paul Ekman, Clifford D. Saron, Joseph A. Senulis et al.,
"Approach-Withdrawal and Cerebral Asymmetry: Emotional Expression and Brain
Physiology," *Journal of Personality and Social Psychology* 58 (1990): 330–341. A review of
research on cerebral asymmetry and the experience and expression of emotion revealed experimental arousal of positive emotions is associated with selective activation
of the left frontal region and arousal of negative emotions with the right frontal region.
See Richard J. Davidson, "Emotion and Affective Style: Hemispheric Substrates," *Psychological Science* 3 (1992): 39–43.

identification of emotions and affects. If emotions and affects are discovered to have noncognitive defining conditions, then the question arises how those differential activities can be assessed as appropriate, rather than as simply having a cognitive response, or as the cognitive response accompanied by some other ANS or CNS activity. Of course, if assessing affects and emotions depends on assessing ANS or CNS activity, the chemistry of tears, or the pattern of left or right hemispheric activity, it looks like we have a reductio ad absurdum of the view that we can indeed assess—at least in the sense of giving type warrant for—affective responses. I concluded in chapter 7 that affectively responding is grounded in features of a literary work that are generally useful for appreciating it. And the fact is that, as I argued in Chapters 3, 4, and 5, we can alter our sensitivities and hence the way we respond in many ways. Learning to appreciate requires developing affective flexibility so that one is able to respond differentially to the various things one reads. The connection between types of responses and qualities of the work is made through developing an account of the work. But, unlike cognitive components of emotions, noncognitive components or characteristics of emotions and affects do not seem to bear any useful relationship to the qualities of the work that generate the affective responses.

There's one other interesting fact to be noticed about the work of Frey and Davidson. Frey, a psychiatrist and biochemist, wanted to determine whether tears generated by eye irritation differ chemically from tears generated by an emotion. It would seem to be just one more step to compare genuine distress tears with tears shed in response to a work of fictional literature (or other work of art) to see how close responses to fiction are to real emotions in this respect. As you might expect, however, Frey had some technical problems in carrying out his research, for it is difficult to capture sufficient quantities of tears in sterilized test tubes from people in the throes of serious emotional distress. (One has images of the professor chasing ambulances and lurking around funerals and hospital emergency rooms.) What to do? He finally decided to collect the tears produced while his subjects cried at sad movies! Thus, his experimental design presupposed that emotional responses to films were sufficiently similar to real-life emotions to warrant speculation and generalization about the role that particular kinds of chemicals discovered in them have in affecting the way we "feel" and in relieving stress in nonfiction cases.[13]

13. Frey, "Not-So-Idle Tears," p. 159.

We encounter a similar phenomenon with Davidson's work as well. A notable feature of Davidson's experimental design is that his correlations between brain activity and distinctive facial expressions indicative of a positive (happiness) or negative (disgust) emotion were derived during electrical monitoring and videotaping of subjects who were watching film clips designed to elicit either a positive or negative emotional response.[14]

Even if emotional and affective responses to fictional literature can be sorted according to the typology developed for ordinary, garden-variety emotions and affects, there is a long way to go before we understand emotions, and especially affects, well enough to develop principles of type assessment for them. In the following section I explore some of the reasons why.

II: Complexities and Subtleties of Experience

My aim is not to show the futility of trying to make assessments of affective responses to fiction. Quite the contrary, I hope to show why we are at a very primitive stage in making them. That is, the lack of progress can be explained by the lack of sufficient understanding of emotions and affects themselves and not necessarily by the impossibility of making assessments of emotions or affects at all. In this section, I discuss how, even if we had all the understanding called for in section I, there are two additional difficulties with assessing affective responses to fiction. First, responses to fiction, echoing our daily emotional lives, often become exceedingly complex. Where to individuate and how to identify individual component emotions raises questions to which, to me, at any rate, there seems to be no clear answer. Such situations raise a question about how to integrate the components of assessment which would apply to neatly individuated emotions and affects in order to assess the whole emotional complex. Second, responses to fiction often have a subtlety and focus that is not captured by ordinary emotion terms. Novel situations call for judgments about the identity of the emotion or affect involved and hence about how to

14. Davidson et al., "Approach-Withdrawal." Though no systematic differences in hemispheric activity was found between positive films as opposed to negative films, other research did establish a correlation between selective activation of the left frontal region with positive, approach-related emotions and selective activation of the right frontal region with negative, withdrawal-related emotions. See also Davidson, "Emotion and Affective Style."

assess its appropriateness. In both areas, judgments about how to assess responses are liable, often with good reason, to affect judgments about how to identify and individuate emotions and affects themselves.

Consider first the complexities of our emotions. The boundaries and identifying characteristics of emotions and emotional responses to fiction are not nearly as neat as we might wish, and if we try to be precise about exactly what sort of emotional response is appropriate to a work of literature, we run the danger of conferring an artificial purity and articulation on what we commonly identify as "the" response. If you took a psychological run through what could pass for an ordinary life, you would rarely find emotions and feelings, or our identifications of them, tidily individuated and separated from one another and their surrounding psychological environments. They grow out of, feed on, reflect, and are absorbed by myriad aspects of mental life.

At one point in George Bernard Shaw's play, "Widowers' Houses," he gives the following stage direction to a character named "Lickcheese": "surprised into contemptuous amusement in the midst of his anxiety." How many emotions would a person have (or how many different psychological states would that person be in) who was surprised into contemptuous amusement in the midst of his anxiety? How many emotions would you have if, when reading the play, you were to empathize with Lickcheese—though with a name like that it may be hard to do, which is no doubt significant. There are four words that have emotional connotations. But is contemptuous amusement one emotion or two? If it's only one, is it amusement colored by contempt or contempt colored by amusement? Is being surprised into contemptuous amusement a single emotion and a different emotion from just being contemptuously amused or is it the addition of a new emotion to one (or two) one already has? Is doing all of this in the midst of anxiety a single new emotion or the addition of a new emotion to one (or two, or three) one already has?

I think a lot of people would find these questions a little silly ("the sort of thing that gives philosophers a bad name"), and it goes to show that identifying and individuating emotions is a pretty messy business. How would we ever know what the answers to these questions are, and what difference would it make? It matters because our answers affect the basis for assessing the components of this emotional stew. Is the warrant for this experiential mixture simply additive of the warrants for the individual components? What about the fact that Lickcheese was experiencing anxiety when he was surprised—doesn't that lead us to assess his contemptuous amusement a little differently?

And because he was surprised, there is less basis for holding him responsible, at least for momentary feelings of contempt.

One of the facts about such complex situations is that we don't need to wait on a science of psychology either to raise the issues or to provide at least preliminary speculations on how to deal with them. Do we really think that a psychological theory is going to determine for us whether the preceding emotion complex is one emotion, or two, three, or four? We all work with a pretheoretical, common-sense identification and individuation of mental states and processes and their relations that has come to be known in the philosophical litera- ture as "folk psychology." Folk psychology is not a scientific theory; it is constituted by sets of ordinary beliefs and assumptions ordinary people make about psychological states and processes. These states and processes include emotions and other affective states, as well as beliefs, desires, and imaginings. Being pretheoretical, the concepts employed may be more or less integrated and consistent but are not necessarily rigorously defined or systematically related. Thus, a chari- table interpretation should be taken towards folk psychology. Some stipulations might be needed to tighten up and render consistent what ordinary folk might assert about various psychological states. Even so, a certain part of philosophical psychology, and of philosoph- ical aesthetics insofar as it attempts to understand emotions and other psychological phenomena occurring in our appreciation of art need not compete with, or be dependent upon advances in, the science of psychology at all.

In fact, it is plausible to think that the kinds of distinctions we ordinarily make are precisely the ones that should be employed when trying to identify what sorts of emotions or other affective responses constitute part of our appreciation of a given work. Literary works of art are functional objects that are written, understood, and appreci- ated by human beings. Objects are identified as artworks in light of the cultural roles they are perceived as playing or are chosen to play. It would be decidedly odd to sit back and ask science to tell us how to individuate the different sorts of responses one might appropriately have to these culturally emergent entities. Do we need the science of psychology to tell us how we are warranted in responding to fiction? Rather, responses should be identified in terms of the accounts human beings give of how the works to which we respond are sup- posed to function.

Nevertheless, if we try to answer these questions using our own common-sense notions of what individuates emotions from one another, the introduction of artificial (i.e., not folk psychological) standards of rigor is inevitable. When our ordinary concepts do not provide us a way of settling where to put unclear cases, we need to start making distinctions where previously there were none or where there were only fuzzy transitions. But distinctions introduce terminology made more rigorous for a purpose: distinctions turn out to be appropriate or inappropriate if one has certain interests. It is not a purely arbitrary matter; there will be presuppositions and implications of drawing distinctions one way rather than another. Even the decision as to whether emotional responses to fiction are emotions in the same sense as real-life emotions turns out to have implications for what kinds of explanations of human behavior you expect emotions to provide. As I suggested, folk psychology may indeed stand in need of some additional rigor, and we need to acknowledge the consequences of the emendations we make.

The second difficulty to discuss in this section concerns what I like to call the waywardness of responses to fiction. Responses to fiction, perhaps even the ones most worth having, tend to have a subtlety and focus that is not captured by standard emotion terms and that is lost in the overworked examples of pity, fear, and sadness. Though appeals to the subtlety of responses is commonplace, it is unfortunately an invitation to obscurantism. There's no vocabulary to name responses; it's difficult if not impossible to describe them with the limited vocabulary one does have unless one is a poet or agile critic oneself; one is forced into the position of just repeating the words that elicited the response, hoping one's reader will respond the same way. This is all very unsatisfactory, and such claims are easily open to abuse. But sometimes they are true.

Not only are they sometimes true but arguably also of the utmost importance. If what I say in Chapter 11 is correct, one of the values of appreciating and learning to appreciate fiction is the stretching and flexing that it entices in the human mind. The stretching is accomplished not through traversing the well-worn territory of familiar emotions but through exploring different affective directions. One way is to have a new emotion, such as litost, an emotion for which Milan Kundera claims there is no term in any language except Czechoslovakian.[15] Empathizing with the protagonist of Chapter 5 of *The Book of Laughter and Forgetting* means the reader will experience

---

15. Milan Kundera, *The Book of Laughter and Forgetting*, trans. Michael Henry Heim (1980; New York: Penguin, 1981), part 5.

litost. Another way to do the stretching is to experience familiar emotions in response to new things. And finally, a third way is when one has
an experience that one identifies as an emotion or feeling but which
one had not individuated as such before. Such feelings and emotions
have no names and will be difficult to describe. These are the wayward
responses. And if we have no prior comprehension of them, how in
the world can we be in a position to defend their appropriateness?

I found Patrick Süskind's *Perfume* evocative of many such responses,
partly because it opens up a world of odors and aromas that provide the
basis for relating to objects in a largely new way. Grenouille, the novel's
protagonist, has a hypersensitive nose: he can smell a person miles
away; he can smell glass and stones; he individuates odors within the
complex barrage to which he is subjected every day; he doesn't need to
see because he can locate objects by their smell. Grenouille makes his
own perfumes, including perfumes from the odors of people. Each one
captures the person's "aromatic soul." The very description of an aromatic soul produces an ethereal, incorporeal feeling, but more the feeling of a ghostly spirit than a lighthearted soul. Yet this soul carries a
sense of being more real than the corporeal world—almost like a
Platonic essence unsullied by vision or touch. When Grenouille kills
the person whose scent he robs, one feels that the body imprisoned
the true essence of the person—the scent—that then lives on when
absorbed away from the useless corpse. In the world of odors things
permeate and penetrate—extend through space—much more than
any mere physical object. Reference to a person's "aromatic soul"
certainly produces a special feeling, or perhaps a complex of feelings,
for which we have no standard vocabulary.

There is a feeling for which I have not been able to discover a
name but which really deserves one. It is the feeling you have when
affectively apprehending a searing insight. It is the closest thing I can
think of to the feeling Clive Bell says he has in experiencing "the cold
white peaks of art." A sentence or phrase pierces with its insight, and
the mind is affected by the perspicacity and just the "rightness" of it
all. It's a shudder of recognition of its uncompromising, forthright
rightness. Though not from fiction, I cannot resist an example from a
memorial notice written by Salmon Rushdie for Angela Carter shortly
after she died. Rushdie describes her as "cackling gaily as she impales
the twentieth century upon its jokes."[16]

16. Salmon Rushdie, "Angela Carter, 1940–92: A Very Good Wizard, a Very Dear
Friend," *New York Times Book Review*, 8 March 1992, p. 5.

David Best describes a set of feelings evoked by a passage from Patrick White's novel *A Fringe of Leaves,* in which a sensitive woman is trying without success to describe her experiences to a military commandant. He tells her, "If it made such an impression on you, I should have thought you'd be able to describe it."[17] The passage conveys more powerfully than any description of him could how pompous, arrogant, and emotionally shallow the commandant is. Loathing of the commandant, sympathy with the woman to whom he makes the insensitive remark, and the sense of rightness of the remark for revealing a multitude of the commandant's psychological qualities fuse phenomenologically in an experience of the work, yet they are discriminable analytically as components of that experience.

The paradigm cases of emotional responses to fiction are very complex phenomena. They depend on taking certain attitudes or points of view, having various beliefs about a work and even about its worth, developing sensitivities to various features of a work—including its formal and expressive qualities—and having a capacity for reflective responses—an awareness of and responses to other responses. Finally, all these must be alterable by reflections on the warrant for or appropriateness or relevance of one's beliefs and responses. These kinds of psychological phenomena depend upon one's having a mind with a very high degree of psychological complexity and power, a complexity and power that is used in the process of appreciation. If we want to understand why affective responses to fiction are an important part of appreciating a work of literary art and why appreciation is something that itself should be fostered and encouraged, then it is most likely that the highly subtle and complex feelings and emotions that arise during the appreciation of a work will be the most revealing. But they will also be the most complex and problematic to defend.

III: A Requirement for Individuating Emotions and Affects

There is one more concern that hovers over the individuation of emotions. Responses may be individuated in a manner that is so finegrained that no two responses of the same type ever occur. This is

---

17. Cited by David Best, *Feeling and Reason in the Arts* (London: Allen & Unwin, 1985), p. 150.

potentially a problem because, for appreciation, some emotions or affects may constitute a partial appreciation of a work. A partial appreciation is different from an approximate appreciation. The former involves having part, but only part, of what is necessary to appreciate a work fully. In fact this is likely the state of all of us all of the time—we don't "get out of it" all that it has the potential to provide. But to approximate being in a given emotional or affective state is different. Does fear approximate terror, or delight joy, or loathing disgust? Approximation involves the notion of similarity, and similarity admits of degrees. Now there is room for this, especially in the notion of simulation. But it is also operative when identifying *affective* states, where we would have to understand how the terms we use for identifying affects are related to one another, so that we can come closer or move further away.

There are theories of the nature of mental states that advocate what I call "experiential holism."[18] It is an "everything counts" view of experience, and its advocates are the new Heracliteans: you can't step twice into the same psychological state. On this view, an experience is defined, at least in part, by the relationships in which it stands to one's past experiences and other psychological states—not just a subset of them but any and all of them. Holism entails that an experience can never be duplicated: if I have read the first sentence of *Pride and Prejudice* before, the very fact that it has been experienced before makes my experience different the second time around.

In Jorge Luis Borges's short story "Funes, the Memorious," Funes keeps accumulating mental data in his memory bank without ever reinforcing any beliefs or other psychological commitments he has formed on the basis of his other experiences. Every experience is literally brand new. He eventually dies of "cerebral congestion": his brain becomes so densely packed because so much stuff has been crammed into it that it eventually suffocates. The absurdity of the idea is not without its point. Memory is, in actuality, enhanced by repetition and cognitive integration of new experiences, not just by

18. Its advocates run the gamut from philosophers to literary theorists. P. F. Strawson suggests experiential holism in "Imagination and Perception," in Lawrence Foster and J. W. Swanson, eds., *Experience and Theory* (Amherst: University of Massachusetts Press, 1970), p. 40, where he refers to Kant as holding there is a sense in which a present perception "would not be just the perception it is" but for past perceptions. Wolfgang Iser hints at experiential holism in *The Act of Reading: A Theory of Aesthetic Response* (Baltimore: Johns Hopkins University Press, 1978), p. 149. See also Stephen P. Stich's view that attributing mental states involves making a similarity judgment, in *From Folk Psychology to Cognitive Science: The Case against Belief* (Cambridge: MIT Press, 1983).

piling up unrelated or uninterpreted data.[19] Some aspects of experience, such as perceptions, images, and the propositional content of a thought, have to be reidentifiable to perform as reinforcers and to integrate information provided through experience. Thus, we need to distinguish different types of mental entities that play roles in "higher-level" explanations that abstract from (relatively) minor variations to achieve the kind of generality necessary for an explanation to serve its purpose. A psychological "explanation" whose application is necessarily restricted to one instance does not enhance our understanding of the phenomenon: it must at least in principle be generalizable over some range of cases.

If experiential holism of the sort I have been describing were true, we could not capture or understand the affect or emotion, much less explain why it is an appropriate or inappropriate response to a work of art, because it is in principle unique and can never be replicated. As long as our whole set of experiences is treated as a seamless whole and not an amalgam of separately identifiable aspects, we cannot even obtain a partial understanding of it. Comparative judgments, such as similarity judgments, are possible only if we can identify and individuate the items among which the comparisons are made.[20] Experiential holism presents us with a new sorites paradox and solves it by endorsing the conclusion that every tiny change in our mental makeup entails that our subsequent affective experience is of a different sort than we, or anyone, have ever had before. Like the old Heracliteans, experiential holists will be reduced to wagging their fingers. If they do use language, they can't use it to describe their responses but as a pointer or in some other way that doesn't have a descriptive function.[21]

Some experiences, as well as emotions and affects, can be similar to others in important respects. Even if they are ultimately different

19. See, for example, John T. E. Richardson, *Mental Imagery and Human Memory* (London: Macmillan, 1980), chap. 7.
20. Equally dangerous and unhelpful is literary theory that holds that the reader's response completes the literary work, so that the work itself—and, at bottom, there cannot even be said to be such a thing—is never quite the same. In that case, different individuals, or even the same individual at different times, would not be acquainted with the same work.
21. Arnold Isenberg seems to me to dig himself into this hole in his justly influential "Critical Communication," *Philosophical Review* 58 (1949): 330–344; repr. in *Aesthetics and the Theory of Criticism: Selected Essays of Arnold Isenberg* (Chicago: University of Chicago Press, 1973): 156–171. See especially his Note at the end. Isenberg is more concerned with the properties of the work than the nature of our experience, but the principle remains the same.

kinds of experiences, emotions, or whatever, our identifications of emotion types should be sensitive enough to capture partial similarities among them. These shades and nuances, whether they constitute separate psychological entities or not, identify significant components of our affective response, as illustrated by the Shaw example. Even if we ultimately do not know where to draw the line between one emotion or affect and another, it is at least necessary to be able to pick out aspects of the experience in relation to which similarities to other emotions and affects can be identified.

Some issues dealt with in this chapter were briefly anticipated in Chapter 6, such as the problem of whether differences in degrees of intensity of emotions and affects constituted differences in kind. The problems of identifying and individuating emotions and affects, however, range far beyond that simple complication. Emotions and affects are defined by psychological theories that explain and, where appropriate, predict human behavior. But psychology has not yet yielded anything like a comprehensive typology of emotions, much less affects. The real progress that cognitive theories of emotion have yielded belies the complex roles played by noncognitive factors, factors that are important for emotions and of the essence for affects. The task of assessment is compounded when the emotions and affects themselves are united and interwoven in experience. Ordinary "folk psychology" is not up to the task of sorting out these complexities and must be made more rigorous by the addition of, of course, theory. Rigor is added at a price; the price comes in the form of the reasons for making theoretical decisions that point in one direction rather than another. These decisions and the reasons for them are likely often to be interdependent with assessments of the reasonableness of particular responses. Outside the realm of existing theory are, for example, wayward responses, those feelings and emotions not named by our folk psychology or our science. They nevertheless may be precisely the sorts of ways it is most important to be able to respond to a literary work.

Chapter Nine

Type Warrant

In Chapter 7 I explored the possibility of aesthetic passional grounding of responses, grounding for having any responses at all. I argued
there that responses could be passionally grounded by features of a
work traditionally considered to be aesthetically or artistically significant, such as diction, sentence structure and narrative voice. Type
warrant, as opposed to passional grounding, provides a basis for assessing the particular type or sort of responses one has. Principles of
type warrant are handicapped by the difficulties of identifying and
individuating emotions and affects, as discussed in Chapter 8. Nevertheless, in this chapter I explore the possibility of type warrant for
responses, in an effort to make some progress in spite of those difficulties. First, I use a distinction between epistemic emotions and factive emotions to differentially assess emotions that fall into these two
categories. This assessment provides an example of one basis for assessing emotional responses to fictional literature as (type) warranted.

Another basis for assessing emotions as type warranted is provided
by a principle that links the way one would be warranted in responding to actual situations to one's being warranted in responding
to a description of that sort of situation in a work of fiction. This is a
"piggyback" principle, in that assessments of responses to fiction ride
on the back of assessments of responses to real-life situations. The
plausibility of this principle depends to an extent on one's theory of
interpretation; it is virtually impossible to keep the form or logic of
type assessments independent of the content of an interpretive theory
concerning the methods, objectives, and principles of understanding

the meaning(s) and import of a work. Yet there is still a point to be made about why such a principle does provide warrant for responses to fiction.

The two bases for assessment discussed in this chapter are indeed only two bases for assessment out of myriads of relevant factors, and if this discussion reveals anything it is how difficult it is to provide type warrant for a response. I have chosen to discuss the former principle, even though it deals with a relatively obscure aspect of emotions, because of its fairly clear independence of interpretive theory. I have chosen to discuss the latter because of the way it relates warrant for responses to fiction to warrant for responses to actual events, and hence because of the way it relates appreciation to how to live a life. One does not have to defend art as a teacher of moral truths or bearer of other insights to take this second principle seriously. It depends merely on seeing that not only do we use our experiences, beliefs, and values to interpret and appreciate fictional literature but also that the warrant we have for affectively responding to actual people, situations, and events serves to warrant affective responses to fiction.

I: Epistemic and Factive Emotions

Any principle for type warrant for responses must depend on crucial identifying features of the responses as the type or sort of responses they are. In this section I deal with a limited range of responses, in particular, emotions (or simulations thereof) involving either beliefs or unasserted thoughts. In *The Structure of Emotions*, Robert Gordon distinguishes two classes of emotions: epistemic emotions and factive emotions. Both emotions have what he calls propositional objects, or emotions that can be substituted in the following formula, "I emote that p," where "emote" is a variable standing for the particular kind of emotion, and p stands for what he calls its propositional object, the belief or unasserted thought providing its cognitive content.[1] Factive

---

1. Robert M. Gordon, *The Structure of Emotions: Investigations in Cognitive Psychology* (New York: Cambridge University Press, 1987). Gordon, however, allows only beliefs to constitute the propositional object of emotions. I have used his distinction for my own purposes, especially for developing the concept of different normative ideals for factive and epistemic emotions, so my analysis parts company with his in various ways. In particular, I do not take the "I emote that p" formula to be as central to the understanding of emotions as Gordon appears to.

emotions are such that, if I emote that p, then I know that p. Examples of factive emotions are anger, embarrassment, surprise, disappointment, and pride. If I am angry that I was fired, then I not only must have been fired, but I must know that I have been fired. If I am surprised that you loaned me the money, then I must know that you loaned me the money; if I am proud that my daughter won the spelling bee, I must know that she won.

One may be angry, where the thought of p constitutes the cognitive content of the emotion, yet fail to fulfill the conditions for being angry *that p*. That is, in believing that I have been fired, I may become angry, but if I don't know that I was fired, I am not angry *that* I was fired. Think, then, of the "I emote that p" construction as expressing a normative ideal for factive emotions, the ideal of knowing that whatever one is angry about is true. Anger and other factive emotions are thus assessed in light of that ideal, either that one knows that p or that one justifiably believes one knows that p.

Epistemic emotions are such that if I emote that p, then I *don't* know that p. Epistemic emotions are appropriate, qua epistemic emotions, when one doesn't know what the facts are. Moreover, it is not merely permitted that I not know that p, but required that I do not know. Examples of epistemic emotions are fear, worry, and hope. Suspicion, as in the stockbroker case, is clearly an example of an epistemic emotion.[2] "I suspect that the stockbroker is untrustworthy" (or "I suspect that he will cheat me if I give him half a chance") clearly entails that I don't know that he will. Furthermore, suspicion does not entail that I believe that the stockbroker is untrustworthy or that he will cheat me. I am suspicious; that does not imply that I've made up my mind about whether he can or cannot be trusted. But I do have, as Greenspan would say, a feeling of discomfort directed towards an evaluative thought, in particular, the thought of him as untrustworthy.

The stockbroker example was introduced as an example of an emotion's being warranted, passionally warranted, even though one is not justified in believing its identificatory thought ("he is untrustworthy.") It is revealing that the emotion that appears in the example is an epistemic emotion, suspicion. For epistemic emotions are precisely those where, by definition, one doesn't have knowledge that p. As far as one's own beliefs and experiences go, rationally speaking, it's up for grabs whether or not p, whether or not the stockbroker is untrust-

2. See Chapter 7, sec. II.

worthy. Passionally, anger would be just as warranted as suspicion, but given the normative ideal of knowledge for factive emotions, anger in particular, that *type* of emotion, is unwarranted.

Responses to fiction arise in many different ways, as explored in Chapters 4 and 5. A reader's anger or suspicion may be empathic, sympathetic, antipathetic; it may be a metaresponse or a garden-variety response trading on our actual values. But whichever sort of response they are, to be *warranted* as factive and epistemic responses, respectively, they must arise out of the appropriate epistemic relation to their cognitive contents. Some instances of empathy constitute exceptions to this principle, however, since one may appropriately empathize with fictional characters whose emotions are unwarranted, even when the reader knows they are unwarranted. This exception reveals the different structure of empathy: the fact that the emotion is empathic is important—reflecting the fact that one is warranted in empathizing with a character even when the character's emotion is unwarranted—and the warrant for it is attendant on its being empathy, rather than the particular emotion being empathized with.

Other instances of empathic anger can nevertheless be assessed as the factive emotion anger. In *Brazzaville Beach*, Hope Clearwater works for Eugene Mallabar's African research team, documenting and analyzing chimpanzee behavior. Hope discovers evidence of violence and cannibalism in chimpanzee behavior that is at odds with Mallabar's published views. He discourages her from pursuing her line of inquiry; he threatens her; he questions her sanity. He ultimately fires her and publishes her findings under his own name. Hope is indignant and angry. The facts are in no doubt; both Hope's anger and the reader's empathic anger, qua factive emotions, are warranted.[3]

Where the warrant available is sufficiently compelling, one will be more warranted in having a factive emotion than an epistemic one. Suspicion, puzzlement, and even hope are inappropriate when the evidence piles up enough to indicate a malevolent will is at work. Continued refusal to draw a conclusion could be a kind of epistemic irresponsibility in that one doesn't see—or appreciate—how strong the evidence really is. Thus, the epistemic *modesty* of the warrant

---

3. In the novel the situation is more complicated. Among other things, Hope signed a contract essentially giving the right to publish research over to Mallabar. Yet only her persistence over Mallabar's efforts to suppress her led to the discoveries, and she was not given sufficient credit for them. See William Boyd, *Brazzaville Beach* (New York: Avon, 1990).

might be undermined or overridden by the greater assurances provided by other factors.

Suspicion is an epistemic emotion whose normative ideal requires that one not have the relevant knowledge. In Julian Barnes's *Flaubert's Parrot*, Ed Winterton, an American academic, claims to have discovered a cache of correspondence between Juliet Herbert and Gustave Flaubert. Winterton owes Geoffrey Braithwaite (the narrator) a favor, and Braithwaite reasonably expects Winterton to sell or even give the letters to him. They would have enormous value to Braithwaite's literary studies, not to mention his reputation. But when Winterton meets with Braithwaite to tell him of his discovery, he is a little coy, a little reticent, and obviously enjoying the enticement. "He paused, and gave me a look which might have been roguish if he hadn't been such a meek, pedantic fellow. Probably he was enjoying my excitement."[4] Braithwaite is consumed by anticipation of seeing these letters. But the reader becomes suspicious of Winterton, that he has made up the story of the letters, and is raising Braithwaite's hopes just for the *Schadenfreude* of seeing his exasperation when they are dashed. Finally, Winterton tells Braithwaite he hasn't brought the letters with him. Why not? In accord with a wish Flaubert allegedly expressed in the letters themselves, he burned them.

Braithwaite is angry, but not clearly angry *that* Winterton destroyed the letters. For it's not clear there ever were any letters. As a reader, I regard Winterton with suspicion. I don't know whether he burned the letters or even whether there were any letters. But there is something suspicious about him, and he certainly enjoys Braithwaite's disappointment. Moreover, I also become angry with him, angry that he treats Braithwaite with such disrespect, angry that he has toyed with him in such a way. This is not empathic anger—I am not simulating Braithwaite's anger over the letter burning—but it is sympathetic anger, in accord with the interests of Braithwaite.

Would we judge anger as type warranted even if we had no more justification for the belief that someone did us an injustice than for the belief that he didn't? For my *anger* that you did such and such to be warranted, I'd better know, or justifiably believe I know, that you did rather than that you didn't do such and such, reflecting the normative ideal for factive emotions as knowledge. In the case of my suspicion of Winterton, the justification I have for believing he is making the whole thing up is more or less counterbalanced by justifi-

4. Julian Barnes, *Flaubert's Parrot* (New York: Random House/Vintage, 1984), p. 44.

cation for believing there really were some letters. Anger (over his burning the letters) is less warranted than suspicion. Epistemic emotions have a normative ideal that is inherently epistemically modest in that they require that one *not* know or *not* be certain of p when one emotes that p. This inherent modesty makes them epistemically *more* warranted as responses to the situation described in the example. The character of the response itself is reflective of the fact that the significance of what one is responding to is unknown. And, in this sense, it is epistemically more warranted than a factive emotion, which does not, in the nature of the emotion it is, capture the epistemic questionableness of its propositional content.

However, the fact that emotions can have unasserted thoughts, rather than beliefs, as their cognitive components raises a question about this principle for assessing emotions as factive or epistemic. If the thought involved in the emotion is unasserted, and hence part of the imaginal activity I engage in in reading the work, does the epistemic normative ideal still apply for warranting the emotion? Suppose I am not angry *that* Winterton burned the Herbert/Flaubert correspondence, but instead a state of anger is induced in me by the thought of him *as* doing this. Reading what he says to Braithwaite makes me think of him as having burned the letters. (Braithwaite's hearing what he says produces the belief, which produces the emotion of anger. In this case, I simulate Braithwaite's mental processes, and hence I empathize with him.) That is, what I read induces the thought but not the belief. The thought makes me angry. Even though I don't believe that Winterton is guilty, I get all riled up—angry—just the same. There is, after all, some reason to believe he burned the letters, and I may go with the thought, emotionally speaking, but not so far as to believe that he did so. Isn't this precisely what we ought to do when reading fiction—engage in a kind of emotional trial and error to see what works? I have argued throughout the book that it is important to approach literature with a receptive and responsive attitude, even at the risk of responding inappropriately or irrelevantly. A certain amount of risk is necessary to "get into it." The way to deal with this risk is not to clamp down on emotions that are not highly warranted but rather to try things out while exercising a sufficient degree of reflectiveness to make sure you don't get too carried away or carried off in the wrong direction.

It is instructive to look at what we might say in the case of real-life emotions. If someone goes around being angry, offended, excited, annoyed, and so on, when these emotions are generated by thoughts of things she has no evidential basis for believing, there is something wrong with her affective system. This is in part because when belief-independent emotions take such a preponderant role, it is likely that one will be responding emotionally more to thoughts than to what one does have good reason to believe. Her fixating on features of the situation that are likely to be significant, even though she has no reason to believe they are (or that they are likely to be) significant in this situation, shows that her attention is not focused on and directed by what does justify beliefs about it. With people whose affective systems are working properly, most of their emoting will be warranted because they are justified in having the beliefs that are components of the emotion, and relatively few of their emotions will be warranted solely in belief-independent ways. It does not follow from this observation, however, that they are *never* so warranted. Responses need to be assessed as a whole, not merely in piecemeal fashion. The affective system is out of line when there are many false negatives or false positives. The system should reflect the right type of attitude; epistemically, it is like seeking out evidence—additional evidence for or against a belief or hypothesis.

Something similar is the case with responses to fiction: if too many of one's responses occur when they are generated by momentary thoughts rather than considered interpretations of the novel, the likelihood is that they will interfere with responsible reading. The reflective component of appreciation enters at this point: a reasonable amount of emotional adventurousness is acceptable—passionally grounded—but type warrant must be considered as well.

There is another wrinkle to the emotions that have unasserted thoughts as their cognitive components. In a sense, a large percentage of our thoughts when reading are unasserted, at least to the extent that we do not believe there are or were such people who encountered such situations. But we may believe fictional characters to be, or think of them as being, say, arrogant, manipulative, or psychologically distressed. In thinking of characters in these ways we may have an emotional response. In what follows I argue that how that response should be assessed depends in part on how much control I have over what I think of (or imagine) the character as being like.

Again it is useful to compare what we'd say about emotional responses to actual persons, so consider again the stockbroker example discussed in Chapter 7. If my anger were generated by, or involved, the belief that the stockbroker was doing me an injustice, it would be the case that I am angry *with* the stockbroker. That anger would be unwarranted unless one had sufficient justification for the belief component of the anger. Even if I don't believe but only think of the stockbroker as doing me an injustice, and I *couldn't help* but think of the stockbroker as being this way, if I don't have sufficient warrant for believing that he is, my anger would be unwarranted. If I can't help but think of the stockbroker as doing me an injustice, I am angry at or with the stockbroker. In either case, my anger is directed at that individual. In these cases it doesn't matter whether the cognitive component of the anger is a belief or an unasserted thought: the anger is assessed according to whether I am justified in believing its cognitive component. Remember the example of the person who has an irrational fear of dogs, discussed in Chapter 3. He is afraid of the dog—of the dog not because he believes the dog is dangerous but because he can't help but think of it as dangerous, and this thought is instrumental in generating the emotion. For the purpose of identifying who one is angry with or what one is afraid of, unavoidable thoughts function the same as beliefs.[5]

If beliefs or unavoidable thoughts identify what we are angry with, we can explain why we want to say we are disappointed in Pip, or loathe Rosamond Lydgate, or pity Anna Karenina. It is because we want to say we believe, of those fictional characters, or can't help but think of each of them, respectively, as an individual who didn't live up to expectations, is arrogant and selfish, or trapped in undeserved distress. With respect to Winterton in *Flaubert's Parrot*, it is not the case that I can't help but think of him as a destroyer of important literary documents. Instead, I "go with the flow," now thinking of him one way (as a letter burner) and responding with anger, and now thinking of him in another way (as a fibber) and responding with suspicion. The emotions do not indicate beliefs or settled thoughts but simply the way I use my imagination, admittedly in response to parts of the text, to think of him as being in various ways and in responding in ways generated by these thoughts. And I can flip back and forth between thinking of him as being one way and as being another.

There is a real-life analogy. I am sitting in my stockbroker's office

---

5. In "On Being Moved by Fiction," *Philosophy* 60 (1985): 82, Don Mannison argues against Michael Weston's claim that we can be moved by thoughts by countering that thoughts are not the objects of our emotions. But thoughts may be the sources or cognitive components of emotions without being their objects. Even so, we can explain, as I do in the following paragraph, why one might want to think of the grammatical subject of one's thoughts as identifying the object of one's emotion.

and once again my imagination is in gear. I see the refocusing eyes; I think of him as untrustworthy; I experience anger generated by that thought. Presumably, I can bring myself "back to my senses," as we say—back to a state where evidence and justification for beliefs dictate my affective condition rather than my imaginings. If I can't bring myself back to my senses, I do have an "irrational eye-focusing irasci-bility," analogous to an irrational fear of dogs: I can't help but think of this guy, whose eyes refocus like that, as untrustworthy. That's irrational, but it's not irrational to engage in imaginings, when the constituent thoughts and hence feelings and emotions are under my control (at least in the sense that they do not occupy my mind obses-sively). It's because my imaginings are under this type of control—I can avoid thinking of things this way if I so choose—that I deny that I am angry at or with the stockbroker. Hence, I do not do him an injustice in thinking of him in this way and having an emotional or affective response of a given character because I think of him as being this way.

Control is something that can be exercised in degrees, and this fact reflects the degree of ability one has to control thoughts and the emotions they generate.[6] Identification of the objects of emotions, however, does not comfortably admit of degrees. In light of this, it seems to me the reasonable thing to do is to resist the blanket applica-tion of the technical notion that emotions necessarily have objects. Sometimes it's just not clear whether you're angry with the person or not: the degree to which you cannot control your thoughts (and attendant emotions) is the degree to which you are angry with the person.

The same can be said of responses to fictional characters. If I can-not help but think of Winterton as doing something sneaky and sly, I am suspicious of *him*. But if I merely think of him *as* being one way, and this thought generates an emotion, and I then think of him *as* being another way, generating a different emotion (or even the same emotion for different reasons), it is not clear that we even want to say Winterton is the object of my emotions. We need to examine whether my responses are generated more by my imagination than by the

---

6. Marcia Eaton has argued that the control we have over fictional contexts (in contrast with real life) accounts for the pleasurableness of our responses to fiction. Though I am not here concerned with the pleasurable dimensions of emotions and affects, control is obviously implicated in thinking of appreciation as an ability, and one often enjoys exercising one's abilities. See Marcia Muelder Eaton, "A Strange Kind of Sadness," *Journal of Aesthetics and Art Criticism* 41 (1982): 51–63.

work. If more by my imagination, the relevance of my responses is compromised, and a fortiori the type warrant for my responses is in question for the reasons described previously: if I am engaging in too much imaginal activity I am less likely to be attentive to what in the work does warrant a response.

In this section I have explained one basis on which type assessments can be made, that is, on the basis of whether the emotion is a factive emotion or an epistemic emotion. This is clearly a very minimal beginning and, as I have shown, requires considerable finesse for its application. In the following section, I consider a more substantive basis for type assessment of a sort more commonly discussed.

II: A Real-Life Principle

Another possible way of type warranting emotions is by appeal to a principle that relates the warrantedness of emotional and affective responses in "real-life" situations to warrant for responses to descriptions of those sorts of situations in fiction.[7] Appreciating fiction requires that we use experiences we have had in life to inform our experiences of the work, both cognitively and affectively in the process of reading. Our own experiences not only will affect our attitudes towards and associations with what we read, but they should do so. The ways in which our own experience contributes to or handicaps— because it distorts—our reading of a work is a large topic way beyond the scope of this book. But in this section I consider one principle for type warranting responses to what is described in the work. In this principle, the nature of what is described, rather than the character of the description or the way it is described, constitutes warrant for a particular kind of response. It takes the fact that we would be warranted in responding to an actual instance of that sort of thing in a particular way in real life as warranting responding in that way to a description of such events in a fictional work.

Responses to good literature are rarely warranted merely by the content of what is described. Nevertheless, this content is one factor going into the mix of warrant for responses, and it would distort the

7. Several versions of such a principle have been hinted at in recent philosophical literature. See, for example, William Charlton, who has argued that "in being moved by fiction we are genuinely applying the same practical principles we apply in ordinary life," (though we are applying them in a different way), in "Feeling for the Fictitious," *British Journal of Aesthetics* 24 (1984): 206–216.

nature of appreciation to leave it out entirely. One may be warranted in responding in many different ways according to this principle, just as one may be warranted in responding to an actual event in many different ways. In addition, such warrant may be undermined or overridden by other factors, like any other type of warrant. Because such a response is warranted doesn't mean that it is ultimately *appropriate*.

Examples not only must abstract from these complications about warrant but also from other responses that are warranted or appropriate. Once again, for the purposes of illustration, I use ordinary emotion terms to try to capture the response in question. For example, in Gabriel García Márquez's *The Autumn of the Patriarch,* the following passage appears: "his mother who had conceived him alone, who had borne him alone, who was rotting away alone until the solitary suffering became so intense that it was stronger than her pride and she had to ask her son to look at my back to see why I feel this hot-ember heat that won't let me live, and she took off her blouse, turned around, and with silent horror he saw that her back had been chewed away by steaming ulcers in whose guava pulp pestilence the tiny bubbles of the first maggots were bursting."[8] Horror and a recoil of disgust are warranted responses to this passage. Why? Because one would be warranted in responding in those ways to an actual event or situation of that type.

Horror seems to provide such clear examples. Consider the following passage from the end of *Perfume*, where Grenouille is being attacked, clawed, and bitten by thieves, murderers, cutthroats, and the like. "But the human body is tough and not easily dismembered, even horses have great difficulty accomplishing it. And so the flash of knives soon followed, thrusting and slicing, and then the swish of axes and cleavers aimed at the joints, hacking and crushing the bones."[9] If anything is clear, it is that one would be warranted in being horrified at a person's being hacked to pieces. The horror is increased by the allusion to being drawn and quartered; the image of horses having difficulty tearing the body apart intensifies the feeling because it implies an excruciating random tearing rather than a swift, clean slice.

An example of an implausible way of formulating a "real-life" principle is the following: whenever a person *S* would (or would tend to)

8. Gabriel García Márquez, *The Autumn of the Patriarch,* trans. Gregory Rabassa (New York: Harper & Row/Avon, 1976), p. 125.
9. Patrick Süskind, *Perfume: The Story of a Murderer,* trans. John E. Woods (New York: Knopf, 1986), p. 309.

respond in real life in way R to the sorts of events described in the work, a description of that sort of event in the work warrants the response. This principle takes the fact that one would respond in way R to a real-life event as making one's understanding a description of that event aesthetically warrant a response to that description. But this principle makes the fact that one *would* respond in a given way, even if the response were inappropriate, unjustified, and unreasonable, warrant such a response to a work of fiction. *That* isn't right. A response of a given kind does not derive its warrant from qualities of mind that are irrational, unreasonable, ungrounded, or otherwise unwarranted. What is unwarranted from one perspective cannot provide warrant from another just because that's the way the person is.

Consider a different form of such a principle, one that I defend. If a reader S is warranted in responding in way R to an actual event of a certain sort, then S is warranted in responding in way R to the description of that sort of event in the work.[10] Let us call this the real-life principle. It makes warrant for responses to fictional literature derive from the warrant one has for responding in such ways to actual events of that type rather than from counterfactuals about readers' psychological tendencies to respond. It does not require readers to believe that they would be warranted in responding to that sort of thing in real life. It merely needs to be true that they would be warranted in responding in way R. Further, whether the warrant they have for responding in way R is moral, epistemic, or something else is deliberately left unspecified. Does it really matter what kind of warrant they have for responding in that way? In any case at all, for any type of warrant, one's having that warrant explains why a response of that type would be warranted by what the fictional work describes. It bears repeating that warrant can be outweighed or undermined by other factors, such as tone, diction, pacing, rhythm, and so on. One of the important things about novels is that appropriate responses may be different from the ones that would be warranted in responding to an actual event of that sort.

If I am warranted in responding in way R to a fictional work by

---

10. I do not have the space here to discuss what would make one warranted in responding in way R to the event-type in real life. For some discussion of this see Ronald de Sousa, *The Rationality of Emotion* (Cambridge: MIT Press, 1987), Patricia Greenspan, *Emotions and Reasons: An Inquiry into Emotional Justification* (New York: Routledge, 1988), Jenefer Robinson, "Emotion, Judgment, and Desire," *Journal of Philosophy* 80 (1983): 730–741, and essays in Amelie O. Rorty, ed., *Explaining Emotions* (Berkeley: University of California Press, 1980).

virtue of the real-life principle I defend, then whatever warrants my responding in that way to that sort of phenomenon in real life also partially psychologically explains *R*. In this way, a reader uses actual experiences in responding to a work. The obvious first criticism to make of such a principle is to question why being warranted in responding emotionally in a given way to certain sorts of things in real life would establish a basis for being warranted in responding in that sort of way to a work of fictional literature. Though horror and disgust, let us assume, are warranted responses to actual cases of dismembering and cannibalizing, it would not seem to follow that descriptions of such things ground such a response. What we need to do is explain what justifies the transfer of warrant for emotional responses from real-life events to responses to descriptions of them in a work of fiction. In the process it will emerge why the existence of a disbelief, or, the belief that what one is reading is fiction, does not count against an emotion's being warranted.

People have a capacity—perhaps even a tendency—to respond to descriptions of events in fiction in the same way they respond to those sorts of events in real life.[11] Having such capacities and tendencies, and having the emotions that occur as a result of them, is not in itself the basis for the real-life principle of warrant. But the fact that it is reasonable for authors to use this fact to make their works effective does explain the basis for the real-life principle. Works of fictional literature are functional objects created by human beings. It is reasonable for authors to use the fact that this psychological capacity exists to accomplish certain things within their works, so that it is built into the institution as a principle of warrant. If it is reasonable for authors to take advantage of such capacities, readers are warranted in responding in ways that make use of them (not to mention, for those more self-reflective readers, being justified in believing that authors will be using this human capacity). After all, that is what is likely to make a work work. That is why responding in a given way is warranted by a description in a fictional work when one is warranted in

11. Compare what happens when one transfers dispositions to respond from actual events in the real world to one's experience of fiction, and what happens when one transfers dispositions to respond from *symbols* or representations of things to events in the real world. One can bring a conceptual schema and emotional associations of a symbol to the actual world, so that experience of the world is highly selective, perhaps in a distorted way, ignoring subtleties and underlying facts. There are all sorts of perceptual and associational features of a symbol that can affect emotional responses and alter responses to actual events in the world because of it. See Paul Ziff, *Antiaesthetics: An Appreciation of the Cow with the Subtile Nose* (Dordrecht: D. Reidel, 1984), chap. 7.

responding to actual events of the sort described in the fictional work in that way. In other words, this is why the real-life principle *is* a principle of aesthetic type warrant.

As I said above, this warrant can be overridden. The tone of a work, for example, or the way the scene is described, may override this warrant for a particular kind of response. Irony in particular, such as that in Swift's "A Modest Proposal," is complex. However, notice that in such cases multiple and complex responses may all be warranted: shock and indignation at the very suggestion we should cannibalize our children to avoid a population explosion, and bemusement at the absurdity of the proposal. Another passage from Gabriel García Márquez's *Autumn of the Patriarch* provides another example. The eponymous patriarch's banquet guests are awaiting the arrival of Major General Rodrigo de Aguilar, who always arrives at midnight. All the guests know that the Major General has offended the patriarch, and they are getting nervous:

> it was twelve o'clock but General Rodrigo de Aguilar was not arriving, someone started to get up, please, he said, he turned him to stone with the fatal look of nobody move, nobody breathe, nobody live without my permission until twelve o'clock finished chiming, and then the curtains parted and the distinguished Major General Rodrigo de Aguilar entered on a silver tray stretched out full length on a garnish of cauliflower and laurel leaves, steeped with spices, oven brown, embellished with the uniform of five golden almonds for solemn occasions and the limitless loops for valor on the sleeve of his right arm, fourteen pounds of medals on his chest and a sprig of parsley in his mouth, ready to be served at a banquet of comrades by the official carvers to the petrified horror of the guests as without breathing we witness the exquisite ceremony of carving and serving, and when every plate held an equal portion of minister of defense stuffed with pine nuts and aromatic herbs, he gave the order to begin, eat hearty gentlemen."[12]

Horror and revulsion are warranted responses to this passage, responses whose warrant is established by the real-life principle. But the description is also laced with a macabre humor, "a sprig of parsley in his mouth," and "stretched out on a garnish of cauliflower and laurel leaves." The image of the general laid out on his silver platter

12. García Marquez, *Autumn of the Patriarch*, pp. 118–119.

with a sprig of parsley in his mouth borders on the ridiculous, and there is a cruel irony in the traditional association of laurel leaves with victory.

It has been my task in this chapter to explain how an emotion or affect of a particular type or sort, as opposed to one of some other sort, might be warranted. I have defended two different bases for warranting particular types of responses. The first explains the warrant a response has in so far as it is an epistemic or factive emotion. The type of response reflects our epistemic relationship to the situation; epistemic emotions are more warranted than factive ones when we do not have enough evidence to be, for example, angry rather than suspicious. Sometimes, however, the evidence is overwhelming so that a factive emotion is more warranted, and epistemic emotions would evidence unwarranted caution.

A second principle states that when one is warranted in responding to a certain sort of actual person, situation, or event in a particular way, then one is warranted in responding in that way to a description of that sort of event in a work of fiction. We use our experiences and knowledge from life to interpret and understand the significance of fiction, in the sense that the warrant we acquire for responding in some way to actual events carries over as warrant for responding in that way to descriptions of that sort of event in fiction. It is part of the institution of fictional literature that such experiences and knowledge are to be used in appreciating fiction. Nevertheless, this warrant too may be overridden by other factors, reflecting again how complex a matter type warrant really is.

Chapter Ten

Temporal Warrant

A characteristic of grounding is that, with the exceptional cases of overriders and underminers, it doesn't matter what one's existing beliefs are or what one's past experiences have been. A response is passionally grounded insofar as one is responsive to the kinds of aspects of a work which are held by an existing theory to be aesthetically or artistically significant. Because works of art are what they are because of the nature of the societies and cultures in which they are made and in which we encounter them, the aesthetic grounding of responses depends on the existence of the relevant sorts of theory. The virtual independence of grounds from the rest of one's belief system enables the responses of general readers—as opposed to professional readers—to gain a foothold. But the foothold is lost without reflection. Grounded and warranted responses, combined with reflective components of appreciation, manifest the kind of "desire to do" that is implicated by a desire to appreciate a work.

My discussion of grounds focused on how responses are grounded, not on whether a person's responding a particular way (or a person's responding at all) is warranted. That is, grounds do not provide personal warrant; they do not provide warrant for the *person's* responding to what one does, as one does. Since appreciating fiction comprises exercising abilities, to assess what a person does in relation to appreciation is to assess that person's activities and sensitivities insofar as they manifest those abilities. Assessing what a person does presupposes that the person has control, at some level, over that action or behavior. As I discussed in Chapter 3, control takes place not at the stage of the response itself but at some stage along the process of "getting into it," where one shifts or slides into a "psychological gear." People develop control over their responses through control over their sensitivities. One is responsible for being in—or getting into—the psychological state or condition—having the sensitivity—rather than for having control over the response per se. Appreciating fiction requires developing abilities to get into the relevant psychological states or conditions—*that* is the level at which one has control over feelings and emotions.

Chapter 3 provided a model for how the shifting of "mental gears" or alteration in sensitivities *can* occur. In this chapter I discuss what in fact *warrants* shifting psychological "gears," or a changing of sensitivities. A great deal of warrant is provided by what I call temporal factors. In the first section I distinguish between temporal and nontemporal factors in explanations and explore how temporal factors explain one's responding as one does. Temporal factors include the timing and sequencing of one's own past experiences. Such factors are notable because they contrast markedly with the sorts of factors that typically figure in assessments of both the rationality of emotions and of beliefs. As explained in section II, sensitivities and responses that manifest them may be assessed as not unreasonable, and not irrational, because temporal factors afford excuses for them. Still, this does not provide any basis for a positive assessment of them. Section III, however, explains how developing sensitivities, and having the responses that manifest them, may be judged to be temporally warranted. This warrant is still in the cognitive or epistemic domain, but it provides a crucial link with aesthetic warrant. In section IV, the notion of aesthetic—as opposed to cognitive or epistemic—temporal warrant is explained and defended.

I: Temporal Factors as Explanations

A sensitivity is the psychological state or condition that makes it the case that one will have a particular kind of response to a certain sort of phenomenon or situation, namely, what elicits the response. A factor that explains why one has the sensitivities one has is *temporal* when it has to do with the timing and sequencing of one's past experiences. Timing includes the (relative) length of time elapsed between the past experiences themselves, and the length of time between them and now. Timing also includes the duration or length of time a given sort of past experience persisted. Sequencing is the order in which experiences of something having a given character occur, such as seeing an object at an increasing or decreasing distance, or hearing a sound of rising pitch or increasing volume. An explanatory factor is nontemporal when something other than the timing and sequencing of one's past experiences explains one's responding to what one does, as one does. Nontemporal factors include relevant parts of one's stock of beliefs, ideas, and experiences—what some think of as "background information" and others label a "cognitive stock." Nontemporal factors—both beliefs and experiences—serve as a pool of information to draw on irrespective of when one acquired them. (The "pool," however, may include beliefs about when one acquired such beliefs and experiences.) Temporal properties of past experiences generally operate together with one's cognitive stock to produce sensitivities and responses.

Consider an example discussed in Chapter 4 where the telephone ringing just at dinnertime the previous two evenings made me sensitive to the situation-type, "at home, just about to sit down to dinner." In this example, I proposed that it was the repeated, recent occurrence of the phone ringing just as I was about to sit down to dinner which placed me in a psychological state such that I would affectively respond to that kind of situation. There may be a temptation to say, in this case, that the temporal features of my past experiences do not lead to my having my current sensitivity, but rather some set of beliefs that I have, such as the belief that I am now about to sit down to dinner and the belief that the phone will ring once again. If so, the alleged role of temporal factors will be eliminated, in favor of the (nontemporal) fact that I have a set of beliefs. This explanation, however, is implausible.

Consider first the alleged belief that I am now about to sit down to dinner. First, I may well have no such *occurrent* belief: I am preparing things for dinner, and I know that, but what is the likelihood that, as I am carrying my plate to the table, I have an occurrent belief that I am just about to sit down to dinner? It is certainly not the norm. Second, might I have a *dispositional* belief? If one is antecedently committed to the view that it is such a belief that establishes my sensitivity and hence triggers my response, one has a reason for positing the existence of such a belief. Is there any other reason for saying such a belief exists? If there were such a belief, it would be a dispositional belief that would be present for a fairly short period of time, that is, the period of time after which the food is prepared and before I start eating. Furthermore, it's not clear when the belief would be formed, since "just about to sit down to dinner" is a logically vague description. Is it necessarily the case that I do form such a belief at some point? At what point must I necessarily have formed such a belief?

However, it is highly probable that I have what Robert Audi calls a disposition to believe that I am just about to sit down to dinner.[1] That is, *if* someone asks me, "Are you just about to sit down to dinner?", or, perhaps, "What are you about to do?", I may well then form the thought, and the belief, that I am just about to sit down to dinner. It doesn't follow, however, that I actually have the belief if I am not asked about it or otherwise prompted to form it. I have a disposition to believe, not a dispositional belief. What gives me this disposition to believe? Lots of things, including my intentions and thoughts about what I am doing, and my actually doing the things that I am doing, such as heating up food and putting it on my plate and such. It is very important not to underestimate the importance of these actions, my actual behaviors as I prepare dinner. They are actions, of course, and not merely "going through the motions." They acquire their identity as the actions they are in part because of the ways I am thinking about what I am doing. But they also acquire their identity in part because of the ways I am actually interacting with my environment—taking food out of the refrigerator, putting it on the plate, sticking it in the microwave, and so on. Indeed, it is conceivable that my apprehensiveness could become "generalized" to "just about to eat" situations when they involve performing similar sorts of actions and not all or only preparations for dinner. For example, it could become generalized to "putting food on a plate" situations, even when one is putting the food on a plate for lunch, or to store it, rather than to heat it and eat it. (Such associations may be at least partially responsible for the phenomenon of déjà vu.) The conceivability of these sorts of generalizations of affective association shows that we think of the responses as generated not merely by thoughts or beliefs but in association with actions and movements.

There has been a tendency to overintellectualize explanations of human behavior by taking only beliefs and thoughts to be the relevant explanatory factors and by emphasizing cognitive contents of desires (i.e., desires that something be the case, as opposed to desires to do, as explained in Chapter 2). But the fact is that understanding a mind

1. Robert Audi, *Belief, Justification and Knowledge* (Belmont, Calif.: Wadsworth, 1988), p. 96.

requires understanding also what goes on in a body. The beliefs involved are not the only crucial factors; the integration of those beliefs with actions and movements, as well as perceptual experiences, is also important to the etiology of the affect or emotion (as shown by its potential for being generalized to different types of situations). The "situation" in the example thus turns out to be a fairly complex phenomenon, carrying a potential for affective effect in many different directions. Those aspects of the situation in conjunction with a subset of my own mental states explain why I have the disposition to believe (i.e., to believe that I am just about to sit down to dinner), and may also explain why I respond with something like apprehensiveness even when I do not form that intermediary belief.

These points reinforce my worries about under what description it should be generally adaptive to attend to the perceptual evidence available, as discussed in relation to the passional grounding of responses.[2] It is not as easy as one might think to identify the description of what it is one attends to, that is, what elicits the response. My point has been here that there is something in the environment that one relates to, physically and psychologically, and it is etiologically significant in generating a response. Put very basically, without having food in some kind of receptacle one can't be in the situation of being just about to sit down to dinner. The way one interacts with the food, physically and psychologically, alters the nature of the situation, which is why the description of it has become so complex. It is a mistake to focus exclusively on the beliefs of the individual agent and ignore the role of factors in the environment with which one bodily interacts.

Now consider the other belief one might appeal to in the complex of beliefs to explain my apprehensiveness, that is, the belief that the phone will ring once again. This belief would certainly be irrational; the phone ringing with solicitations two nights running does not justify a belief that it will ring again the third night. If I do have such a belief, and it is responsible for my apprehensiveness, then my apprehensiveness is indeed irrational. However, no appeal to such a belief is necessary to explain my apprehensiveness. It can be explained, as could the irrational fear of dogs discussed in Chapter 8, by attributing a *thought* to me (either occurrent or dispositional) rather than a belief. Why do I have such a thought? Because, on the previous two evenings, as I was doing the sorts of things I was doing on the third

2. See Chapter 7 for discussion of this point.

evening, the phone rang. This set of recent past experiences, *as* recent past experiences in a similar type of situation, explains my having the sensitivity to my current situation. The timing and sequencing of certain kinds of experiences may well explain *why* one had the thoughts one did, as well as why those thoughts are affectively linked with certain kinds of responses.

Virtually every fictional work makes use of timing and sequencing, simply through the ordering of the sentences that tell the tale. It is not irrelevant to appreciation to read the first sentence first, and so on. There are reasons why authors sequence the telling the way they do. Of course the set of sentences builds readers' cognitive stock or storehouse of ideas and beliefs to draw on in interpreting the work, but the sequencing of the sentences is important for responses, including when readers know or figure out what they do and how they respond in light of that knowledge.

Some authors play with narrative voices in ways that use the timing of the shifts to affect how we respond. In Penelope Lively's *Moon Tiger,* the narrator shifts fairly frequently among different persons, often from paragraph to paragraph. Though the device is disconcerting at first, one fairly quickly becomes comfortable with it (especially since shifts are heralded by a blank line between paragraphs) and even looks forward to hearing the different perspectives expressed by different characters about the same situation. Claudia is very close to her brother, Gordon, and has never gotten along with Sylvia, his wife. Towards the end of the novel, Gordon has a terminal illness. The three of them are riding in a cab, and Gordon and Claudia are heatedly discussing some topic of politics, as they have done all their lives. Sylvia hears Claudia exclaim, "Rubbish"; Sylvia seethes. How can she be so callous to argue with Gordon when he is, well, *dying?* Tears begin to well up. Then it's Claudia's perspective, reflecting in the third person on her own remarks, " 'Rubbish!' . . . It sounds vehement enough; it sounds almost as though she means it."[3] The arguing, the banter, the often rehearsed positions they take in opposition to each other are all part of their established intimacy, reaffirming their bond, even in this difficult time. Sylvia is the one who is behaving improperly: "Sylvia, [Claudia] sees, is weeping again. Not quite silently enough. If you don't stop that, thinks Claudia, I may simply push you out of this taxi."[4] And then we read Gordon's

3. Penelope Lively, *Moon Tiger* (New York: Harper Perennial, 1987), p. 185.
4. Lively, *Moon Tiger,* p. 186.

point of view. "His eyes meet Claudia's. 'Rubbish,' she says. 'I've always given theory its due.' " He continues in a like vein to report the substance of their discussion.[5] Their arguments are important to him; he thrives on them. But soon Claudia will be lost to him. "Rubbish," which stung Sylvia like a lance, almost disappears for Gordon in the waves of argumentation and debate.

The rapid juxtaposition of these different points of view makes it possible to get a "feel" for very subtle contrasts in attitude, delicate changes in how each participant perceives the wording of the conversation. This subtlety would be lost, or at best made very obscure, if the passages had been further removed from one another. The contiguity also reinforces how distanced Sylvia's mentality is from that of the two siblings. The sense of hopelessness and regret over the inability of two people who both love the same person ever to understand each other is made painfully immediate. Fresh from hearing Sylvia's legitimate concerns for Gordon, we are impatient with Claudia's irritation over Sylvia's emotionality. We then realize, in hearing Gordon's side, that despite many years of marriage Sylvia really doesn't understand what is important to him and how intellectually suffused his emotional bond to his sister is. We also admire the way Gordon performs an emotional balancing act between the two important women in his life.

II: Temporal Factors as Excuses

Explanation is not a normative notion; excuses and warrant are. What explains why Paul was driving recklessly (he was roaring drunk) does not excuse or justify his behavior. Sometimes special sets of recent (or perhaps even remote) past experiences not only explain but also excuse behavior, and they may excuse our having certain sensitivities, responses, or a lack of responsiveness as well. Sometimes excuses completely absolve one of responsibility (my hands were literally tied), and other times they simply mitigate how negative the assessment should be, showing that I shouldn't be taken to be quite the noxious and irrational brute I may otherwise seem ("I was under a lot of stress and had very little sleep for days"). We recognize that people are often affected by things that, logically (or morally) speaking, we

5. Lively, *Moon Tiger*, p. 186.

shouldn't be affected by. And though such things don't *justify* a response, they will sometimes excuse it, because they excuse the *person* for responding in that way on a given occasion.

Excuses exist in a context where a *negative* assessment of a belief or action has already been made. If I have acquired ample evidence for believing that *p*, and in fact do believe that *p* on that basis, and the same for *q*, and *p* and *q* pretty obviously entail *r*, it appears, if the issue of whether *r* is true comes up, I *should* believe *r*. (I say "if the issue comes up" because it is unreasonable to expect one to draw *all* the consequences of everything one believes. Doing so is not epistemically required, even though it would be epistemically justified, albeit an impossible task.) But if the issue arises, then we rationally expect one to summon the cognitive tools one already has to do the job, that is, to draw the logical conclusion.

But if it's been a long time since I was exposed to the evidence for *p* and *q*, and I haven't thought about one or the other or both for a long time (not having had any reason to have done so), my failure to draw the conclusion *r* when the issue comes up, though not justified, would perhaps be *excusable*, given the lapse of time. I still believe *p* and *q*, but they're in sufficiently "deep storage" that I don't readily retrieve them. Yet I am excused for not putting *p* and *q* together. Notice that this is not a situation where there is either competing evidence or where something is cognitively more deserving of my attention. Admitting that time is an excuse is due simply to our being realistic about human beings' forgetfulness, and adjusting accordingly the conception of what constitutes being epistemically responsible.[6]

The narrator of Jorge Luis Borges's "Funes, the Memorious" tells us that he "had begun, not without some ostentation, the methodical study of Latin."[7] Shortly thereafter the narrative tells us he receives a telegram that tells him his father was "in no way well": "God forgive me, but . . . the desire to point out to all of Fray Bentos the contradic-

---

6. Respects in which we should be realistic when describing a person's epistemic responsibilities are explored by Alvin I. Goldman in "Epistemics: The Regulative Theory of Cognition," *Journal of Philosophy* 75 (1978): 509–523. Memory has separate storage and retrieval components. Simply saying "I forgot that *p* and *q*," obscures whether that information is no longer "encoded" in your mind, or whether it is there but you're just not accessing it. Either may be excusable after a long period of time.

7. Jorge Luis Borges, "Funes, the Memorious," in *Ficciones* (New York: Grove, 1962), p. 109.

tion between the negative form of the news and the positive adverb
. . . distracted me from the possibility of anguish."[8] We all know how
one's attention can be focused by recent, intense concentration directed in a particular way. In studying Latin, the narrator clearly is
attuned to and sensitive to word order and grammatical construc-
tions, so instead of responding to the content of the news with anguish (which would presumably be an appropriate response to the
message) he responds to the way the words are used to convey the
message. We may think of this as cold and callous, yet it is explicable
and indeed excusable because of his recent concentration on studying
Latin. In reading this passage, a sympathetic response, perhaps even
empathy with the narrator, is warranted by passages immediately
prior to the report about the telegram that enable us to know his
mental state and how his attention had been focused.

If the response of Borges's narrator is not very intense, however,
(and hence his sensitivity not so deep that it can't be controlled by
shifting his attention to other things), we might consider his response
to be not unreasonable. "Not unreasonable" also seems a plausible
verdict if the sensitivity "decays" fairly quickly over time. A sensitivity
with a relatively short "half-life," even when it is developed with so
little provocation, would be more reasonable than one that persisted
forever. Both the intensity of the response and the longevity of the
sensitivity are factors subject to assessment. But these assessments
entail only that low-level responses are permitted, not unreasonable,
but not that there is, as it were, anything to recommend them.

That we would find it somehow "natural" to be influenced emotionally or affectively by temporal factors is an interesting phenomenon.
Nevertheless, the sequence in which one experiences events, and the
proximity of them to one another and to the current moment, can
and often does affect how one emotionally or affectively responds
and what one responds to. This fact is one basis for charges of irrationality against emotions, precisely because the response is conditioned
or explained by the timing or sequencing of recent experiences,
rather than by virtue of one's existing set of beliefs or an assumed
background of belief and experience that constitutes a pool of information from which one should draw on any given occasion. From a
nontemporal point of view, recent experience simply adds to the pool
of information.

8. Borges, "Funes," p. 110. Other things contributed to his distraction, but to make
the example manageable I consider only this one.

Thus, in relation to the phone example discussed earlier, one might judge me to be overly reactive insofar as I have developed a sensitivity to this particular sort of situation so quickly, since the phone rang on only two occasions out of the last several years. But this judgment clearly employs a nontemporal basis for assessment—as if what matters is how many times the phone has rung at dinnertime in relation to how many times it has not rung—and not what has happened recently. With emotions, too, we do take the timing and sequencing of experiences not only to explain but also at least sometimes to excuse a person, presumably because we take the influence of some things to be so compelling that it would be verging on the supererogatory, rationally speaking, to resist them completely. Mitigating circumstances, though not providing justification, are taken to undermine what would otherwise lead to a judgment of cognitive or affective irresponsibility.

For one's emotional and affective responses to be conditioned only or even primarily by *recent* past experiences by virtue of their proximity to the current time, is just one step better than being stimulus-bound and certainly not illustrative of the cognitive control we expect of a fully rational creature. Our rational faculties presumably enable us to dissociate ourselves from accidental coincidences of experience so as to respond and make judgments on the basis of the totality of evidence available and not just on the basis of what happens to have hit you lately. A willingness to accommodate the recentness (or remoteness) of experience as an excuse reflects the extent to which we view it as nearly impossible for humans to function as fully or ideally rational creatures. It would be quite different to say such factors, at least sometimes, function as warrant for sensitivities and responses. But this is precisely what I do wish to say with respect to both *rational* and *aesthetic* warrant: that is, the timing and sequencing of past experiences sometimes aesthetically warrant one's responses because they warrant one's becoming sensitive to a particular sort of thing—that is, they warrant one's developing a particular sensitivity.

III: Rational Temporal Warrant

If something that has never happened to me before happens two days running, that recent set of experiences does not provide sufficient justification for believing that something about the world has changed rather than that it was just a coincidence. Two instances are not suffi-

cient to conclude there is a pattern, but it is something that an epistemically responsible and alert person may take note of in some way. It
could be part of a pattern. That is, it's certainly reasonable for one's
sensitivity to this kind of experience to be enhanced. The sensitivity
need not take a cognitive form, manifesting itself in a belief, or even
a thought, that this might signal a change. It might instead manifest
itself in feelings of tension or uneasiness, given the epistemic uncertainty over what role these new experiences are to play. Psychologically, it is a well-established fact that human beings' attention is drawn
to strongly contrasting elements of an otherwise relatively homogeneous array. Visually speaking, contrasts are often boundaries of objects, and our natural tendency to attend to them serves the
epistemically valuable purpose of picking out objects from their surrounding spatial environments. The same principle may apply when
we pick out contrasting elements from their temporal environments.

Not every visual contrast indicates an important aspect of our environment, but given the likelihood that such contrasts are significant,
that we are sensitive to such aspects of our environment is an epistemically valuable aspect of the human visual processing system. It
would be irrational to jump to conclusions on the basis of limited
perceptual input. That is, it would be irrational if this experience
alone, without supporting evidence, affected our beliefs about what
is the case. Contrasts within a visual array are insufficient grounds for
forming a belief that there is an object out there, but they do provide
grounds for believing that there might be an object out there. It
would be a mistake to conclude from this that the only way experiences of these spatial contrasts can be rationally assessed is if they
figure as grounds for some belief that we form, whether it is a belief
about what is the case or about what might be the case. For they can
also be rationally assessed insofar as they generate a change in cognitive sensitivity: it serves our epistemic purposes well if our psychological processing of sensory input changes in a way that affords such
things increasing importance. The changes can be experienced in
affects, such as uneasiness or mild discomfort.

Analogous points can be made about affective responses to temporally emergent features of our environment. Not every temporal contrast will be indicative of an important change (or lack of contrast an
important temporal continuity) in one's environment. Nevertheless,
it is plausible to think that at least some of the sensitivities one has to
these changes, exhibited in, for example, feelings of tension or

uneasiness, are epistemically, and hence rationally, valuable. It would be an epistemically desirable feature of people to be constructed in such a way that certain kinds of temporal features of experience alter their sensitivities and hence make an affective difference. Being constructed in this way could be especially valuable since it means people can respond to systematic changes—or what might be systematic changes—in their environment. Two phenomena, occurring in rapid succession, could be coincidence. But there is sufficient possibility that it is not a coincidence for one's sensitivity to the phenomenon, exhibited by one's affective response, to be assessed as reasonable. Rationally speaking, it is not desirable to forestall any changes in one's mental system until sufficient evidence has accumulated to justify a belief about whether things are different. Beliefs are ill equipped to deal with the gradual accumulation of evidence, but affects, especially given that they occur in degrees, are well equipped for this.

In Chapter 4, section III, "Simulation and Qualia," I discussed a proposal that the qualitative aspects of affective experiences may have to do with the *way* information is processed—the ease with which a conclusion is reached or a belief held in light of the evidence and other beliefs, the tensions or collusion among beliefs, desires, memories, and plans. If that hypothesis is on the right track, recent changes in one's environment will rationally warrant tension when (a) these experiences don't fit entirely comfortably with one's existing set of beliefs, yet (b) they aren't sufficient to justify a new belief. One might respond by saying that they would justify a belief that things might have changed, but, of course, such beliefs are almost always justified. Whether one's environment has changed or not, things might be different; we rarely have absolutely conclusive evidence for the state of things beyond the point when it is being directly examined. One thing affects can do is reflect the increasing cognitive tensions, the increased weight of the evidence, which is not easily captured by a proposition expressing a belief. One might then respond by saying that probabilities can be quantified, or at least indicated, by a belief that "there's a little more probability than usual that things have changed" (and then when the event occurs again, "there's a little more probability still," and so on). It is not at all clear to me, however, that this is, rationally speaking, a better way to go than just to alter the "computational weight" of the input, something manifesting itself in affective experience, rather than to form elaborate propositional beliefs about degrees of probability.

These considerations echo some of the points made in Chapter 7 with respect to passional grounding of responses. Indeed, they make it understandable why, in some cases, it is easier to show that an affective response that is not an emotion is warranted than it would be to show that (a factive) emotional response is warranted. The problem with warranting affects, remember, is that they do not have cognitive components. What basis, then, might be available for rationally assessing them? Precisely the kind of circumstance envisioned above. That is, feelings of tension or uneasiness might reflect difficulty in integrating a new experience into one's existing set of beliefs, even though it doesn't come anywhere close to providing sufficient evidence to alter those beliefs. The feeling reflects the cognitive dissonance between an existing set of beliefs and a new experience.

Furthermore, an emotion that has a thought, rather than a belief, as its cognitive component may be similarly warranted. In the telephone example, my apprehensiveness may be due to my having the *thought* of the phone ringing once again rather than to my having a *belief* that it will ring. My having the thought is explained by my experience of the phone ringing the previous two evenings just at dinnertime; it has been cognitively conditioned. There is a sense in which my having the thought is warranted by what happened the previous two evenings. This warrant would serve, then, as warrant for the emotion, apprehensiveness, insofar as it has the thought, "the phone will ring again," as its cognitive component.

We don't generally think of having thoughts, as opposed to having beliefs, as warranted or not. One would think that it's epistemically permissible to have whatever thoughts one has. But sometimes it is appropriate to assess the thoughts one has, to see if they reflect something important that's going on in the world or whether they are genuinely "idle." Sometimes the thoughts that enter our heads do so "for good reason." The danger in not allowing assessments of them is that we will then automatically negatively assess whatever emotions or affects arise out of or in conjunction with them. If we do not allow having thoughts to assume some of the burden of assessment, emotions and affects must assume the whole burden. The irrational part does not lie in having the emotions; it lies in reading too much into them, as if they manifest beliefs or as if they manifest grounds for beliefs. If having thoughts is temporally warranted then those temporal factors also serve to warrant the emotions or affects to which they give rise.

IV: Aesthetic Temporal Warrant

For various gadgets, tools, machines, or instruments, you have to do the right things to get them to work. With fiction, as I argued in Chapter 6, part of what readers should do with a work is to "use" aspects of it progressively encountered to effect changes in their sensitivities so that they become sensitive to something read subsequently. This is (part of) how works of fiction are supposed to work. Parts of a literary work, like parts of a gadget, are supposed to work together, to coordinate with one another to accomplish their functions. Making the work work requires using the various parts to do what they are supposed to do. Some parts of a work should function to alter our psychological condition so that we become sensitive to this or that. Other parts should be producing emotional or affective responses—making use of the sensitivities readers are warranted in having. With gadgets, we push buttons and pull levers; with fiction, so to speak, we push our own "psychological buttons," so that our minds shift or slide into different psychological "gears."

One develops an account of a work and how it is supposed to function in part by knowing how to use similar sorts of works (where knowledge and experience partially warrant one's sensitivities) and in part by trying it out, becoming attentive to what it does do, and figuring out how its doing that can figure into an account of what it is supposed to do. The more effectively one uses, for our purposes, one's past experiences and beliefs in the formation of new beliefs about and responses to works of fictional literature, the more warranted one is in believing and responding as one does.

The temporal character of reading does and should structure the very possibilities inherent in the medium (see Chapter 1). The temporally sequential nature of narrative—the fact that there is a canonical mode of presentation for literary fiction (or perhaps more than one canonical mode for a given work)—is crucial to the character of temporal assessment.[9] Parts of the work are made accessible to an audience (perceiver or reader) in a fixed temporal sequence. It is of course true that our access to all things exists in time; however, an important fact about narratives is that there is a canonical mode of access to

9. See Jerrold Levinson and Philip Alperson, "What Is a Temporal Art?" in Peter A. French, Theodore E. Uehling, Jr., and Howard K. Wettstein, eds., *Midwest Studies in Philosophy*, vol. 16. (Notre Dame: University of Notre Dame Press, 1991): 439–450.

portions of that sequence. Literature is unlike painting in this respect: with painting, there is no canonical mode of access to the various parts of a painting; no ordering of presentation of parts so that a perceiver is given access to some parts prior to others.[10]

An author's actual control over how a reader accesses parts of a work, however, is limited. Some people read the last page first and then go back to the beginning. Serialization provides an author with more control but enforces a temporal gap between installments (unless the reader collects several or all before starting to read, thereby once again usurping the author's control over the sequencing of readers' access). It is also the case that in other media where there is a canonical mode of temporal access to a work, technology has usurped the artist's control over how we do access it. A portion of a piece of music can be played out of sequence—on an instrument, on tape, on a CD player—and the same is true of films on a VCR. Advanced technology makes it easier for us to take parts of a film or recording out of their context, and we can examine them in light of new juxtapositions or as (relatively) isolated phenomena (something that facilitates the postmodern sensibility). So also that major technological advance in mid–fifteenth century Europe—movable type—eventually made printed books more accessible and hence removed the control a storyteller had over hearers' access as it exists in oral traditions. Repositioning of parts can also be accomplished in the nontemporal arts: you can cut a painting into pieces and rearrange them, or you can turn the painting upside down. None of this affects my claim, of course, that there are canonical modes of presentation for any given literary work. The temporal relationships within the presentation of elements in a work of fictional literature are just as important to its identity as the spatial relationships of the parts of a painting are to its identity, though parts can be—often fruitfully—examined out of their canonical spatial or temporal contexts.

There are novels where readers are supposed to rearrange the pages as they wish. This *seems* to deprive those novels of one identifying temporal characteristic, a specific canonical sequence of certain (page-length) chunks of text. This deprivation (if you want to call it

---

10. Some qualification is needed here, of course. I grant that temporal factors are *sometimes* in force with painting. Some paintings are arranged as part of a sequential ordering, such as those presented in series, for example, along the walls of a church or public building. But even there, one's access is hardly as specifically controlled as it is with fiction. Temporal factors have greater relevance to appreciating Chinese scroll paintings, where scenes are exposed as one unrolls the scroll.

that) is crucial to identifying them as the kind of novel they are. In Kendall Walton's terms, such works have a property that is contra-standard, that is, one that tends to exclude them from being members of the category of novels.[11] Yet the sequencing within the page-length chunks of text is retained, sustaining at least this much of a canonical ordering. It also does not follow that the sequencing is aesthetically insignificant just because it is aleatory. Clearly, authors of such works are quite self-consciously stretching the boundaries of the concept of a novel and challenging readers to adapt their reading skills to this new artistic environment. Hence they have a characteristic that, insofar as we perceive the work as being in that category, stands out as a focus of attention.

Literature is also unlike theatrical performances, film, and music—and oral recitation, which was more common in earlier times—in that fictional literature does not have a fixed rate of presentation. The fact that a given rate of presentation is not imposed on the reader can be enormously influential on affective responses. This influence is not due only to the fact that readers must exercise choices, or to the fact that they can put the novel down for a long time before they get back to reading it. The speed or pace of one's reading can have enormous affective implications, just as it can in music. Speed is part of what distinguishes, in Paul Ziff's memorable examples, the way you drive an XKSS and the way you drive a hearse, the way you drink brandy and the way you drink beer.[12] Henry James is literary brandy, to be sipped and savored, but Henry Miller, James Michener, John Barth of *The Sot-Weed Factor,* and Thomas Pynchon are literary beer, meant to be swigged and gulped.

Authors make use of the narrative potentialities of fiction for affective response by exploiting the canonical temporal access we have to its parts. Of course, different aspects are used—or exploited—in different ways in different works, borrowing from and contrasting with other works, which themselves provide a kind of context for experience (though not necessarily one having a fixed order of presentation). In some respects, other works of literature function as something like an assumed background, or "pool" of information. One can draw on knowledge of those other works, but they may or may not temporally warrant developing or sustaining various sensitiv-

---

11. Kendall Walton, "Categories of Art," *Philosophical Review* 79 (1970): 334–367.
12. Paul Ziff, "Reasons in Art Criticism," *Philosophic Turnings: Essays in Conceptual Appreciation* (Ithaca: Cornell University Press, 1966), p. 71.

ities by virtue of the proximity of one's act of reading of those works to one's act of reading of the current work.

In some cases, "real-life" experiences with temporal proximity to one's reading may figure in the temporal warrant for a given response to what one reads, particularly when one reads a novel or short story recently after its publication, when it is related to current events while they are still fresh in mind. There may be differences in one's experiences between reading a novel when it is first published—when it may be assumed that it is read against recent experiences of specific actual events—and reading it thirty or a hundred years later (or, in some cases, even ten years later, when its datedness may be even more striking). This difference is not just because for the contemporary novel one has a larger pool of information to draw on. The contemporaneity of the experiences can heighten, dampen, or in other ways alter the novel's effects. (Unexpected turns of events can as well provide great potential for irony. There can be an interplay between the novel and the evening news.) Cries for "relevance" in literature may well be motivated in part by a desire to make one's own experiences temporally relevant, not merely nontemporally relevant.

It is clear that makers of fictional literature and other temporally presented artworks exploit the fact that the sequencing of the presented elements and the relative proximity of some elements to others can make a difference in how people respond to it and to what aspects of it people respond. The temporal sequencing of elements is a way of setting up the context for experiencing each element in the sequence. This truth is perhaps most obvious in music, where changes in speed, dynamics, and tonality affect the emotive power of a work. Jerry Levinson has provided a very succinct analysis of how this phenomenon occurs in arguing that a certain passage of Mendelssohn's "Overture to *The Hebrides*" expresses hope.[13] According to Levinson, the proximity of two passages leads us to experience them as being linked together, and when the themes are temporally distanced from each other we also psychologically distance them from each other. With psychological distance they lose a sense of urgency they have when juxtaposed.[14]

In this chapter I have described the nature of temporal explanations and distinguished them from nontemporal explanations. In

---

13. Jerrold Levinson, "Hope in *The Hebrides*," in *Music, Art, and Metaphysics: Essays in Philosophical Aesthetics* (Ithaca: Cornell University Press, 1990), esp. pp. 366–371.
14. Levinson, "Hope," pp. 368–369.

fact, temporal factors are often cited as excuses for one's responding, responding in a given way, or for not responding in a way dictated by strictly cognitively rational considerations. Nevertheless, I argued in section III that temporal factors do sometimes provide a rational basis for one's having the affective responses one does, especially when those responses are not emotions. Emotions have cognitive components either in the form of a belief or a thought. But non–emotion affective responses, precisely because they lack the cognitive component, are especially amenable to this type of warrant: they manifest what is going on within one's mental processing that beliefs or thoughts cannot represent, or at least cannot represent so easily or efficiently, or in quite the same way. Aesthetic temporal warrant utilizes our affective capacities, temporally and nontemporally. We can shift psychological gears, putting certain concerns "off-line," desensitizing ourselves to them, or putting them "on-line," so that they play a role in the way we respond to what we read. The distinctive contribution of *temporal* factors has been ignored in favor of the sorts of factors that can be expressed in propositions and hence can constitute the content of beliefs and be subjected to a fairly straightforward rational assessment.

Chapter Eleven

Values

I promised to provide some notion of the values inherent in appreciating fictional literature as works of art, in light of my analysis of the role of affective responses in appreciation. It's time to pay up.

Appreciating fiction involves exercising a set of abilities. One doesn't have to be a connoisseur or professional scholar or critic to have these abilities, though increased value can be expected to coordinate roughly with increases of abilities.[1] Simply to describe something as an ability is to endow it with a certain normative weight. However, there are virtually useless abilities and abilities to do harm. In this chapter I argue that there is a value of developing and exercising abilities to appreciate fictional works of literature as works of art which we can reasonably think of as an aesthetic value: it develops and maintains a psychological *capacity* that I call "affective flexibility." This capacity is in turn valuable, in that it underlies both imaginative potential and emotional control.

In the first section of this chapter I sort out differences between capacities and abilities and distinguish two kinds of capacities, additive and preconditional. In the second section I argue that developing and exercising abilities to appreciate fiction enhances the preconditional capacity of affective flexibility. Note that this section deals with the value of appreciating fiction, that is, the value of *developing and*

---

1. When an ability becomes "professionalized," however, it is not at all clear that it affords the same benefits to the individual as it does to an amateur who pursues the activity in moderation.

exercising abilities to appreciate. In section III I describe one reason why having an enhanced capacity for affective flexibility is desirable: as expanded potential for affective or experiential imagination. In section IV I describe another reason why having such a capacity is desirable: as a condition for developing control over one's emotional and affective life.

That the arts, in their distinctively aesthetic capacity, both utilize and expand our range of imagination and feeling is an old idea. I intend my defense of learning to appreciate fictional literature to qualify as a distinctively aesthetic defense precisely because of its connection with imagination and feeling. I emphasize that what I argue here is only one defense, but an important one that has been largely overlooked and unexplored. Thus, it is rather different from standard defenses that appeal to the phenomenogical quality of the experiences themselves, the pleasurableness of these experiences, or the knowledge or moral understanding gained thereby. Instead, I argue that appreciating fiction expands one's imaginative capacity and one's capacity for emotional control.

I. Capacities and Abilities

Abilities are powers to do things, in particular, powers to control and direct successive states and movements of our bodies and minds. Not all abilities involve movement: "playing dead" requires staying very still, something not everyone has the ability to do, and some abilities require being relatively inactive, such as the ability to remain calm in the face of sudden calamity. *Capacities* are underlying conditions enabling one to acquire, acquire more easily, or perfect an ability to a higher degree. Strength and flexibility, coordination, endurance, and quick reflexes are all different sorts of physical capacities. My position is that *a* value of developing and exercising abilities to appreciate a variety of fictional works is that it enhances the mental capacity I call affective flexibility. Affective flexibility is a capacity, an affective analogue of the physical flexibility underwriting physical abilities to perform various practical and athletic movements, and the intellectual flexibility underwriting abilities to understand different points of view.

Unfortunately, our descriptions of capacities emphasize what they enable one to *do*—flex, coordinate, endure, react quickly—rather than the condition of one's mind or body that makes it the case that one can flex, coordinate, and so on. Thus it is difficult to draw a line between capacities and abilities. But there is a rule of thumb. One acquires abilities through learning to do whatever one comes to have the ability to do; conversely, an ability is lost when one forgets how to do it. Capacities, however, are not increased or enhanced by learning, and they are not lost by forgetting. Capacities can be increased by training, as strength and endurance can be enhanced by the right kinds of exercise. You can learn techniques, like mind control, to enhance capacities, such as endurance, and such techniques can become embedded through habit. That is, you can learn to do things that in fact enhance your capacities. But you don't learn the capacities, say, to become more flexible, or to have greater strength. Similarly, strength and flexibility may be lost, but they are not forgotten.

As I argued in Chapter 1, appreciation is an ability. You learn to appreciate, and how to appreciate, a work of fiction. Essential to this ability, I have argued, is making the psychological shifts and slides and having sensitivities that are implicated in having affective responses to fiction. Moreover, learning to appreciate does not involve learning merely one technique or method for appreciating everything. Different sensitivities are called for by different works: for example, an ability to appreciate late eighteenth-century English novels will not necessarily entail the ability to appreciate early twentieth-century modernist novels. Not only is a very different knowledge base required for the two, but different sensitivities to prose styles and content are called for. The various psychological shifts and slides require that one have sufficient affective flexibility, that one have a psychological capacity for shifting in various ways.

Two kinds of flexibility occupy the poles of a continuum. At one end is additive flexibility and at the other is preconditional flexibility. In the additive sense, becoming physically more flexible is constituted simply by acquiring capacities to perform specific movements, one by one. For example, I have been told that there are people who can play specific pieces on the piano, such as "Moon River," without knowing how to play the piano in the usual sense. That is, they have learned the sequence of keys and phrasings necessary to play a given piece, but they have no general knowledge of piano-playing. Their skills are not extendable to playing other pieces, except insofar as other pieces contain fragments of the pieces they can already play. *This* acquisition of the ability to play "Moon River" is valuable for whatever reasons being able to play that particular song is valuable—because one likes to hear the song, because one can entertain others at parties by playing it, and so on. Hence, the value of having this specific added flexibility is confined to the value of the ability specific to it.

Compare this with learning to perform certain gymnastic movements, such as doing a backbend and touching your toes with your fingertips without bending your knees. Each of these is an ability (or something one is *un*able to do, as the case may be). Suppose I can't do a backbend, but I work at it, gradually loosening and stretching my body in appropriate ways, so that I acquire this ability. This week I work on backbends, and the flexibility required for making that movement is increased; next week I work on touching my fingers to my toes, and the flexibility required for that movement is increased; and the following week I work on the splits. In one sense, the additive sense, I am certainly now more flexible than I was. I acquire, bit by bit, more range of motion and varieties of sustainable positions, and in this piecemeal addition to my kinematic repertoire I become more flexible.

But there is another way to think about flexibility—indeed, probably a more accurate way to think about it in relation to the gymnastic physical flexibility just discussed. To be able to do backbends and touch your toes with your fingertips may stretch or realign your muscles, tendons and bones so that you become able to make many *other* movements and perform other actions, even those you have not practiced or even attempted before. You also come to be able to perform your current repertoire more gracefully and assuredly. That is, acquiring these specific abilities makes it easier to acquire other abilities or to develop existing abilities to a higher degree. Acquisition of the additional abilities changes something "deeper down" in one's bodily condition, something that is a *precondition* for acquiring other abilities or acquiring abilities to some considerable degree. Thus, the flexibility acquired would not be ability-specific but a general condition of one's body that underwrites a variety of actual and potential abilities, that is, a preconditional capacity.

An increased capacity of this sort, a preconditional capacity, increases a variety of abilities one already has in ways that don't depend on practice or additional learning. Strength is such a capacity. Weight training for football players increases their strength that, one plausibly assumes, enables them to block and tackle better. But the effect need not be so direct. "Strong hands" enable one to play the piano better, not so as to hit the keys harder, but because that strength makes it easier to control how you hit the keys and makes it possible to use effort and attention that would otherwise be diverted to other purposes. Similarly, changing an underlying psychological condition may effect an improvement in the exercise of a number of mental abilities. Additive and preconditional capacities vary in degree; some capacities are relatively restricted in their contributions to the acquisition of abilities and quality of performance, and others are more far-ranging.[2] In the following section, I explain how appreciation enhances a preconditional capacity, i.e., affective flexibility.

II: Punching Bags for the Mind

Appreciating fiction stretches and flexes the human mind; it provides us with exercise that both sustains and enhances a capacity of our imagination called affective flexibility. Its value is usefully thought of as an analogue of the value of physical exercise, the stretching and flexing engaged in during a good workout at the gym. Unfortunately, Nelson Goodman has wittily parodied this view: "Aesthetic experience becomes a gymnasium workout, pictures and symphonies the barbells and punching bags we use in strengthening our intellectual muscles."[3] I think the parody is unfortunate, of course, because what he parodies is very close to a position I want to defend.

I shall argue that a value of learning to appreciate fiction, and of exercising that ability, is that it develops—not our intellectual muscles —but affective flexibility, a flexibility that veers decidedly towards the preconditional end of the spectrum. Thus, it is not the intellectual or cognitive merits of fiction for which I argue; neither is it strength implied by the analogy with muscles. My argument concerns the affective side of our minds, rather than the intellectual, and its flexibility rather than its strength.

How do we know that appreciating fiction sustains and increases preconditional affective flexibility? We know this in part because of what is involved in a desire to appreciate, as described in Chapter 2. As a desire to do, it manifests itself by engagement. The engagement is in turn characterized by adaptability, responsiveness, experimen-

2. Abilities might also be additive or preconditional. The fundamentals of education —reading, writing, and arithmetic—are best thought of as preconditional abilities rather than preconditional capacities: having these abilities has a very broad-ranged utility as a precondition for acquiring other abilities. The example of learning to play "Moon River" is actually an example of an additive ability whose effect on one's capacities is further along the additive part of the continuum than other kinds of musical exercises that underlie musicianship in general.
3. Nelson Goodman, *Languages of Art: An Approach to a Theory of Symbols* (Indianapolis: Bobbs-Merrill, 1968), p. 256.

tality, and an affective willingness to "try things out." These are the touchstones of a desire to appreciate, pushing the boundaries of one's affective potential. In particular, appreciating fiction requires having four kinds of affective adaptability. One must adapt affectively (1) to what are traditionally characterized as aesthetic features of a work, (2) in ways that are temporally warranted as a work proceeds, (3) to what is different about different sorts of literary works, and (4) in using different theories of criticism or approaches to reading. Appreciation is not merely experiment, but requires reflective and sustained patterns of responsiveness in each of these four ways.

Sensitivities to imagery, subtle connotations and associations, rhythms of language, diction, style, voice, and vocabulary are hallmarks of approaching fiction as art. These are not the *only* sensitivities one should have towards fictional literature to appreciate it, and in some theories, the significance of these features is seriously minimized. However, developing these sorts of sensitivities constitutes the unique sort of contribution appreciating fictional literature as works of art makes to an expansion of affective flexibility.[4]

Furthermore, a sensitivity to these sorts of features is often precisely what enables us to experience empathy or sympathy. A sensitivity to sentence structure enabled me to empathize with Mr. Ramsay in the passage cited above from *To the Lighthouse*. "[Mr. Ramsay, stumbling along a passage one dark morning, stretched his arms out, but Mrs. Ramsay having died rather suddenly the night before, his arms, though stretched out, remained empty.]" The fact that the sentence is bracketed, that "out" is placed at the end of a clause, that numerous phrases protract the sentence thereafter, all leave the reader feeling rootless and alone. This is one reason that appreciating fictional literature as art is not necessarily politically reactionary; it does not necessarily reinforce a status quo that valorizes the point of view of members of privileged classes who have the leisure to acquire the ability to appreciate fiction as literature. For a sensitivity to narrative voice and style enables one to have experiences that reflect attitudes or points of view critical of privilege, or in sympathy with the disenfranchised, such as the hypocritical shield of respectability that covers the aristocracy's moral decay in the novels of Ivy Compton-Burnett. ("The Drydens were a pale, tall brother and sister at the end of their twenties, both with auburn hair and wide hazel eyes, and a look of coming of a stock that had become worn out without ever being

4. See Chapter 7, sec. III.

much.")[5] In contrast, a sensitivity to the plain-spoken, simple, and idealized style of John Steinbeck enables one to sympathize with the undeserved indignities foisted upon migrant workers and the value of friendship for those unable to take care of themselves. (" 'He's a nice fella,' said Slim. 'Guy don't need no sense to be a nice fella. Seems to me sometimes it jus' works the other way around. Take a real smart guy and he ain't hardly ever a nice fella'."[6])

This is not to claim that only works of art can be experienced with what we might think of as specifically literary sensitivities, nor that all works of art will in fact be affectively expansive. One can read all sorts of things "aesthetically," including the list of ingredients on the side of a soup can. (This principle informs "found poetry," which presents verbal materials so that a different attitude from the usual is taken towards them, transforming them into a work of art.) There are, however, good and bad works of art, and one relevant factor for distinguishing between the two is whether a work is formulaic or whether it breaks new ground. Innovativeness in this realm is not decisive, but it is definitely a relevant factor.

Works of certain kinds are generally considered not to be art, even when they are well written, because, as a genre, they do not tend to exhibit high literary values. Mystery novels constitute such a genre.[7] As much as I enjoy reading Sue Grafton, I would not classify her mysteries as literary works of art. Sarah Caudwell comes a little closer. In her *The Sirens Sang of Murder,* Julia describes to friends her use of what she calls the "Alcibiades strategy" on someone in whom one has a sexual interest: "to make no advance oneself but to find ways to make it clear that one would be happy to receive one."[8] But, in Julia's case, it proves unsuccessful. "He sat on a chair and talked about currency investment. I recalled, however, that Alcibiades had not allowed himself to be discouraged by Socrates continuing to talk about the nature of virtue and truth and so forth, but had decided, when all else failed, to express himself with perfect candour. So I said that I would not by any means wish him to feel obliged to make any

---

5. Ivy Compton-Burnett, *Brothers and Sisters* (1929, London: Allison & Busby, 1984), p. 44.
6. John Steinbeck, *Of Mice and Men* (1937; New York: Bantam, 1955), p. 45.
7. Hugo A. Meynell, *The Nature of Aesthetic Value* (London: Macmillan, 1986), argues that in good detective novels, everything is supposed to be subordinate to working out the plot, so "an elaborate literary style will be annoyingly intrusive" (p. 56).
8. Sarah Caudwell, *The Sirens Sang of Murder* (New York: Bantam Doubleday Dell, 1989), p. 69.

advance to me if he were not inclined to do so, but that, if he were, then in view of the lateness of the hour, it would perhaps be a pity to delay further."[9] The fare is still very light, but there is a dry wit to her writing that starts to breach the boundaries. I know people who feel the same about Reginald Hill. But neither Caudwell nor Hill comes anywhere close to having the literary skills of Angela Carter, Carlos Fuentes, or Milan Kundera. And when a literary giant such as Henry James takes on a task akin to writing a mystery story, such as "The Turn of the Screw," the story clearly transcends its genre, in that appreciating it involves an affective expansion beyond the rather mundane abilities involved in reading mystery novels.[10]

The second way in which appreciating fiction expands affective flexibility concerns the adaptiveness that is required as a work proceeds. I explored this kind of adaptiveness in detail in Chapters 9 and 10. The fact that responses are warranted rather than grounded shows that one must be flexible enough to have different responses in altered contexts, considered in relation to either temporal or nontemporal factors. Nontemporally, it is a commonplace that the same features in different contexts and different works warrant very different kinds of responses.[11] Only the most naive and simple-minded theories will give formulas for how one is to respond: for instance, rules of the form "When a work is written in the first person one is to empathize with the narrator," or "Long sentences are supposed to produce a dreamy, trance-like feeling," or "One should identify with the female characters." Any plausible theoretical approach will require that readers have a certain amount of affective flexibility.

With regard to temporal warrant, the timing and sequencing of the words constituting the work are supposed to affect how one responds to what one reads: curiosity builds, tensions are resolved, anxieties are sustained. Words and sentence structures that warrant a response in one context may not warrant it in another; how a passage functions depends in part on what has gone before, precisely because it has gone *just* before, or because there has been a temporal gap and it is

---

9. Caudwell, *Sirens*, p. 70.

10. These considerations help to explain why the question "Is it art?" should not always be expected to have a simple "yes" or "no" answer. ("Is it art?" provides a distressingly ubiquitous opportunity for the "simple answer fallacy.") The importance of the role of artistic literary values for any given novel or short story occupies a point on a continuum, reflecting the degree to which, in this respect, we should consider it to be art.

11. See Frank Sibley's lucid explanation of this phenomenon in "General Criteria in Aesthetics," in John Fisher, ed., *Essays in Aesthetics: Perspectives on the Work of Monroe C. Beardsley* (Philadelphia: Temple University Press, 1983), esp. pp. 6–7.

not as fresh in one's mind. In Heinrich Böll's "Murke's Collected Silences" the fact that the phrase "I prayed for you at St. James' Church" appears fairly early in the story and then again at the end temporally warrants a somewhat different response at the end from what would have been warranted if it were still fresh in our minds. As it stands, it produces a feeling of being reminded of something one had forgotten, perhaps because of having had at the time no reason to think it especially important. Sensitivities to factors that operate over time reflect abilities to respond in ways that are temporally warranted. Developing these abilities requires the flexibility to respond in accord with temporally relevant features of a work.

I am of course not claiming that it is desirable for one's sensitivities to shift and change uncontrolled or uncontrollably during the course of reading. If they did, one would not be exercising an *ability* to appreciate. But there is no more reason to believe that affective flexibility will result in uncontrolled emotional fluctuations than there is to believe the body of a very flexible gymnast will flop around in an uncontrolled manner. Capacities are not incapacities; increased flexibility does not handicap our imaginative lives, but is a precondition for their expansion and control.

Exercising abilities in novel circumstances—in relation to an expanding range of authors and types of fictional works—expands one's capacities. The value of appreciating fictional literature is enhanced when one appreciates a fairly wide variety of works of fictional literature, and not just one particular author, genre, or period. These expanded capacities, in turn, make it easier to appreciate new fictional works, that is, easier to exercise the ability to appreciate, and to exercise it to a greater degree. As a preconditional capacity, affective flexibility makes it easier to exercise one's affective or experiential imagination in general, whereas a lack of flexibility consigns one to the dictates of one affective "gear." Different sensitivities and frames of mind are required to appreciate the refined irony of Jane Austen's *Sense and Sensibility,* as opposed to the biting sadistic sexuality of Angela Carter's *The Infernal Desire Machines of Dr. Hoffman,* or the idealistic seriousness of John Steinbeck's *Of Mice and Men.* One goes into a "high-gear" romp through Smollett, Fielding, Barthes, and Pynchon; one goes into a low-gear meander through Henry James.

Affective flexibility also allows us to respond differently on different occasions to the same work. To train people to appreciate literature by teaching them a formula would be like teaching piano students to play everything in the same style something like what happens with muzak: rock, jazz, classical—it all comes out as "easy listening." It doesn't get to the foundation of what lies behind and beneath the ability to play, or appreciate, *music*. For this reason, the idea that there is a single theory of interpretation or appreciation that one can learn and then apply to all literary works is pernicious. In the terms introduced in Chapter 2, perhaps somewhat paradoxically, it doesn't manifest a desire to appreciate.

There have been innumerable theories of criticism through history, and our own age has seen the proliferation of not only theories of criticism and interpretation, such as formalism, structuralism, herme-neutics, Marxism, feminism, and new historicism, but also theories of reading, such as reader-response theory, and theories of "de-inter-pretation," such as deconstruction. The proliferation of theories tends to overwhelm, which, in turn, tends to lead to the "simple an-swer fallacy": if there's no *simple* answer to our questions (What does this work mean? How am I supposed to respond to it?), then there's *no* final answer, and one may just as well respond however one does. On the other hand, if we recognize affective flexibility as a value or benefit of studying literature, we should not only welcome the chal-lenges to our ingrained sensitivities that new works provide but also the challenges provided by new theories, calling for mental shifts and altered patterns of sensitivities. If what I say in this chapter is correct, we should expect a changing network of theoretical approaches. They will not all be equally successful or rewarding, but they test the flexi-bility that is at the heart of a desire to appreciate. Theories of reading and interpretation are themselves up for assessment, and a failure to assess them reflects the lack of a desire to appreciate, just as the absence of any reflective component in appreciation reflects the lack of such a desire.

Developing and exercising abilities to appreciate (good) fictional literature enhances the preconditional capacity, affective flexibility. But why is it valuable to develop this capacity? If it were valuable for no reason other than making it possible to appreciate fiction more easily and to a greater degree, it would be a relatively additive rather than preconditional capacity. However, appreciating fiction, includ-ing its affective dimension, does not draw on capacities whose poten-tial is restricted to that one activity. To suppose it does is part of the noxious residue of aesthetic experience theories of the sort Clive Bell proposed, theories that isolate the ability to appreciate art from other sorts of abilities. Affective flexibility that underlies appreciational abil-ities also underlies other aspects of our affective lives. Nevertheless, appreciating fiction should not be seen as a means to some other end. The following section describes how affective flexibility expands our imaginative potential, and section IV describes how affective flexibility is a precondition for emotional control.

III: A Foundation for Affective Imagination

The benefits of physical capacities, like the benefits of intellectual or cognitive capacities, are these days not often questioned. Their general usefulness is clear. But the importance of developing underlying capacities in relation to our imagination and emotional lives is not generally recognized. We need to rethink the value of fictional literature as equipment for exercising our minds, just as we have developed new attitudes towards equipment for exercising our bodies. Amplifying capacities is good, capacities of affective imagination as well as physical and cognitive ones. The simple fact is that developing one's potential to a higher degree—physical, epistemic, affective and imaginal—is a desirable thing to do. It is good to develop all the resources of one's mind, including the affective and emotional capacities of imagination, and not merely the epistemic or practical ones.

I have argued that appreciating fictional literature, that is, exercising the ability to appreciate, sustains and enhances affective flexibility. In this section I explain one reason why it is valuable to have this ability: it expands our imaginative potential with respect to generating affects, so that it is possible to *imagine* a wider variety of possibilities, for instance, what it is like to *do* this or that, to be a certain sort of person, or to be in a certain sort of situation.

I quoted Nelson Goodman's parody of the view that appreciating art develops our "mental muscles." A part of the view he criticizes is that appreciation of (symbolic values in) the arts develops our mental muscles *for the further purposes* of, in his words, "survival, conquest, and gain." [12] But the goodness of developing one's appreciational abilities and mental capacities does not have to be predicated on the assumption that it enhances our ability to survive, conquer, or gain, or even that it provides pleasure, knowledge, or moral enlightenment, any more than the goodness of the development and exercise of our physical capacities must be predicated on the assumption that doing so enables us to handle these aspects of life better. Goodman,

12. Nelson Goodman, *Languages of Art*, p. 256.

though roundly rejecting that symbolizing in the arts has the purpose of serving these other practical ends, nevertheless argues that symbolizing serves cognition as an end in itself. As he puts it, "The drive is curiosity and the aim enlightenment . . . what compels is the urge to know, what delights is discovery."[13]

Responding to fiction requires that we make imaginative use of emotional control, in the sense that the emotions and affects, moods and attitudes, play a role in projects of the imagination, as ends in themselves, rather than for practical, moral, or epistemic purposes. Being able to shift sensitivities in these ways of course may carry its own pleasure, simply in the exercise of the ability, and it may provide knowledge of what it's like to experience something. But its value lies not simply in that pleasure or knowledge and not simply in the exercise of that ability. Furthermore, the development of particular sensitivities may not have potential benefits in any other sphere. The value of shifting sensitivities lies in the development of one's imaginative, affective capacities—one's flexibility.

The value of a capacity is generally explained in terms of how it enables one to develop more and greater *abilities*. So it is in the case of fiction: enhanced capacities are valuable because they enable one to develop abilities. This may sound circular: one should develop and exercise the ability to appreciate a variety of fictional works because it enhances a certain capacity, and it is valuable to develop this capacity because it is a precondition for developing and exercising abilities. However, this argument is circular only if they are the same abilities in the two cases. There is nothing circular about this situation: developing and exercising abilities M, N, and O enhances the mental capacity C, and in having capacity C one is able to develop abilities M, N, and O to a greater degree, but also R, S, and T to a greater extent and more quickly. Developing a capacity through developing an ability enables one to expand and extend one's abilities and to develop the same, original ability to a higher degree. But if it were merely for the sake of further development of the original ability, the capacity wouldn't have independent worth beyond its role in producing those original abilities. This is one reason I stressed the difference between additive and preconditional capacities. Preconditional capacities have the potential to affect a wider range of abilities and performances.

13. Goodman, *Languages of Art*, p. 258. Interestingly, given Goodman's conventionalist views about knowledge, my view is closer to his than my reluctance to attach the value of appreciation to cognitive or epistemic benefits would indicate.

Two confusions invite themselves at this point. First, I am not arguing that expanded imaginal capacity is useful as a *means* for developing certain specific abilities. As Christine Korsgaard reminds us, "things can bear other relations to good ends besides being their causes or tools for their production."[14] Capacities are not a means for developing abilities but a precondition or foundation for developing them more quickly and to a greater degree. Furthermore, a means is typically a means to a specific end or set of ends. The absence of a specific set of ends is an indicator that we don't have a means to an end at all, but a *precondition* for obtaining a perhaps unlimited variety of possible benefits.

A second possible confusion may arise over whether an expanded capacity is desirable even if it is never used. The issue is moot with respect to the capacities I am discussing for two reasons. First, it is unlikely these capacities will never be used. Ask an analogous question of other mental capacities, such as quickness to learn and a good memory, and physical capacities, such as strength and endurance. Are these valuable even if never used? By their very nature, if one needs to know anything, or ever thinks about anything, or ever does anything, the state of one's capacities is implicated. Only if one were comatose or catatonic would no mental or physical activity trade on one's capacities. Similarly, if one ever thinks of or about anything, the state of one's imaginal capabilities is implicated. If someone is comatose, questions about the value of appreciating fiction would hardly be an issue.

There is another reason why the question of the value of unused capacities is moot. Capacities are typically developed and maintained through engaging in the relevant types of exercise, that is, through the exercise of certain abilities one already has, through pushing oneself a little farther, and through efforts to obtain other abilities. There are cases where people enhance (or try to enhance) capacities through vitamins, steroids, and mind-expanding drugs, but even these are typically taken as supplementary to the relevant types of exercise, rather than as a replacement. If capacities are developed and sustained through engaging in activities, then the question whether a capacity would be valuable if never used requires denying a condition (the use of a capacity) that actually is involved in its maintenance and growth. Thus, the question leads us to imagine an impossible

14. Christine M. Korsgaard, "Two Distinctions in Goodness," *Philosophical Review* 92 (1983): 172.

counterfactual situation, in that it supposes the denial of a circumstance required for the counterfactual to be the case.

In Chapter 4 I described how the simulation account of empathy provides at least some structure for explaining when responses to fiction constitute *knowing* what it is like to be a certain sort of person or in a certain sort of situation. The connection between appreciating a fictional work and this sort of knowledge is not automatic. If appreciation can take place without knowledge, one's defense of the ability to appreciate should not rest on epistemic grounds. If appreciation enhances affective flexibility, as I contend, this flexibility may be useful in a number of ways. One can, to an extent, know what it is like to experience a certain sort of situation. But appreciation does not ensure knowledge. An author may successfully communicate to the reader, via the work, a certain kind of experience, even though it is not an experience of what that experience is represented as being an experience of in the work. For example, in the essay entitled "Blindness," Jorge Luis Borges criticizes a line from Shakespeare that attempts to provide an insight into what it is like to be blind. Borges writes, "People generally imagine the blind as enclosed in a black world. There is, for example, Shakespeare's line: 'Looking on darkness which the blind do see.' If we understand *darkness* as *blackness,* then Shakespeare is wrong."[15] According to Borges, being blind is not like having a black or dark visual experience; it is rather not to have any visual experiences at all. The line from Shakespeare may prompt one to imagine being blind, but it doesn't enable one to know what it's like to be blind.

Understanding the relation between imagining and knowing is complicated by the fact that there is a sense of "imagining" that is veridical.[16] In the veridical sense, one simply isn't imagining being blind or what it is like to be blind unless one is simulating what goes

15. Jorge Luis Borges, "Blindness," in *Seven Nights,* trans. Eliot Weinberger (1980; New York: New Directions, 1984), p. 107.
16. Michael Tye strongly endorses the veridical sense of imagining in "The Subjective Qualities of Experience," *Mind* 95 (1986): 1–17. Paul Taylor uses imagination in a nonveridical sense that also strikes me as being quite consistent with ordinary language. See "Imagination and Information," *Philosophy and Phenomenological Research* 42 (1981): 206, where he says imagination is not necessarily meant to portray the world as it actually is. (Taylor's view, however, includes the peculiar position—perhaps linked to his commitment to the nonveridical sense of imagination—that experiential imagination produces quasi-experiences, rather than actual experiences.) However, Edward S. Casey's view that "apart from negligible exceptions, we cannot *not* imagine what and how we want to" is far too permissive. See *Imagining: A Phenomenological Study* (Bloomington: Indiana University Press, 1976), p. 6.

on, mentally, in someone who is blind. One may not be imagining what one thinks one is. One may, however, imagine what it's like to be such-and-such without realizing it. For the imagining to play any significant role in appreciation, one needs to be cognizant of what one is doing and reflect on its appropriateness or warrant, factors that may in turn affect how one responds subsequently. The veridical sense of "imagining" further emphasizes the fact that imagining, including imagining that carries emotions or affective responses along with it, is an ability, and also that one may be more or less skillful in exercising that ability.

An unfortunate drawback of using "imagining" in a veridical sense is that it cannot account for the fact that even if one's imagining doesn't simulate a mental process that constitutes what it is like to be such-and-such, one still may be imagining something. What are we to say of these imaginings? Some might be unsuccessful attempts at imagining what it is like to be a certain way or in a certain situation. But others may simply have their own character, or an amorphous sort of content, just as many feelings and affective experiences do not lend themselves to ordinary descriptions. These amorphous imaginings may be well within the scope of the sorts of experiences a fictional work appropriately produces. Certainly a fictional work need not always have the function of getting one to imagine or know what it's like to be such-and-such. Such experiences account for some of the "indescribability" of our experiences of art. It would hence not be possible to describe them to ourselves as part of the reading process. But unless we attribute an identity to them, we cannot defend them as warranted or appropriate, since otherwise there is no determination of what it is that is supposed to be warranted or appropriate. Whether these experiences have names, or constitute knowing what something is like, they still expand affective flexibility.

IV: A Precondition for Emotional Control

In section III I argued that increased affective flexibility is desirable as an expansion of one's mental potential and should be viewed as desirable just as we view the expansion of other capacities—intellectual and physical—as desirable. But there is another reason to see the expansion of affective flexibility as desirable: it is a precondition for acquiring and maintaining control over one's emotional life.

The idea that we can develop control over our emotional lives is contrary to many received views of emotions as *passions*, as things that happen to us rather than as things we do. Undramatic though it may be, the truth lies somewhere in between. Emotions are automatic to a degree, but we also can exercise certain kinds of controls over them. The kinds of controls we can exercise are precisely those discussed in relation to abilities to appreciate, where one psychologically shifts into different gears, and where various sensitivities are brought "on-line" or taken "off-line." The benefits of the affective flexibility we develop in learning to appreciate fiction need not be restricted—like a mere additive capacity—to the arena of literary appreciation. We exercise abilities in appreciating and hence in responding to fictional literature but also in responding to people, objects, and events in our daily lives. Thus, the second reason it is valuable to sustain and increase affective flexibility is that it is a precondition for developing control over our emotions and feelings.[17]

Affective flexibility, being a capacity, not an ability, does not in itself provide control. It is a precondition for acquiring control, because, without it, only one affective option would be open, whatever emotion or affect one has. The notion of control is applicable only when more than one option is available. Other options are available when it is within one's power, at least to some extent, to respond differently. Affective flexibility ensures that several different possible attitudes, points of view, or orientations are psychologically available to inform one's experiences of and responses to a phenomenon. With the development of the ability to shift psychological gears, to bring various psychological states on-or off-line, one develops some control over one's affective life.

There are those who think that emotions and affects are beyond our control, that people are "passively" overcome by emotions and feelings, and that there's nothing we can do about them. This point of view would deny, of course, that having affective responses to fiction has anything to do with developing an ability to appreciate fiction. In Chapter 3 I argued that on a particular model of mind there are various mechanisms that explain how abilities to feel can be developed and how one can come to develop some control over one's own mind in these respects. One learns to shift into different "emotional gears." Claims that it's not possible to gain control over emo-

---

17. B. J. Rosebury argues that "a vision of mastery over the chronic disorder of our feelings" is one reason we enjoy art. See *Art and Desire: A Study in the Aesthetics of Fiction* (New York: St. Martin's, 1988), p. 13. I am not making claims about enjoyment but about a value we may or may not recognize and enjoy.

tions are refuted by the myriad ways responsible people do in fact gain control over them.

The situation is exactly analogous to physical flexibility. Physical flexibility is a precondition for controlling one's actions, for if one is so inflexible that one can't move in any other way, one literally has no choice. Without choice, without the possibility of doing otherwise, one doesn't have the power—or potentiality, or capacity—to control one's actions in the relevant sense. Similarly, affective flexibility is a condition for being able to control one's emotions and affects, moods, and attitudes. Without flexibility, one is not able to respond differently from the way one does. That is a handicap—a limitation on one's power over one's own affective life—because of the lack of options. Emotions and affects play roles in many aspects of our lives—aesthetic, moral, interpersonal, intellectual, and imaginative—and hence there are many arenas wherein this power is useful. Far from showing how inconsequential emotional control is, it shows how important, complex, and difficult it is to know how one ought to respond.

Affective flexibility may at times seem like a handicap, just as seeing too many different sides of a story may seem like an intellectual or cognitive handicap, since it makes it more difficult to figure out what to believe. It is psychologically so much easier and less stressful simply to assert one's belief or perform a commonly acceptable action at the expense of understanding the complications and the merits of alternative views. Other points of view "get in the way" if understanding them makes it more difficult for us to make up our minds. Affective flexibility, similarly, can make our responses more tentative and conflicted. It's so much easier just to react without having to think about it.

Throughout this book I have been emphasizing how mere reactions do not count as appreciation. It would seem that they might, since the desire to appreciate is a norep desire, a desire that does not involve a specific mental representation of what one will be doing in doing what one desires. Appreciation does require experimentation and trying things out psychologically. Properties of a work that have traditionally been taught as important for appreciation, such as narrative voice, diction, and style, provide passional grounding for responding at all. That is, affective responses are warranted by those sorts of features. One may respond inappropriately, but simply responding to such features is part of what is involved in the ability to appreciate a work.

Yet for reactions to count as a manifestation of a desire to *appreciate*, one must reflect on the relevance, appropriateness, and warrant for those responses. Moreover, the various psychological shifts and slides one makes are not mere stretchings and flexings of the mind but informed by what one has read previously in the work and by past experiences with similar works. They manifest abilities to appreciate, abilities wherein affective responses are informed by such factors.

Appreciation is a temporally extended ability involving interaction with an external object, a text. That there is a canonical temporal order of access to the text ensures that the ability is a temporally extended one. The timing and sequencing of one's access to the text can serve both to explain and warrant responses. One does not just accumulate information as one reads, but sensitivities change in light of the sequencing of what one reads and in light of how remote or recent one's experience of parts of the text was. Becoming able to alter one's sensitivities in accord with these temporal factors is part of learning to appreciate fictional literature.

Making assessments of responses is complicated by a variety of factors. There is no well-developed typology for emotions and especially not for affects. Some responses, "wayward responses," don't have ordinary names or descriptions. Responses are typically complex and follow one another with great rapidity. Works may have a variety of functions and even within a given account different responses to the same passage may be warranted or appropriate. But we should not conclude therefore that warrant doesn't apply to affective responses to fiction. Responses are in principle assessable as long as they are being considered as manifestations of abilities to appreciate.

What, then, do you get for developing and exercising these abilities? I have not argued here for the intrinsic value of appreciation itself, nor have I argued for appreciating literature as a source of knowledge about oneself, various kinds of human character, one's own or someone else's cultural heritage, or what it's like to live under certain conditions. I have instead emphasized what one might call a distinctively aesthetic benefit of having abilities to appreciate fictional literature. They won't necessarily save the world, but they do enable a person to develop more fully a certain capacity of one's own mind, a preconditional mental capacity I call affective flexibility. Such flexibility expands one's capacity for imaginative and emotional life and is also a precondition for emotional control.

Index